TWELVE DAYS OF GRACE

Twelve Days of Grace

by

G. Derek West

Darf Publishers Limited
London
1989

FIRST PUBLISHED 1989

ISBN 1 85077 212 6 (hard)
1 85077 214 2 (flexi)

Printed in Great Britain by BPCC Wheatons Ltd., Exeter

Twelve Days of Grace

List of Illustrations

Foreword

I HAVE always liked that anecdote about the traveller, who penetrated into the very heart of Fiji some time around the end of the nineteenth century. During his exploration, he encountered an elderly chief, whose tribe had only recently abandoned the practice of cannibalism, and who still looked back with fond regrets to the good old days. These representatives of two vastly different cultures struck up an acquaintance, and the chief invited the adventurous traveller to enter and inspect the interior of his simple dwelling. Of particular interest was the mural decoration, consisting of a pair of oleographs depicting two bearded white men, whose appearance was instantly familiar to the explorer. One of the subjects was the then Prince of Wales, later King Edward VII; the other, more imposing in all his hirsute splendour, was W. G. Grace.

The chances are that portraits of W.G. have become much rarer in the far-flung quarters of the globe to-day and, for that matter, probably in Britain also, though he was generally acknowledged in his lifetime to be one of the most important inhabitants of these islands. In a first-class career lasting over forty years, during which he eventually found himself playing with or against the sons of men who had once been his team-mates or adversaries in his younger days, W.G. was responsible for bringing about a revolution in the technique of batting. Before he came on the scene, most batsmen had been much more limited in their defensive tactics and the range of their scoring strokes. They were either back-players or forward-players, but the Champion changed all that by combining the best aspects displayed by the contemporaries of his youth into a complete and unified method. As K. S. Ranjitsinhji (or more likely C. B. Fry) said, with an elegant turn of phrase, "He turned the old one-stringed instrument into a many-chorded lyre."

Because of his extraordinary genius and his immensely long career, as well as his physical stature, W.G. towered like a colossus over the other cricketers of his time. One of the most popular and universally recognized personalities of the Victorian age and several years beyond, his fame has endured to this day, even though he died in 1915. In England, that is, though he is still accorded some reverence by enthusiasts in other cricket-playing countries as well. I cannot remember the last time anybody looked at me with blank incomprehension when I mentioned the name of W. G. Grace. Come to think of it, I don't believe that I have ever come across a single person in England, who had not at least heard of the celebrated doctor. So great has been the adulation of him, that you have difficulty in resisting the impression that he existed in a kind of vacuum, dominating a succession of faceless nonentities, who spent their time bowling for the purpose of providing him with opportunities to score centuries, or who batted in order to swell the number of wickets he took. An understandable error, I suppose, but W.G. was far from being surrounded by a horde of grey mediocrities. Take, to start with, his own family. He was the fourth of five brothers, and all but one of them played in first-class cricket, the exception being the second boy, Alfred, the longest-lived and the only smoker among them, though perhaps we should refrain from drawing any conclusion from that. The third was christened Edward Mills and was almost always known by his initials. For a brief period, until the advent of the Champion, E.M. looked like acquiring some of the renown accorded later to his younger brother. Nor must we forget the baby of the family, George Frederick, whose cricketing talents might have come fairly close to rivalling W.G.'s. Poor Fred, alas, died young in 1880, at the age of twenty-nine, when he seemed destined for a long career as a brilliant all-rounder.

So, we have the Grace brothers, who between them dominated the world of cricket for more than forty years, with E.M. and G.F. making an indelible mark in the earlier part of the period, and W.G. omnipresent throughout most of the time. But what of the other cricketers encountered by members of the Grace family at Lord's, The Oval, Prince's, and other grounds of nineteenth-century England? What of the many professionals who were contemporaneous with one or more of the Graces and also enjoyed considerable fame in their day? At the time of writing, no separate Life of Fred Grace has been published, but there is one of E.M., and while the Champion has been the subject of several biographical studies, few of the great professionals of the Victorian age have received similar treatment. In their lifetime, perhaps, there was an inadequate supply of competent ghost-writers, and not enough material has survived after their death beyond a set of statistics. This somewhat skeletal condition, however, does not apply to all of them. On the basis of brief reminiscences as well as the testimony of contemporaries, both fellow cricketers and spectators, it is possible to form an image of how they looked and behaved, and arrive at some conception of their methods of batting, bowling, and fielding. So, let us now praise famous men, who hitherto have been honoured with little or no memorial—men who achieved glory in their own time only to suffer undeserved oblivion in the succeeding generations. No longer mere cardboard characters, let them assume their rightful place as some of the leading personalities of the Days of Grace.

This book, then, presents biographical sketches of twelve professionals, whose careers overlapped or ran parallel with those of the Grace family. Some earned recognition for their prowess at batting, some for the virtuosity of their bowling, and others for their outstanding merits as all-rounders, while one was the leading wicket-keeper of his day. You could easily pick quite a formidable team, on condition that one of the bowlers pure and simple should be nominated as twelfth man, otherwise there would be an inordinately long tail. You would have three specialist batsmen, one of whom could bowl, if required (a career record including over 200 wickets); two excellent all-rounders, who are known to have opened both the batting and the bowling for England against Australia; another good all-rounder; a wicket-keeper/batsman, who was one of the first cricketers to reach 1000 runs in a season; a fast right-hander, who was a competent, forcing batsman; a fast left-hander, who barely knew one end of the bat from the other; three more bowlers giving variety to the attack, slow left-arm, off-break, and leg-break. For reasons which will become apparent on reading his biographical sketch, you would doubtless omit the leg-breaker from the side. This is no mere modern prejudice against a wrist-spinner. All things considered, you would probably feel it would be safer to leave him behind in the dressing-room and take the risk of putting him in charge of the drinks tray.

Complaints are occasionally heard that there are no real "characters" among the cricketers of our own times, coupled with the belief that the last genuine article in this respect gave up the first-class game over twenty years ago. Those who make this assertion may well have some justice on their side, but certainly no such criticism could be levelled against the individuals portrayed in the following pages. Twelve good men and true would not be an entirely appropriate description of them: as human beings, they had their fair share of weaknesses as well as strengths, like the rest of us. Few of them could claim to be unblemished paragons of virtue, and one or two, while possessing some redeeming features, were far removed from being models of decorum. None, however, could be dismissed as dull and commonplace, judging by their exploits both on and off the field and by the many stories told about them, whether authentic, exaggerated, or, possibly, even invented. Like W.G. in particular and other members of the Grace family with whom they were associated in varying degrees, all were united by the common bond of their dedication to cricket.

In addition to dealing with the careers and characteristics of the twelve players in this book, I have endeavoured to relate some of their outstanding performances and include brief details of their records. When comparing these with the statistics of modern cricketers, the averages for both batting and bowling seem rather low, and one would usually have to double the former and certainly increase the latter to arrive at a rough equivalent of to-day's standards. Conditions, as I have indicated in the biographies, were far less favourable to the batsmen in the second half of the nineteenth century, especially in the earlier part of the period. The care and maintenance of pitches left much to be desired; most hits had to be run out; the over consisted of only four balls, being changed to five in 1889. A noticeable increase in scoring in the last twenty years or so of the century was the product of the improvement of playing surfaces and the introduction of boundaries, though a six was only awarded when the ball was hit out of the ground.

For details of the score cards in most first-class matches, I have relied mainly upon the excellent books compiled and published by the Association of Cricket Statisticians, and in most instances I have used the big *Who's Who of Cricketers* and county booklets issued by the Association for the career records of individual players. I have also consulted *Scores and Biographies*, particularly for the details of early and minor contests. Whenever a reference is made to a particular match, I have usually inserted the place and dates for the convenience of those who may wish to look up the full score.

Several years ago, I contributed shorter articles dealing with various aspects of some of the twelve players to *The Cricketer, The Journal of the Cricket Society*, and *Wisden Cricket Monthly*, and I am grateful to the editors of those publications for giving me permission to incorporate some of the material in these more developed biographical sketches. The chapters concerned are three and eight (*The Cricketer*), one, five, and one or two portions elsewhere (*JCS*), and twelve (*WCM*).

More than one person has rendered me invaluable assistance in locating information relating to the subjects of the sketches and their doings on and off the cricket field. A special word of thanks goes to Stephen Green, the Curator and Librarian at Lord's, who has never failed to help me in my research; Tony Woodhouse, who has more than once carried out some investigations for me, and who came to my aid when some essential material was not available to me; and Peter Wynne-Thomas, who over the years has received my questions and come up with the answers. Nor must I forget the courtesy of the staff of the British Library Newspaper Library at Colindale.

To Roger F. Mann I owe a particular debt of gratitude for the part he has played in the compilation of this book, above all for selecting and providing a goodly proportion of the illustrations to accompany the text.

Caversham, Berkshire, 1989 G. DEREK WEST

Note on Money, Weights, and Measurements

Sums of money mentioned in this book are given in the old coinage, one pound consisting of 20 shillings (1s = 5p). A guinea was one pound one shilling (£1.05).

Weights are expressed in stones (1 st = 6.35 kg) and pounds (1 lb = 0.45 kg), one stone consisting of 14 pounds.

Height is given in feet (1 ft = 30.48 cm) and inches (1 in = 2.54 cm), one foot consisting of 12 inches. A yard was 3 feet (0.91 m).

CHAPTER ONE

William Buttress *"The Father of Break-bowling"*

FEW cricketers could boast of a longer or more varied career than Edward Mills Grace. Recording over three hundred appearances in first-class matches in more than thirty years (1862–1896), he also took part in myriads of minor affairs before, during, and years after that period. His experience of the intricacies of the game was rivalled only by his now more famous brother's, and his knowledge of the skills exhibited by team-mates and opponents stretched, like W.G.'s, far away into infinity. A man, you would not hesitate to agree, whose views demanded a ready acceptance without demur. In all those years spent at the crease facing up to countless bowlers of every variety and pace, he was able to formulate a sure-fire judgement of the qualities of that host of adversaries perpetually striving to claim his wicket. According to the belief of his biographer, E.M. "gave a very high place indeed to Buttress" among all those whom he encountered. The basis for this opinion is not elaborated, nor can E.M.'s experience of that apparent nonesuch of bowlers have been extensive. Perhaps, as a youthful teenager, the future "Coroner" had two opportunities to watch Buttress in action at Cirencester in the mid-1850s, while the bowler was assisting the local team against the All England Eleven. On both occasions, E.M.'s brother Henry, already an adult, was playing for the home side, and it is well within the bounds of possibility that the youngster might have persuaded the famous professional to give him some batting practice during the dinner interval. All this, of course, is mere conjecture in an effort to rationalize the claim advanced by his biographer, but we do not have to rely solely upon the word of E.M. Grace for evidence of Buttress's genius. Other contemporaries, both players and onlookers, have testified to the extraordinary and, for that day and age, virtually unique prowess he displayed at the height of his powers.

William Buttress was born into a family of humble origins at Cambridge, on November 25, 1827. His formal education was brief and ceased not so very long after it had begun, presumably out of the urgent necessity of making a contribution to the meagre family income at the earliest possible moment, seeing that he left school at the age of about twelve or thirteen and obtained employment as an apprentice gasfitter. This may not have seemed the most desirable and fulfilling of occupations to him, but Billy Buttress, as a native of Cambridge, enjoyed certain distinct advantages not then available to others of his age group, except at Oxford. Cricket was a thriving sport in both of the old university towns, where there were many gentlemen undergraduates and a few young college fellows anxious to improve their talents, especially their batting. The slight figure of the juvenile gasman soon became familiar on the playing fields of Fenner's Ground and the more central Parker's Piece, and, in the process of earning a few extra pence as a practice bowler after hours, he discovered and developed those abilities, which were to bring him fame and even notoriety, but little in the way of fortune, easy living, or security.

Of no more than medium height, Billy Buttress had little to boast of in the way of physique, weighing less than 10 stone at the outset of his career and not very much more in his prime. Wiry rather than robust and broad in the shoulders, his slender frame lacked the brawn and muscle essential for the making of a determined batsman intent on forcing the pace. He possessed no hitting powers and was equally deficient in the ability to defend his wicket. Batting was the department of the game to which he paid the least heed, causing the editor of one of the early cricket annuals to pen the sniffy, acid comment that "He is no bat, therefore ought to practise with it." The literary style of this succinct observation may leave something to be desired, but we are left in no doubt as to the meaning. Perhaps Billy's constant employment as a practice bowler left him little opportunity to develop his batting, which remained permanently addled in the shell. Although he occasionally managed to get into double figures in minor contests, his highest score in first-class cricket was 9 not out, and he attained a career average of no more than 3.82. There *have* been worse records, but you would have to wrap your brow in a cold towel and burn the midnight oil in your lengthy search to find one. Even Jemmy Shaw, the fast left-hander of Nottinghamshire, notorious for his absymal incompetence at the crease, just succeeded in achieving a batting average slightly better than Billy's. Truth to tell, the latter experienced no thrill of joy or pleasurable anticipation in grasping the handle of a bat. The briefer his sojourn at the wicket the better, as far as he was concerned, and even more so if his innings could be avoided altogether. According to one story—and Billy was the type to attract tall tales—he was playing in a match at Lord's in the days when there were far fewer buildings but more in the way of flora on the ground. When the time came round for his turn to bat, Billy was nowhere in sight. An anxious search party sallied forth and eventually located him sitting in the branches of one of the lime trees. Asked what he thought he was doing perched up there in that incongruous and precarious position instead of taking his innings like everybody else, Billy was overcome by a flood of pessimism, saying, "What's the good of me going in? If I miss 'em I'm out. If I hit 'em I'm out. Let's start the next innings!" The story may well be apocryphal, since Buttress appeared only seldom at Lord's, probably no more than three times in all, but he was of that genus of eccentric characters, who readily found a niche in the anecdotage of cricket. Certainly, his distaste for batting was widely known. One writer, in recalling the events of a famous, hard-fought match, which Billy's side eventually won by the slender difference of two wickets, hazarded the conjecture that "No doubt Buttress sat shivering in the dressing-room praying anxiously that his batting services might not be called upon."

There was nothing particularly remarkable about Buttress's fielding. No story of a blindingly brilliant catch or a heroic feat of vital run-saving is connected with his name; no tale of long, accurate throws to the stumper survives to embellish his reputation. The position allocated to him in the field was usually short-slip or somewhere else fairly close to the wicket. His hands were probably a little safer and more reliable than those of the above-mentioned Jemmy Shaw, but that, after all, is no great shakes as a recommendation of surpassing excellence, since *everybody* was better then Jemmy.

With the ball in his hand, however, and a batsman to outwit, Billy Buttress was transported to a higher plane. Superb as a bowler and one, moreover, a long way ahead of his time who "could almost make the ball speak," he was remembered with awe by many of those who had the privilege of seeing him perform. He belonged, of course, to the round-arm period, since the legislation permitting the bowler to deliver the ball above the level of the shoulder was not sanctioned until his day was almost done. In accordance with the current trends, many of the round-arm bowlers of his time were fast or fast-medium. Often going round the wicket for choice, they were accustomed to relying upon their action to make the ball move with the arm away from the batsman. Should speed prove ineffective, captains would call upon the services of their lob–bowlers to try their luck with "the slows". Buttress, however, was almost unique among his fellow-trundlers: his round-arm bowling was slow to medium, with an occasional quicker ball sent down with no apparent change of pace or action. Of even greater moment was the fact that he was a genuine leg-breaker, probably the first known in the history of cricket, other than lobsters. Spin bowling was in its infancy at this time, and we would give much to know more about how Buttress and others arranged the position of the fingers in relation to the seam, but such exact details are depressingly difficult to discover. Richard Daft, one of the most outstanding batsmen to live in the age of the evolution of round-arm to over-arm, was of the opinion that Buttress was able to get as much break on the ball as any other bowler he had ever encountered—and their name was legion, since Daft was playing cricket of one sort or another for nearly forty years. Take also the views of William Caffyn, who was even more emphatic in his judgement, saying without qualification, "I never saw a man in my life able to get more work on the ball." One of the gentlemen undergraduates whom Buttress tutored in bowling on Parker's Piece or Fenner's Ground praised his "very easy and deceptive delivery" and maintained that he "was really the father of break-bowling," a sentiment echoed, incidentally, by Richard Daft. Another of his Cambridge pupils extolled his virtues as a bowler in even more lavish terms. This was none other than Henry Mayers Hyndman, who always believed that there was gross injustice in the university captain's failure to award him a blue, and who later in life achieved a certain measure of fame as a sort of early champagne socialist. In Hyndman's eyes, the Cambridge wrist-spinner "was the only really scientific bowler I have ever known" and he even went so far as to characterize him as "a genius," whose methods ought to have been carefully studied and practised by others.

Although the precise particulars of Billy Buttress's grip may elude us, it is nevertheless possible to establish some of the features of those methods so extravagantly admired by Henry Mayers Hyndman and all the others who were acquainted with him. "The father of break-bowling" had especially long, thin fingers, which "went all round the ball." This physical peculiarity gave him a distinct advantage in the matter of control, but the nails, deliberately left untrimmed on his right hand, gave an even greater purchase to his grip. At the end of a day's play, it was by no means uncommon to find that the surface of the ball had been lacerated and scarred by Billy's long nails. He achieved the twist in from leg by imparting spin to "the leathern sphere" with his middle finger, which made the ball leave his hand "just as a top spins." Pitching on a length, the ball rose again sharply from the responsive turf to veer away abruptly in the direction of the off bail and the expectant fielder crouching with predatory hands at short-slip. Woe betide the unwary or injudicious batsman who wilfully scorned the protection of batting gloves! He was always in grave danger of having the tender skin knocked off his bare knuckles when facing Billy Buttress.

A perfect control of the ball based on a happy blend of length and spin was not Billy's only asset, for "the father of break-bowling" was a careful and penetrating student of the game—or rather of the aesthetics of bowling, since, as we have seen previously, his knowledge of and interest in the other departments of cricket were merely minimal. He was quick and eager to worm out the weak points of any batsman. Although he always relished the supreme ecstasy of hitting the stumps, like many another trundler of any age—a goodly number of his victims suffered this mode of dismissal—he was always prepared to buy his wickets by deliberately bowling for catches. Hyndman had a vivid recollection of one match at Cambridge, when Buttress was pitting his wits against those of Mr H. "Peter" Bagge, one of the undergraduates. The state of the pitch on that day swung the odds very heavily in favour of the batsman, and Bagge, whose defensive play bordered on the unbowlable, was nonchalantly preserving his wicket intact and defying all comers. Thwarted by these safety-first tactics, Buttress abandoned any idea of slipping the ball past that barn-door bat and concentrated on the alternative method of getting rid of his adversary. In spite of his predilection for the stubborn dead bat, "Peter" Bagge, as Billy was only too well aware, was often loath to deny himself the satisfying exhilaration of a big hit. "The father of break-bowling" set about luring him to his doom with a series of choice deliveries. At first, by a supreme effort, Bagge succeeded in mastering his instincts and refrained from bringing about his own downfall. He was hovering near the barbs of the hook, however, and it was all more than ordinary human frailty could withstand. At precisely *the* right psychological moment, Billy, like a veteran angler, dangled the bait once more. Unable to resist the temptation any longer, "Peter" Bagge committed himself to a mighty heave-ho to leg. Before the stroke was even completed, Buttress threw up his hands in unconcealed delight, crying, "That's got him!" and he smugly watched the ball coming down safely into the hands of square-leg.

Buttress was, in fact, what used to be called "a head bowler," and his outstanding ability to bewilder his opponents was founded on the principle of varying his attack from one moment to the next. Although the spinning, twisting leg break was his chief weapon, he was never averse to mixing in a few innocuous-looking straight deliveries. Possessing also the artistry to make the ball move in to the batsman from the off with no apparent alteration in his action, he was dispensing the occasional googly long before B.J.T. Bosanquet came on the scene. Confronted by this scheming sorcerer's spells, many an opponent's bat failed to make the slightest contact with the ball. On one occasion, Surrey's William Caffyn, one of the best batsmen of his age, shaped for what he judged to be a perfect gift for a comfortable leg-hit only to suffer the agonizing mortification of being bowled round his legs. Nor was Caffyn the only one of Buttress's victims to be dismissed in this fashion. Dubbed for obvious reasons "the artful dodger," Billy was always remembered by more than one of his contemporaries as *the* most difficult of slow-medium bowlers that England ever produced. Maintaining an immaculate length while bowling leg breaks demands a high degree of physical and mental fitness and extraordinary powers of concentration. Highly impressed by "the father of break-bowling's" virtuosity, one of the earliest writers on cricket asserted that Buttress, "as a bowler, in his best days, is second to none at the present day." As will be seen, there is an ominous ring to the conditional praise implied by the reference to "his best days."

Sleight of hand with a cricket ball was not the only form of deception practised by Buttress on the innocents of an unsuspecting world. He was a talented amateur ventriloquist with a speciality for imitating the various sounds made by a cat. Sometimes, when travelling by train to take part in a match, he would make a point of arriving early at the station in order to secure a seat in an empty compartment. Once installed, he produced from his hand luggage a stuffed cat with a long piece of string attached to it, and quickly stowed this dummy out of sight under the carriage seat. After the compartment had been filled with other travellers, preferably the elderly of the opposite sex on their way to market with heavily laden baskets, Billy would surreptitiously begin imitating cat noises while at the same time jerking the string to make the stuffed animal bump against the passengers' legs. If any of the unfortunate butts of his practical joke attempted to reach under the seat to drive the offending nuisance away, Billy usually contrived to escape being unmasked by mimicking an enraged feline spitting and swearing at an intruder. Humour, of course, tended to be rather more cruel in those somewhat unsophisticated days, but Billy's efforts in that line were not confined to tormenting ingenuous old ladies. On the cricket field, he was not slow to exploit an opportunity to play to the gallery and, possessing "a keen sense of the ridiculous," he would often attempt to raise a laugh by fielding "after the custom of cripples." This indulgence in playing the buffoon, however droll, was not always appreciated by everybody and may well have caused him some trouble in later days. Put it down to whimsicality, if you like. William Caffyn, who knew Buttress almost as well as anybody else, described him as "one of the most eccentric characters that ever played cricket."

According to more than one account, Billy Buttress often operated with a high delivery by raising his bowling arm above the level of the shoulder. His contemporary, the ubiquitous Caffyn, as good a bowler as

H. H. Stephenson and W. Caffyn

he was a bat, asserted that this was done by "nine out of every ten bowlers of that time, " and further admits that he himself was often guilty of contravening the then Law X of the code, and often escaped without suffering any penalty. Beyond this possibility of an occasional high delivery above the shoulder, there is absolutely nothing to suggest that Buttress's arm was not straight and his bowling action anything but impeccably fair and correct. Off the field, however, he had a reputation for bending his elbow all too frequently. If Billy could have been transported in a time machine from the Victorian age to a more modern era, who can doubt that, at the very least, he would have been an ardent supporter of CAMRA, and, at the very most, a founder member of that organization? He was afflicted with a fatal "failing for 'pints'," though I don't suppose that Billy would have thought of it as an affliction. While paying a generous tribute to the excellence of his bowling, one of his former pupils at Cambridge was sorry to say that he was "rather too fond of glass." There was a slight attempt to instil some Christian charity in these words of condemnation, coming as they did, from a pillar of the established church, but a layman, also tutored in cricket at Cambridge by Billy, was less restrained in his language, referring to his former coach as "a drunken old chap," adding, "The difficulty was to keep Buttress sober."

Undergraduates were not the only gentlemen to benefit from Billy's bowling. At one time, he held a temporary engagement at Eton, perhaps at the instigation of Fred Bell, a Cambridgeshire professional, who held the post of permanent coach there for several seasons in the early 1860s. Billy's fame as a bowler had preceded him, and it was rumoured that his undeviating accuracy enabled him to pitch a ball on a shilling. When put to the test, he failed to live up to his reputation, much to the disappointment of his pupils. This incident may have taken place in 1861, or thereabouts, when Billy certainly had some connections with Eton. By then, having already squandered some of his talents at the ale-house, he was no longer so good as in the days of yore, but something other than cricket was evidently absorbing his interest. One of the boys, who later wrote a book of memoirs, put his finger unerringly on the spot, saying, "I think his thoughts were too much taken up with the numerous bottles of beer he had tied to a stone in the river, as he said, to keep cool, to do really well in the bowling way." It is only fair, of course, to speculate on the number of total abstainers who would be capable of pitching a ball on a ten-pound note, let alone a shilling.

English cricket is notable for having given rise to numerous hoary legends of the "We'll get 'em in singles, Wilfred" variety, which, delightful though they be and hallowed by constant repetition, are dissipated on closer examination of the hard facts. One flight of fancy would have us believe that Alfred Shaw was the first man to suggest that the creases should be marked with whitewash instead of being cut in the turf with a knife at Lord's, when the idea had already been mooted before he had even become a ground bowler at headquarters. Another favourite concerns John Willes, a pioneer of round-arm bowling in the early years of the nineteenth century, when the standard delivery was under-arm. The story tells that he first became aware of the possibilities of the alternative action on the day when he persuaded his sister to give him some batting practice at his home, in Sutton Valence, Kent. Since, we are informed, she was wearing a long-skirted crinoline dress with spreading hoops, she was unable to bowl an orthodox under-arm and was compelled to deliver the ball from around the level of her waist. Miss Willes was evidently a remarkable young lady: crinolines did not become fashionable until many years later.

As befits a bibulous eccentric blessed or cursed with a perpetual thirst, Billy Buttress was, as we have seen, another character around whom legends were woven. One anecdote relates that he was taking part in an important match at Lord's, and it was realised at the end of the second day that his side would not stand a chance of winning, unless Buttress could produce his best form the next morning. But how to keep him away from the copious draughts of ale he would surely imbibe? A hasty plot was hatched, with the conspirators spinning him a yarn about a cellar in the basement of the old pavilion or tavern. This cellar, they assured him, possessed some remarkable feature, architectural or otherwise, which he shouldn't fail to inspect. Duped by the plausibility of their story, Billy accompanied them to the cellar. He entered first, whereupon the door was slammed shut behind him and securely locked, leaving him to spend the night in total darkness and—more serious still, as far as Billy was concerned—deprived of the merest drop of his preferred beverage. His release was delayed until shortly before the start of play on the following day. Furious at the treatment he had received, the parched leg-breaker "worked off his anger at the expense of the opposing side, who could make no stand against him, and were easily beaten."

This highly entertaining anecdote of Buttress's incarceration is riddled with improbabilities. Put yourself in Billy's place. If you had been imprisoned in a cellar, wouldn't you make such a racket that somebody would be bound to hear you and come and let you out? Were the whole personnel at Lord's, from the President of MCC down to the most junior employee, privy to the plot as well as Billy's team? The opposing side would certainly have heard about these machinations. Who can doubt that one of them would have been only too happy to set the prisoner free, point him in the direction of the nearest bar, and even stand him a few pints! Even more important is the fact that Buttress seems to have played only three times at Lord's, and the circumstances of the matches do not fit easily with the story of the long night of enforced abstinence. If the stories of Billy's visits to Lord's be true, he had an unusually hectic time, what with having to climb a tree to escape from batting on one occasion, and being locked up in a cellar to keep him dry on another.

Only a fairly limited amount of first-class cricket came off during Buttress's career, especially in the early part of his playing days. He participated in no more than 17 matches at this level, the first in 1849 and the last in 1861, taking 37 wickets at an average of 15.08. This, however, is not the full story. The details of the bowling analysis have not been preserved for nearly half of those 17 games, during the course of which he obtained 46 more wickets. His record might have appeared more formidable if certain other contests had been accorded first-class status. Whereas encounters between the Cambridge Town Club and Undergraduates of Cambridge have been deemed worthy of admission to that honour, those between Players engaged at Cambridge and the Undergraduates have been excluded—a decision which seems passing strange, considering that the Players' team usually had the services of some excellent professionals and the Undergraduates fielded sometimes as many as nine of the eleven appearing in the varsity match the same season. A brief biographical sketch of Buttress contains the following interesting sentence: "It is considered (by good judges) strange that he has not been chosen oftener in the great contests of the day." A few fleeting appearances in first-class matches were recorded in the early part of Buttress's career, but he was never called upon to assist the Players against the Gentlemen. On the whole, with the gift of hindsight, one would point to his reputation for boozing as the most obvious reason for his frequent omission from "the great contests of the day." Exactly how wide-spread this reputation may have been is a perplexing matter. The author of the sentence just quoted makes no reference, however oblique, to it, and as a cricketer himself, he possessed an encyclopaedic knowledge of the amateurs and professionals of his time.

In common with some of his professional contemporaries, Billy Buttress earned his living largely on what might be called the periphery of cricket by exploiting his mastery with the "leathern sphere." Around 1850, he was engaged for two or three years to fulfil the duties of coach and practice bowler to the Bagge family at King's Lynn, Norfolk. He held similar posts with other private employers in subsequent seasons, though, for reasons which may not be too hard to fathom, none of these seems to have lasted for any appreciable length of time. Hired as a practice bowler at Oxford University in 1854, he performed the same role at Cambridge on a more or less permanent basis for several years, certainly from 1856 to 1863. For the season of 1859, he was engaged as a professional by the Bradford Club. It may be imagined that the local connoisseurs of the finer points of cricket in that northern city were delighted to witness the spectacle of Billy Buttress dispensing his artful twisters in partnership with Bradford's own favourite son, Isaac Hodgson, the first of that famous line of slow-medium left-handers produced by Yorkshire. Finally, in 1864 or 1865, he was signed on by the Peterborough Club, but this engagement, like some of the others, was not apparently of very long duration.

In addition to the positions he obtained with individuals and clubs throughout a season, Billy Buttress was frequently in demand as a "Given Man," the term used in those days to denote a player, almost without exception a professional, engaged for an agreed fee to assist a club or team in one particular match to strengthen the bowling resources. He is found in this sort of employment as early as 1848, and few were the seasons up to the early 1860s when he did not appear as a Given Man. It was in this role that he achieved much of his fame, and one of the earliest of many outstanding performances occurred during the time of his sojourn at King's Lynn. At Swaffham in the same county, early in September 1850, he made a major contribution to Norfolk's victory by six wickets over a strong MCC team in an eleven-a-side match by taking 8 wickets in the first innings and 4 in the second. In the following season, he played twice for the Gentlemen of Leicestershire against MCC, achieving still better figures in the second encounter by claiming 14 of the 20 wickets. And so it went on for more than a decade, year by year, when his services were at a premium, especially when a local team, usually a twenty-two, required assistance in contests against the All England and United All England Elevens.

Between 1850 and 1865, Buttress was opposed to these two famous itinerant elevens in at least forty-three matches, very occasionally as a club professional but more often as a bona fide Given Man in the vast majority of the encounters. All England were the opponents on thirty-two occasions and the United on eleven. Billy made his debut in these matches by playing for 22 of Peterborough against the AEE at the end of August 1850. Taking 10 wickets in all, he disposed of the redoubtable George Parr, All England's champion batsman, clean bowled in each of the innings. This feat he repeated the next season. Bowling unchanged throughout the match, as he did on a number of subsequent occasions, he claimed 10 wickets again, hitting the stumps no less than nine times. In spite of all his outstanding qualities, George Parr seems to have experienced considerable difficulty in coping adequately with Buttress's perfidious twisters, nor was he by any means the only first-rate batsman to succumb to Billy's artful dodging: George Anderson and William Caffyn were frequently to be found among his victims on the score-sheet. A veritable scourge of the Two Elevens of England in the first half of the 1850s, he achieved some amazing performances. For 22 of Huntingdonshire against the All England Eleven in 1851, he bowled without relief in the first innings, delivering 24 four-ball overs, of which 15 were maidens, and capturing 8 wickets for the cost of only 15 runs. Another remarkable exploit was recorded when he was engaged to play for 22 of Preston against the All Englanders in 1852. Operating unchanged throughout the whole match this time, he proved particularly lethal in All England's first innings, when he returned an analysis of 19 overs, 14 maidens, 5 runs, 7 wickets!

"The father of break-bowling" reached his apogee as a Given Man against the Two Elevens of England in the middle of the decade, with 11 engagements in 1854 and 10 in 1855. Thereafter, his services were sought after much less frequently, perhaps because his fingers were becoming more accustomed to gripping the handle of a tankard rather than the seam of a cricket ball. The decline in the effectiveness of his bowling around this time is noted in that early cricket annual mentioned previously, which castigated him for being careless and lacking steadiness and finally deliverd the following magisterial rebuke: "from want of attention, and more care, has somewhat lost his once excellent abilities as a bowler." His final appearance against an itinerant eleven was recorded at the beginning of July 1865 and, rather strangely, the team he assisted was identical to the one for which he had first played, namely 22 of Peterborough. As far as can be ascertained from the surviving records, which, more's the pity, are not one-hundred-per-cent accurate, he took 190 wickets at an average of slightly over 8 runs each, when opposed to the All England and United All England Elevens. To these must be added 108 for which there is no analysis, so that, in all, he fell just short of a total of 300 victims. He marked his best performance at Shaftesbury, on August 3, 4, and 5, 1854, when he assisted 18 of Dorsetshire against the United Eleven. The home side employed only two bowlers, and Billy's match figures were 16 wickets for 74 runs (7–46 and 9–28)!

Although never a permanent member of either the All England Eleven or the United for any length of time, Billy Buttress was sometimes employed to fill a vacancy in both teams, making his first appearance when he turned out for the UAEE against 14 Undergraduates of Oxford, on June 26, 27, and 28, 1854. The busiest and most lucrative season was 1855, when, in addition to securing ten engagements as a Given Man, he also played ten times for the AEE, including eight consecutive matches. His continued presence in the All England team may have been partly a stopgap measure, as some kind of substitute was required for William Clarke, the crafty purveyor of under-arm twisters, who was absent ill for several weeks. It is fair to assume that Billy's confirmed failing for "pints" was by now giving rise to some concern, because the next two seasons were completely barren. All England hired his services for four more matches in 1858, but never again, since his performance was inconsistent and, in the last contest, he failed to take a single wicket in either innings. Two more seasons elapsed, and then, in 1861, came a brief and unhappily all too short-lived resurgence with the United All England Eleven. Appearing in a total of 20 contests for the Two Elevens, he took 121 wickets (plus 22 for which there is no analysis) at an average of slightly over 7 runs each. His best individual performance occurred at Enville Hall, Staffordshire, on July 9 and 10, 1855, when the Earl of Stamford's formidable 22 inflicted an innings defeat on the All England Eleven. The latter tried four bowlers, and Buttress was by far and away the most successful of them, capturing 15 wickets for 78 runs.

With the number of engagements apparently dwindling in inverse proportion to the increase in his consumption of ale, Billy was probably compelled to fall back on other sources of income, just as he had done during the darkness of successive winters. He did not, it is believed, resume his boyhood trade of gasfitter, but worked instead as a lamp-lighter at Cambridge, which, all things being equal, was of less danger to the community at large. Had I been a resident of the town at that time, I don't think I would have had a great deal of confidence in the safety factor of any gas-pipes connected up by Billy Buttress.

After lingering like a not entirely guiltless scapegoat in the wilderness on account of the reputation of being a man "whose society was not to be trusted," our hero was presented with a golden opportunity to rehabilitate himself and regain that position to which, on the grounds of his undeniable talents alone, he was entitled. Finding themselves at the last moment short of a bowler for their match against the AEE, at Lord's, beginning on Monday, June 3, 1861, the United Eleven sent Robert Carpenter post-haste to Cambridge to secure the services of Billy Buttress, his fellow townsman. The match provides a masterly illustration of how an evil reputation can give rise to all kinds of fantastic tales. The memories of some of his contemporaries were evidently no more trustworthy than Billy's "society," since in some versions of the event even the result of the match is incorrectly reported! We are asked to believe that the thirsty leg-breaker was "committed to the safe custody of Caffyn" to keep him away from the taproom—which may contain a grain of truth, though Caffyn does not mention it—and made to practise for *several* days—which is demonstrably false, seeing that the invitation for Buttress to play was issued only twenty-four hours before the match began.

Having won the toss, All England took first innings, and Buttress opened the United bowling from the Nursery end, with Caffyn, his temporary guardian angel, operating from the other. In about two hours, the All Englanders were back in the dressing-room, dismissed for only 74. Caffyn took 5 wickets for 41 runs, "and but little could be done with the artful, dodging, trundling of Buttress," who captured 4 for 29. The United's reply was even more feeble. Not one member of the side managed to get into double figures, the top score being 8 by three of them, and Buttress only just succeeded in breaking his duck by contributing a single to the total of 61. All England went to the wickets once more, and at the close of play the score stood at 56 for 5. Three of these wickets were taken by Buttress, who had again opened the attack with Caffyn, and it was during this period of the hard-fought contest that the Cambridge leg-breaker performed one of his most famous exploits. In his fifth (four-ball over), with two batsmen already gone, he clean bowled Tom Hayward with the first ball and George Parr with the third, thus disposing of two of the crack All England batsmen in one over for 5 and 0.

Two of Buttress's former pupils at Cambridge related with gusto that, by way of celebrating his triumph that evening, he indulged in a bender of monumental proportions. According to one of them, "he could not bowl a bit" the following morning, while the other maintained that "he was in a state of hopeless imbecility" for the next forty-eight hours, which implies that Billy was awash with ale. Events belie these accusations. When play was resumed on the Tuesday, Buttress was once more bowling in partnership with Caffyn. First success fell to the latter, when the sixth wicket went down in the thirteenth over, the bowlers having delivered eight maidens between them. This suggests that Buttress could hardly have been operating in an alcoholic haze, and he took the next wicket not very long afterwards. Then, suffering the demoralizing effect of two catches being put down, the bowling lost its edge, and the United captain brought on the changes. Billy's progress, however, was not finished, and he returned to wrap up the innings, bringing his plunder for the day to two wickets—not easy to accomplish if you're suffering from a blinding hangover. His analysis was 5 for 66, and he proved to be the United's most successful bowler with match figures of 73 overs, 37 maidens, 95 runs, 9 wickets, whereas Caffyn came next with 66.3 overs, 33 maidens, 94 runs, 7 wickets. Billy, it must be confessed, bowled the only wide of the innings, but anybody can commit such a peccadillo when he's cold sober.

On the final day, the United needed 37 runs to win, with 3 wickets still standing, and the stage was set for an exciting finish. The proceedings were delayed by rain for a while, but shortly after the start another wicket fell without addition to the total. Then, with fortune favouring the batting side, a determined stand was made. The atmosphere became so tense that John Wisden, the United captain, was assailed by an attack of the fidgets. As he paced anxiously to and fro, one of his team-mates, in contrast, sat completely motionless, unable to move. George Parr, the All England skipper, standing at short-slip, betrayed his excitement by constantly doffing his hat and rubbing his head—a well known habit of his at times of stress. The ninth wicket fell to a catch at mid-on with only 6 runs wanted to win! Buttress, as last man, took up his position at the non-striker's end. Off the next ball, the other batsman made an on drive and called for a run. Bemused as usual at the prospect of having to bat, poor Billy, who had failed to back up, hesitated, set off, and was a goner: before he could make his ground, the ball was in the gloves of the wicket-keeper, "who disturbed the timber," and the match was over.

We could not really quarrel with one reporter's view that Buttress had still much to learn in batting and fielding, but there was no stint to the praise for his bowling. In the eyes of another journalist, "Buttress is a distinct acquisition to The United: may he see the policy of the following it up." He did—for a while. Assisting the United in two "odds" matches in the same month, he took 19 wickets in the first and 9 in the only innings of the second. Playing as a Given Man against All England, however, he was not so successful, and he failed to come off for Cambridgeshire against Kent immediately after his triumph at Lord's, taking only 1 wicket in each innings. At The Oval, on June 27, 28, and 29, 1861, his first-class career came to a lamentable termination. In a high-scoring contest, Cambridgeshire eventually defeated Surrey by 2 wickets. So wretched was Billy's form, so minimal his contribution to the victory, that one can only conclude that he was drunk throughout most of the match. In the first innings, he took 1 wicket for 34 runs in 14 overs. In the second, "bitterly bad did Buttress bowl," wrote an alliterative-minded journalist: conceding 24 runs of 24 balls, he was taken off for good. Evidently considering that he had become little more than a liability, Cambridgeshire dispensed with his services, as did also the United All England Eleven. A slim chance for a return to the first-class game surfaced the next season, at the beginning of July. Cambridgeshire, contending against Nottinghamshire, at Trent Bridge, found themselves reduced to ten men, when Fred Bell was unable to leave his coaching duties at Eton. A message was sent to call up Buttress, but he failed to arrive in time. No other such opportunity was destined to come his way again.

From then onwards, it was a slow but relentless descent into oblivion. Buttress still operated as a practice bowler at Cambridge for a while, but he rarely obtained employment as a Given Man. His last engagement was at Peterborough in 1864 or the next year, and he assisted the local twenty-two against the United All England Eleven, on July 6, 7, and 8, 1865, making a predictable pair and taking 3 wickets, two of his victims being Tom and Dan Hayward, both former team-mates in the Cambridgeshire Eleven. The final act of his egregious folly was staged at Peterborough, where "he was faithless to the good citizens; his sojourn had an unpleasant termination, and he returned to Cambridge to dwindle away and die."

Whatever offences he committed (drunk and disorderly, or worse?), it must be said in palliation that Buttress might have sought relief in even heavier drinking to try and forget the onset of a mortal disease. Though still under forty, he was ageing rapidly and bore the appearance of a man over fifty. In dire poverty and distress, weak and ailing, he took to his bed. The end came on August 25, 1866, at his home, 11 Eden Street, Cambridge, where he died at the age of 38, a victim of phthisis and debilitating intestinal disorders. Some aid was rendered to him in his final hour by Mr John Walker, captain of Cambridge University in 1848, the head of the famous Walker brothers of Southgate, and a well known benefactor of cricketers fallen upon evil times. The deeds of Billy's golden days are preserved in the record books and in the memories of his fellow cricketers and former pupils, and he even received the distinction of a brief mention in the works of a minor poet, who was in residence at the University in the 1850s.

Eden Street in Cambridge, where "the father of break-bowling" lived and died, connected with a narrow road called Melbourne Place, leading only a minute's walk away to Parker's Piece, the ground where some of the undergraduates practised their cricket and were coached by professionals such as Buttress. At the Eden Street end of Melbourne Place stood a public house conveniently located on Buttress's way to and from Parker's Piece. This house, which was still there the last time I was in Cambridge some years ago, was called most appropriately *The Cricketers' Inn*. Was it ever haunted, I wonder, by the thirsty shade of Billy Buttress seeking one of his favourite "pints"?

CHAPTER TWO

James Southerton "The Evergreen"

In the phraseology of the modern educational psychologist, Jimmy Southerton would have been called a late developer. Born at Petworth, in Sussex, on November 16, 1827, he was getting on for forty when he finally made his mark in first-class cricket. A much travelled man, he spent a few years of his boyhood in Lincolnshire before moving with his family to Mitcham, in Surrey. In the 1860s, he resided at Southampton for several years, after which he settled permanently at Mitcham for the rest of his days, apart from two visits abroad. Small of stature, no more than 5 foot 6 inches tall, he weighed less than 12 stone, even at the end of his career. His countenance was pleasant rather than handsome, the expression of his eyes frank, serene, and open, though the semblance of good-natured innocence masked the workings of his calculating brain, for Jimmy, on the cricket field, was ever a schemer. Neat and unostentatious in his attire, he was usually to be seen wearing a cap or a flat-topped, broad-brimmed type of billycock hat. Beneath this covering, his receding hair-line eventually became little more than a mere memory. As if to compensate for the onset of baldness, he cultivated a magnificent pair of bushy, mutton-chop whiskers, descending from each ear to the corners of his mouth. These facial adornments, together with his longish, pointed nose, gave him the appearance of a kindly version of Beatrix Potter's Foxy Gentleman.

Courteous, equable by temperament, and rarely moved to an open display of anger, Southerton was popular with both amateurs and professionals for his civil demeanour, sterling honesty, and sense of duty. His knowledge of the many facets of cricket was developed to the utmost degree, and if he had any failing, it was a strong streak of obstinacy in clinging to his own opinions, which, however, he usually succeeded in expressing without giving offence. He had, of course, his own private feelings on personalities and events, but these he generally took care to keep to himself, confiding them only to the diaries he kept from time to time. A glutton for work, be it on the field of play, at practice or elsewhere, he was rarely to be seen taking his ease after stumps were drawn. In the twilight hours, even at the conclusion of a full day's play, he would often return home and spend a couple of busy hours in his barber's shop, earning for himself the nickname of "The Mitcham Figaro." In the same town also, from about 1875 onwards, he assumed the role of "mine host" of *The Cricketers' Inn.*

Known facetiously as "that man of many counties," Jimmy Southerton followed the occupation of professional cricketer in no less than three of the southern shires. He made his first-class debut at Brighton, on September 28 and 29, 1854, when he played for Surrey, by virtue of his place of residence, against his native county of Sussex. The latter, however, claimed him in 1858, and from that year through to 1872 he was usually regarded as a Sussex man, if required, whenever a conflict of loyalties arose. There were, nevertheless, times when Southerton did not seem altogether at ease in his relationships with the powers that be in the county of his birth. Between 1861 and 1867, he decided to live at Southampton, where he was engaged by the Hampshire County Club as a practice bowler, match professional, and groundsman. During this period, he turned out thirteen times for his new employers before severing his connection with Southampton. In the 1860s also, when he was not required by either Hampshire or Sussex, with whom he had resumed his ties, he began playing more frequently for Surrey. This anomalous situation reached a peak in 1867, when he accomplished the extraordinary feat of assisting Hampshire, Surrey, and Sussex all in the same season. The multiple problem was resolved from 1873 onwards, when a new code of county qualifications came into force, stipulating among other things that no player, be he an amateur or a professional, should be permitted to assist more than one county during the same season. As far as Southerton was concerned, this meant that he could now choose to renounce his connections with Sussex and dedicate himself exclusively to the fortunes of the county in which he had established his permanent residence. He never went back on this decision and remained an out-and-out Surrey player until the end of his time in 1879.

At the beginning of his career as a professional cricketer, Southerton was what might be termed a useful odds-and-ends man. Regarded as "a splendid field anywhere," his versatility extended even as far as taking over the duties of wicket-keeper in an emergency during his service in Hampshire, and the statistics of his first-class record include 3 stumping victims. Batting, if anything, seemed at first likely to be the department in which he would distinguish himself. Possessing a strong and resolute technique of defence, he betrayed at the same time no inclination to settle for merely grubbing about the crease but displayed a commendable eagerness to attack the bowling. For a man of lowly stature and nothing to speak of in the way of a robust physique, he was capable of astonishing the onlookers with the power and variety of his punishing strokes all round the wicket. In later days, his batting came to be regarded as of only minor importance to the sides he represented, but his skill did not entirely desert him, and at times he made some useful contributions to the total. He never succeeded in reaching three figures in first-class cricket. His best performance occurred in the match between Surrey and MCC, at The Oval, on July 20, 21, and 22, 1871. Going in at number 9 in the home side's first innings, he kept up his wicket for two hours before being run out for 82. This was the third and last time he managed to pass the half-century, long after he had gravitated to the position of a tail-ender. The decline in his batting powers became apparent around 1860 and may be attributed in part to a prolonged bout of ill-health, which severely limited his appearances on "the tented field." Another possible contributory factor was the time he had to devote to tending the old Antelope Ground at Southampton as a portion of the responsibilities of his engagement as the Hampshire club professional in the early 1860s.

During the course of these early years, Southerton had few pretensions to establishing his claim for any recognition as a bowler of outstanding merit. He turned his arm over occasionally as part of his duties on the ground at Southampton, employing the statutory round-arm delivery, but he was not often called upon to perform in this role in matches of importance. In his record of the encounter between Surrey and Sussex, at The Oval, on June 11, 12 and 13, 1863, the compiler of *Scores and Biographies*, exercising all the advantages of hindsight, was moved to subjoin a comment, saying, "It is very remarkable that Southerton had not yet begun to distinguish himself as a *bowler*, though he was now 35 years of age." Jimmy appeared for his native county in this match, and in the home team's only innings Sussex employed six bowlers, but he was not among them. It is fair to surmise that, like other cricketers of the time, he may have been inhibited to some extent by the necessity of conforming to Law X of the contemporary code, requiring all bowlers to raise their arms no higher than the shoulder at the moment of delivery. This unnatural action imposed some excessive strain on the physique—much more so than under or over-arm—and many a bowler was apt to infringe the law and take his chance with the umpire by sending down the occasional ball with his arm above the shoulder. Such tactics, either to obtain some momentary relief or derive a nefarious advantage by resorting to the deliberate practice of unfair play, would have been alien to the innate honesty of a man of Southerton's stamp. Liberation from these shackles was soon to come, however, when MCC issued a newly worded version of Law X in 1864, abolishing all restrictions on the height of the bowler's arm. In the following season, Southerton laid the foundations of a new career by coming out as a bowler, and in 1867 his genius burst into full flower, when he captured 132 wickets at an average of 14.14. There have been few individuals in the history of cricket who began making their mark for the first time at the age of thirty-nine!

The manipulation of genuine spin and turn to the ball was a task that defeated most of the trundlers operating in the round-arm days. Many of them, bowling round the wicket, contrived movement away from the batsman by relying on the natural direction produced by the action of the arm. One noted exception was the wayward Billy Buttress of Cambridgeshire, who, as we have seen, was almost unique in his time as an authentic leg-breaker long before his subtle craft was practised more widely by his successors. Anybody who has ever experimented with round-arm bowling will readily agree that the ability to send down an accurate delivery breaking back from the off is given to few. The action, especially if you are going over the wicket, must of necessity be open-chested, and any spin imparted to the ball is produced solely by the purchase of the fingers. H.H. Stephenson, the Surrey professional and captain of the first English team to tour Australia (1861–62), was a fine, forcing batsman and one of the best wicket-keepers of his time. An all-rounder in the truest meaning of the term, he was at one time always willing to divest himself of pads and gloves in order to augment his side's attack. There was, nevertheless, a difference which set him apart from many of his contemporary speed merchants. He discovered the secret of how to employ his long, powerful fingers to bowl a fast off break. The strain imposed by the constant use of this manœuvre became physically intolerable, and Stephenson, deprived of his principal shock weapon, became a rather ordinary fast bowler. After a few seasons, he decided to concentrate on his batting and, when required, his wicket-keeping. By the time that the over-arm action became legal, Stephenson's bowling had, to all intents and purposes, practically deserted him, so that he derived little advantage from the new legislation.

It would probably be inaccurate to maintain that, in 1864 and the next few years, *all* the bowlers in the country immediately abandoned the habits and methods to which they had become accustomed and began to deliver the ball with an almost perpendicular arm. A period of transition supervened before the complete over-arm delivery gained wide-spread acceptance, and the term "round-arm bowler" continued to appear in cricket literature well into the 1870s. One of the forerunners in the process of evolution was James Southerton. It has been said that he emulated the famous F.W. Lillywhite by practising the art of bowling in a barn. Like Old Lilly, Southerton had a physique which militated against any prolonged success as a fast man without shortening his career, and so he prudently came out as a slow bowler. In his essay, "A Few Wrinkles on Bowling," published in the early editions of *James Lillywhite's Cricketers' Annual*, he went on record as favouring the old methods ("The arm should be kept as level as possible with the shoulder"), yet he had no hesitation in admitting that some of his contemporaries achieved their most successful onslaught with a high delivery. Nevertheless, whatever views he may have expressed in print, there is little doubt that he raised his arm higher than many of the bowlers in the second half of the 1860s. His approach to the wicket and his action were smooth and unlaboured, enabling him to perform unchanged for long periods. He could turn the ball a little from the on to the off and was never averse to slipping in a straight one, whenever spin proved unavailing. The off break, however, was his chief weapon, and it was the popular belief that he could "break a yard." For a few years, until Alfred Shaw began to claim some of the laurels as a slow-medium bowler, Southerton reigned supreme, since many of the batsmen had never encountered anybody quite like him. These two famous bowlers were by no means dissimilar in style, but whereas Shaw relied mainly on accuracy of pitch and a change of pace, Southerton was more inclined to give precedence to break. Exactly how the latter achieved what he elegantly called "the rotatory motion of a ball" is obscure, because he confessed he was unable to account for its mysteries in detail, beyond applying the tips of the fingers tightly to the seam. In a wet season, supported by the assistance of an expert stumper, he was a positive menace to his opponents, and when the conditions were less favourable to his cause, he was still one of the most formidable forces to be reckoned with in England.

Towards the end of his career, Southerton was unable to enjoy a well earned retirement, because Surrey were weak in bowling resources, and he was still to be found wheeling away at The Oval when he had turned fifty. One of the cricket annuals published in 1879 contained the comment that his "delivery is very like a throw now." While Southerton realized that a combination of arm and wrist in addition to the correct grip of the ball was essential to yield the turn, it would be doubtful if a man of his acknowledged probity and sense of honour would have resorted to the shady tactics of an intentional throw. The fact remains, however, that his action did not satisfy everybody, and W.G. Grace, for one, referred to it as "doubtful." This suspicion of an unacceptable jerk became more pronounced in the 1870s, after the country's leading batsmen had become more familiar with his style, and, in order to escape heavy punishment, he began to quicken his pace at the expense of break and spin. Yet, if W.G.'s memory is to be trusted again, Ted Pooley, the Surrey wicket-keeper and "The Mitcham Figaro's" principal coadjutor at The Oval and elsewhere, was much more outspoken in his belief that Southerton "never *bowled* a ball in his life".

It is not unknown for a bowler to find himself thoroughly mastered by one particular batsman and to develop a phobia about the outcome of future contests with his [illegible] opponent. Any slow [illegible] like Jimmy Southerton, who was prepared at times to subordinate exact precision of pitch to prodigious break, was liable to lay himself open to severe treatment at the hands of a punishing hitter, whose physical strength was comparable to the keenness of his eyesight. W.G. could hold his own with most contenders, when it came to administering a rough handling to some of the legions of bowlers he encountered, but, scientific batsmanship apart, the opponent Southerton dreaded above all was the legendary hitter, C.I. Thornton. In the fixture between Gentlemen and Players, at Hove, on August 14, 15, and 16, 1871, arranged for the benefit of the veteran John Lillywhite, Mr Thornton broke a personal record in his second innings by amassing 34 runs off nine deliveries—7 fours, 1 six, and a dot ball. Each of the first four deliveries from Southerton was smashed away to the boundary. At the conclusion of this slaughter, the hapless victim, betraying the rivalry existing between south and north, approached his conqueror, saying, "For goodness' sake, Mr Thornton, do serve M'Intyre the same way." The jubilant amateur did his best to oblige, though the Nottinghamshire fast bowler succeeded in exacting some retribution by holding on to a stinging return catch. Southerton had a poor match, taking only 1 wicket for 102 runs, but picked up a crumb of comfort by dismissing W.G.—but not until the Champion had scored 217!

On more than one occasion, the duel between Southerton and his personal Nemesis was re-enacted with the ritual flaying of the slow bowler. Once, at The Oval, in the early 1870s, Mr Thornton achieved a sublime combination of physical strength and perfect timing by clouting the ball far away into the blue and out of the ground. As he watched its soaring flight with a jaw dropping in disbelief, wicket-keeper Ted Pooley yelled down the pitch to Southerton, "So 'elp me God, Jimmy, I believe it's gone on to Brixton Church!" After this or some other instance of brutal mauling, poor Jimmy, it was alleged, became a temporary victim of insomnia and used to lie sleepless in bed, wondering what would happen if Thornton were to drive the ball straight back at him.

C. I. Thornton

Southerton's idea of Hell, one imagines, would have taken the shape of finding himself condemned to be bowling in perpetuity at Charles Inglis Thornton. Happily, his encounters with batsmen attempting to knock the cover off the ball occurred only at irregular intervals, and the statistics of his first-class career indicate that he was one of the most successful trundlers of the Victorian Age. As a slow bowler, of course, he was able to keep going much longer than his contemporaries of a brisker pace or less temperate habits, or both. Still in action at the age of fifty and more, he seemed to have become a permanent fixture on the cricket fields of England [illegible] after qualifying for the nickname of "The Evergreen." When he finally decided to yield to the relentless advance of Anno Domini at the close of the 1879 season, he had taken 1,681 wickets at an average of 14.44. Only five bowlers, whose careers ended no later than 1900 (Attewell, Briggs, Lohmann, Peel, and Alfred Shaw) claimed a higher aggregate of victims, and but two of them recorded a more economical average than Southerton's. "The Evergreen's" most successful season occurred in 1870, when he captured 210 wickets, averaging 14.63, and in 10 consecutive years (1867–1876) his tally of dismissals went beyond the hundred mark, a figure equalled only by Attewell and exceeded only by Briggs. Other indications also point to the remarkable achievements of "that man of many counties." In the matter of taking 5 wickets in an innings, Briggs (200 times) beats Southerton into second place by a fairly narrow margin (192), but when it comes to that supreme mark of excellence and consistency, 10 or more wickets in a match, Southerton comes top of the six with 59.

"The Evergreen" performed the hat-trick once in first-class matches, when he assisted the South against the North, at Bramall Lane, on July 26 and 27, 1869. He never managed to secure all 10 wickets in an innings, but came close to it in the North *v* South contest, at Lord's, in 1875. The match was arranged for the benefit of the MCC Professional Fund, but the takings at the gate were limited by the extraordinary performance of Southerton. The North, it must be admitted, could not claim to be fully representative, seeing that some of the leading players were prevented from taking part by other engagements. On the other hand, the conditions were not overwhelmingly in favour of the bowlers, when the match began on May 17, "A gloriously fine Whit-Monday." Scheduled to last three days, it was all over on the first, thanks to the magnificent and exceptional bowling of "The Evergreen," who took 9 wickets for 30 runs in his first essay—number 11 for the North was run out—and 7 for 22 in his second, achieving his best ever figures in an innings and a match. The mind boggles at the thought that any bowler, even one whose pace was as slow and undemanding as

Southerton's, should record his finest performance at the advanced age of forty-seven!

Although he was still able to hold his own in the bowling department around the time he established his personal record, "The Evergreen" was becoming rather stiff in his joints. With the inevitable departure of the spryness of his distant youth, he was compelled to husband his strength, especially when fielding to his own bowling, and he found it increasingly arduous to stoop down quickly to retrieve the ball. The onset of this patently obvious bodily failing was maliciously but perfectly legitimately exploited in a minor one-day match at Beddington Park, in Surrey, on July 24, 1876. Beddington Park, for whom Southerton had been engaged to play, were contending against the Harrow Wanderers. The home side took first innings and were put out for 143, with Southerton, as third top scorer, making 19. This, as it happened, was his only success in the match. Harrow Wanderers began their reply by sending in A.N. Hornby and A.J. Webbe, two excellent amateur batsmen, who earned an enviable reputation on the county circuit and even represented England against Australia, though without distinguishing themselves. When stumps were drawn, the visitors had reached 162 without losing a wicket, with Hornby 103 not out, and Webbe 56 not out. The latter, generally speaking, was a good-natured soul, whereas Hornby, one of the fastest runners between the wickets at that time, rarely neglected the opportunity to make the most of any advantage coming his way. Adapting his technique to the dictates of the situation, he repeatedly dead-batted the ball gently down the pitch towards the weary, helpless bowler and ran through for a safe single, "to the intense disgust of poor old Southerton." The match came to an end at this stage, because the Wanderers were engaged for a similar type of fixture on the next day, which doubtless acted as a salve to the torment of Jimmy's aching limbs.

Some of the success earned by "The Evergreen" as one of the supreme wicket-takers of his day arose out of his long association with the Surrey stumper, Edward Pooley. Beginning in 1866 and lasting until Southerton's retirement from first-class cricket in 1879, this combination—one of the most famous in the history of cricket—presented an unusual blend of superficial similarity and deep-rooted difference. Viewed from a distance, they had certain physical features in common, since both were small, slight, bewhiskered men, and they shared an abiding devotion to cricket, particularly Surrey cricket, but not far beyond that the resemblance petered out. Southerton, as the older man by over ten years, and though generally cheerful by disposition, was predictably the more serious and sedate half of the pair. Upright, strong-minded, and abstemious, he was mentally and physically equipped to resist the temptations beckoning from the bar of his own hostelry. By contrast, Ted Pooley—was Ted Pooley, the last man in the world to be entrusted with the responsibility of keeping an inn on a profitable basis. To be fair, though, he seems to have organized his life-style in such a way that it did not interfere with his duties as a wicket-keeper. With Pooley behind the three sticks, Southerton could rely upon receiving the best possible service, and roughly one-sixth of those 1,681 wickets fell to the Southerton-Pooley combination, with the stumpings exceeding the catches.

The partnership with the predatory Pooley extended far beyond the first-class game and flourished in a whole array of minor matches. Both of them were members of the United South of England Eleven, playing regularly in the 1860s and 1870s. Southerton began assisting the United South in 1866, and he appeared frequently in the ranks of the team for over a decade. A few of the contests rated the status of first-class, but the overwhelming majority of the fixtures consisted of "odds" matches against local twenty-twos. The opposition he encountered in most of these affairs stood little comparison with the quality of the batting displayed at The Oval and other first-class grounds. More often than not, the full analysis showing the number of runs conceded by the various bowlers was not kept, or at least not recorded for posterity. As might be imagined, "The Evergreen's" wily trundling was often pretty lethal whenever he confronted opponents whose limited skills were inadequate to cope with the problems of twist and turn presented to them. Although the complete statistics are not to hand, it can be maintained with absolute confidence that, in something like 100 matches, Southerton took well over 1,000 wickets. One of his most outstanding exploits occurred at Edinburgh, on May 23, 24, and 25, 1872, when the United South were contending against 22 of the Carlton and Edinburgh Clubs. "The Evergreen" captured 30 wickets (15 in each innings), but this herculean effort was all in vain, since the home team won by 64 runs, thanks to some rather spineless batting by the majority of Southerton's team-mates. Early in September of the following year, he luxuriated in a brief spell of glory in two consecutive matches. Against 22 of Lincoln, he took 15 or possibly 16 wickets in the first innings—the successful bowler's name is missing in one instance— and 11 in the second. Either the same night or the day after the conclusion of this match, the United South headed north for a brace of fixtures in Scotland. First port of call was Inverness, but the tedious, prolonged journey seems to have refreshed Southerton: against 22 of the North of Scotland, his match figures were 23 wickets for only 83 runs (10–49 and 13–34). He had his unproductive days at times, like anybody else, but he was one of the United South's most successful bowlers.

The United South of England Eleven was founded in the autumn of 1864, primarily with the object of yielding additional summer wages for the cream of the southern professionals. At times in the early years, the occasional amateur was invited to make up the numbers. The managers of the United South pulled off a dazzling coup, when they persuaded W.G. Grace to play for them, and later still, the Champion's younger brother, G.F. The Gloucestershire pair, joined subsequently by their cousin, W.R. Gilbert, became regular members of the Eleven, which was gradually transformed into a vehicle for providing a steady income for the highest paid amateurs in cricket. Consequently, Southerton and some of the other professionals whose appearances were frequent established a firm relationship with the members of the Grace family. "The Evergreen," in fact, was photographed with the two brothers in 1873. Dwarfed by the mighty figure of W.G. standing beside him, Southerton is grasping a ball in his right hand, which is resting lightly on the shoulder of the seated Fred Grace. There is a determined, no-nonsense look about the bewhiskered features beneath the brim of the hat. Doubtless, Jimmy was proud to pose with such eminent gentlemen, but he gives the impression of not feeling at all embarrassed at finding himself in their company.

Always civil to his social superiors, Southerton did not, however, conceive it necessary to kowtow slavishly and surrender his cherished principles. This independence of mind could easily be transformed into a spirit of stubborn obstinacy and a refusal to accept any other opinion but his own. Although feeling a certain amount of affection for the little genius of the off break, W.G., acting on the spur of the moment, was unable on one occasion to resist the temptation to play a trick upon him. Batting at number 9 for Surrey in the encounter with MCC, at The Oval, on July 25 and 26, 1870, Southerton slashed at a widish delivery outside the off-stump, and the ball rebounded from the turf into the hands of W.G. at point. Fully aware that the off-breaker sometimes shut his eyes when he was making a hit, the Champion indulged in a little joke, which unfortunately went wrong. Throwing up the ball, he called out, "That's a hot 'un, Jim!" and returned it to the bowler. To everybody's amazement, Southerton strode away from the wicket, ignoring the assurance of one of the fielders that he was not out. Ted Pooley, the non-striker, uttered a piercing whistle to attract his partner's attention, but W.G., rather unwisely, persisted with his little joke, saying, "Keep quiet, Pooley, and we'll have the laugh at him." The humour, sadly, turned rather sour in the end. All pleas and remonstrances to the departing batsman were of no avail. Southerton, in his own mind, was apparently convinced that he had given a legitimate catch and adamantly refused to continue with his innings.

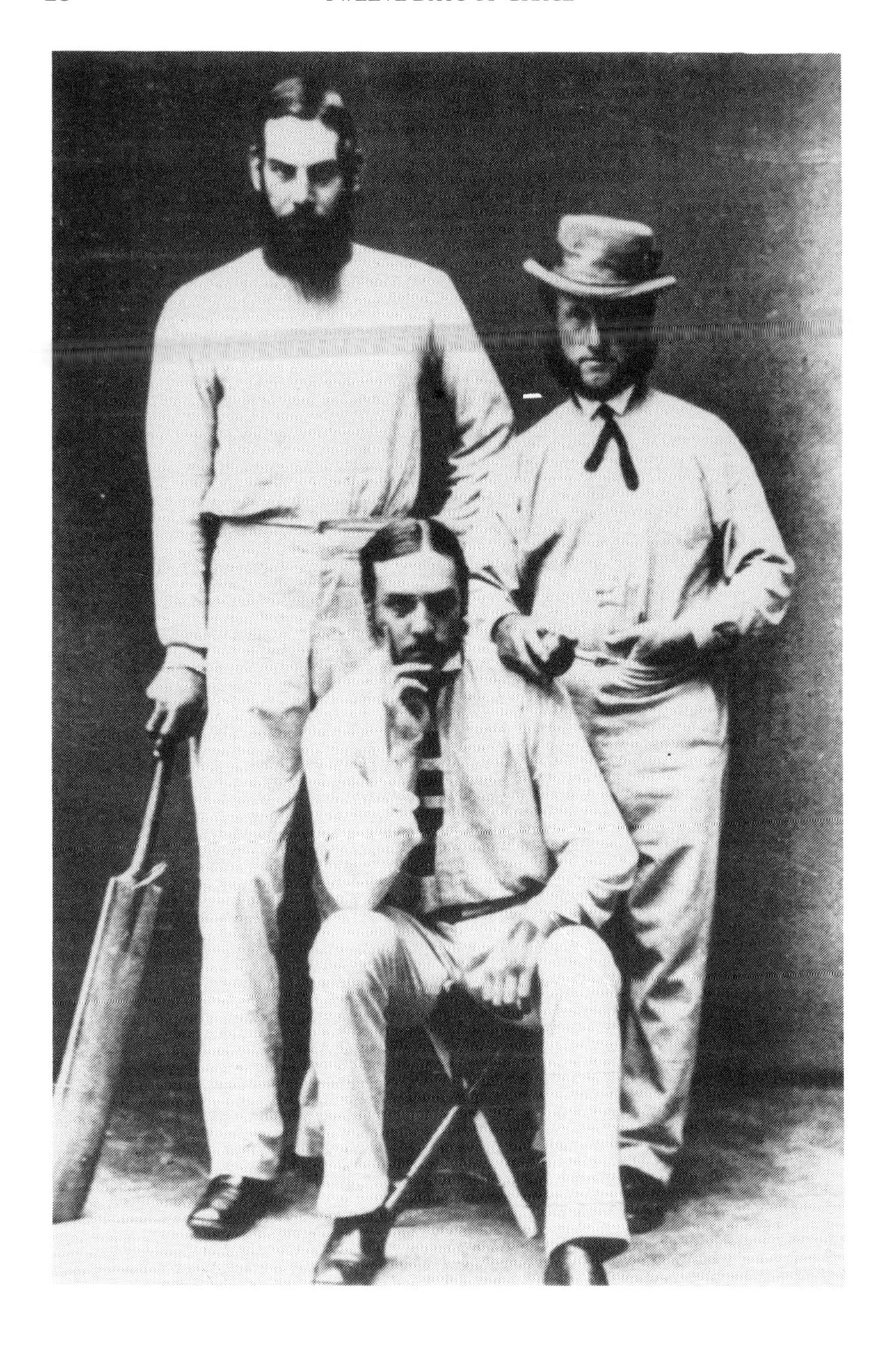

W. G. Grace, G. F. Grace, and James Southerton
Courtesy Roger Mann

The mode of dismissal varies in different score-sheets, the most apt being the version in *Scores and Biographies*, which reads "retired, thinking he was caught, 0."

Once, on a visit to Cambridge, W.G. was spending an hour or two in the company of several cricketing friends, and the conversation eventually narrowed down to the topic of the ideal method of countering a ball breaking back from the off, as bowled by Alfred Shaw and, with a greater twist, by James Southerton. The Champion, the acme of fluency with a bat in his hand, but not far from being a non-starter at speechifying and holding up his end in an abstruse discussion, sat silent as the air was filled with the babble of verbose theories. All at once, the room fell still, and one of the speakers turned to the Grand Old Man and asked him for his opinion on the weighty subject. The company hung on W.G.'s lips, hoping for a lucid explanation of the problem. They were not disappointed. Without any flim-flam or superfluous trimmings, the oracle opened his mouth and delivered a pearl of wisdom, saying, "I think you ought to put the bat against the ball."

When you are facing a foxy trundler like Southerton, putting the bat against the ball with reassuring confidence was sometimes easier said than done, even if your name were W.G. Grace. During the first fifteen years of the latter's career, he had many encounters with "The Evergreen" and did not always succeed in coming off the best, and there is ample evidence that Jimmy was well worthy of a place of honour in that select band of bowlers whom Grace found to be the most formidable. Only two of Southerton's contemporaries, it is believed, took the Champion's wicket on a greater number of occasions—his rival, Alfred Shaw, and Tom Emmett, the fast, left-handed, Yorkshire humorist, both of whom had the advantage of several more years to accomplish the task. "The Evergreen" disposed of W.G. thirty-two times, including 8 clean bowled. There were 19 catches and 1 stumping, and one-third of these stand to the account of the reliable old firm of Southerton and Pooley. In the match between Surrey and Gloucestershire, at The Oval, on June 7 and 8, 1875, the Champion's mode of dismissal in both innings reads "c Pooley b Southerton"—and for an aggregate of only 27 runs. Jimmy was well on the mark in this Surrey victory, with match figures of 12 wickets for 102 runs.

Ted Pooley, at loggerheads with the powerful authorities at The Oval in 1873, was not in his usual position behind the stumps, when Surrey had taken the field against Gloucestershire, at the College Ground, Clifton, on August 25. If only he had not strayed from the narrow paths of righteousness, he would have had the opportunity of witnessing at close range one of the more unusual bowling feats performed by his partner. The visitors' captain won the toss but put the home side in first, and the formidable pair of E.M. and W.G. Grace opened the batting. Almost immediately, the brothers were separated, when E.M. was dismissed "hit wicket" by Southerton for no score. W.G. enjoyed a better streak of luck and managed to reach 48, whereupon he suffered the same fate as E.M. It was no untimely accident, either, such as stepping too near the wicket or inadvertently nudging off a bail. The Champion's bat struck the stumps so hard that he smashed one of them clean out of the ground. "Hit wicket," it might be added, was a mode of dismissal rarely suffered by W.G.

The series Gentlemen *v* Players was a graveyard for the reputations of many a bowler, and some batsmen too, for that matter, and Southerton was no exception. He made his debut at The Oval, in 1870, at the age of forty-two, and was selected for the next six matches up to the end of 1872. Alfred Shaw had appeared also in four of them, but from 1873 onwards it was he who was chosen to assist the Players regularly, usually to the exclusion of Southerton, even for the fixtures at The Oval. "The Evergreen" was picked to play in the contest at Prince's Ground, on July 22 and 23, 1875, and made his ninth and final appearance at the same place, in 1877—aged forty-nine!—when his rival was laid low with illness throughout much of the season. In comparison with his career average of 14.44, Southerton showed a striking decline in the contests with the Gentlemen, taking 31 wickets at an average of 26.12. He recorded only one outstanding performance—in that match at Prince's Ground, in 1875, when he was teamed up with Shaw again. Operating unchanged throughout the whole proceedings, with Alfred as his partner at the other end, apart from one over, Southerton achieved match figures of 12 for 77 (6–38 and 6–39). This was the only occasion in the series when he reached 5 wickets in an innings and 10 in a match. He dismissed the Champion three times, twice by catches to the wicket-keeper, and once clean bowled.

It was the best of all possible worlds for W.G. Grace in the English winter of 1873–74: newly wed and on his honeymoon, he took his bride with him to Australia on the third tour of an English cricket team down under. The party, consisting of five amateurs and seven professionals, was far from being representative of the old country's real strength, since W.G. had experienced some difficulties and set-backs in making up the numbers, when several first-rate players were unavailable or declared themselves unable to agree to the terms offered to them. Among those professionals who accepted the engagement was James Southerton, who, with James Lillywhite, junior, the slow-medium, left-arm trundler from Sussex, received a lion's share of the bowling. The programme consisted of fifteen matches, none of which was first-class, against teams of fifteen, eighteen, twenty, or twenty-two opponents. Being minor affairs, the statistics have not been adequately established and show some slight inconsistencies in different accounts, but Southerton probably took 147 wickets at an average of a little over five and a-half runs each. As regards overall performance throughout the tour, Lillywhite had the edge with a larger tally of victims and a slightly lower average, but "The Evergreen" surpassed his partner on two notable occasions. Against 22 of Tasmania, at Launceston, on February 26, 27, and 28, 1874, he was by far the most successful bowler, with match figures of 23 wickets for 72 runs (13–33 and 10–39). This, however, was only his second best achievement with the ball. Earlier in the tour, against 22 of Warrnambool, in the middle of January, he took 24 wickets for only 58 runs (14–35 and 10–23), bowling unchanged with Lillywhite, and during the course of this match "Southerton earned the hat for three wickets in three successive balls."

Southerton would of a certainty have attained a higher aggregate of wickets if he had not stood down from the side to officiate as one of the umpires in two matches. He possessed the mental toughness necessary for the post and an excellent knowledge of the game, but he was a little vague about the niceties of some of the Laws. In the first of the two matches, at Castlemaine, in February 1874, it had been agreed that a hit going under the boundary rope would count four runs, and over five. W.G. played a towering stroke and had gone down the pitch once, when a fielder in the deep caught the ball but fell over the rope. Southerton flatly rejected the appeal ("it was out of bounds when he caught it") and was equally adamant in his albeit strange decision that W.G. should have only the single he had run added to his score rather than the five to which he felt he was entitled. The Champion knew his man and, after lodging one protest to Southerton, decided it would be politic to hold his peace, "for I should not have been surprised if he had changed his mind and given me out."

When recalling the famous incident of the bump ball catch at The Oval (1870), C.W. Alcock, the secretary of the Surrey Club, referred to W.G. Grace as one of Southerton's "great friends." Outwardly, the two may well have seemed on the best of terms, but there were evidently times during the 1873–74 tour of Australia when the off-breaker became disenchanted with the Champion. The evidence for this is preserved in the pages of a diary, which Southerton kept during the months he spent down under. One of the entries refers to an incident when the party were about to return by sea to Melbourne. Before the ship had even set sail, Grace, who was three sheets in the wind, took up a position in the stern and drunkenly blazed away with a gun at the gulls flying around him. This distasteful and even dangerous episode was not the only thing to arouse Southerton's disapproval. He was severely critical of the general behaviour of the amateurs in the party, and his private opinion on the quality of W.G.'s leadership went far beyond any simple absence of enthusiasm ("a damn bad captain").

In 1887–88, two separate English teams went on tour in Australia. This ticklish situation was nearly anticipated in 1876—77, but Fred Grace's arrangements to get up a side fell through, leaving the way clear for an all-professional Twelve to undertake an ambitious programme at the Antipodes. Four of them, including Lillywhite and Southerton, were veterans of the Champion's party of 1873–74. Remembering, perhaps, the amount of work imposed upon himself and Southerton under W.G., Jim Lillywhite, as captain and manager, took with him a team a little short on batting but rich in bowling resources. There were, in fact, too many bowlers, as Southerton, for one, was to discover to his cost. Of the twenty-three fixtures fulfilled, only three were first-class, the remainder being against various teams of "odds" in Australia and New Zealand. Southerton was included in the team in all but the first encounter of the tour against 22 of South Australia, at Adelaide, during the third week of November 1876. Here, however, he performed a useful auxiliary function, being entrusted with the preparation of the pitch. The Adelaide authorities were reluctant to use a roller lest the grass should be damaged and killed, but "The Evergreen," as usual, stuck to his guns. Persuading them to borrow the local Corporation roller with its team of four, he took hold of one of the horses by the head and guided the whole contraption out to the centre of the ground, producing a pitch that "was good, and played well throughout."

New South Wales provided the opposition in the initial first-class encounter, which took place at Sydney, on January 15 and 16, 1877. England won the toss and batted first, making 270. The home side, dismissed for 82, were compelled to follow on and had lost 6 wickets in their second innings, when play came to an end. Southerton's contribution to the proceedings consisted of 16 not out with the bat and one catch. Lillywhite employed six bowlers all told, but "The Evergreen" was not one of them.

The other first-class contests, which came off at Melbourne in the third week of March and a fortnight later, constitute the first two Test Matches between the two countries, resulting in one victory each. Once again, Jimmy Southerton could have had grounds for complaining that he had been largely left out in the cold, since he was put on in only one innings in each contest. His bowling figures in Test Matches were 7 wickets for 107 runs (average 15.28). When he took the field in the first encounter with Australia, "The Evergreen" established a record which still stands, and, moreover, is extremely unlikely ever to be taken from him. At the age of 49 years and 119 days, he is the oldest player to make his debut in Test cricket.

For this second tour of Australia, Southerton kept a diary once again, but that was not the limit of his literary endeavours, since he sent home reports of matches and events to *The Sportsman* as well. These talents for authorship, expressed also in his contribution to *James Lillywhite's Cricketers' Annual*, were inherited by his son, S.J., who achieved recognition as a journalist and statistician with the Cricket Reporting Agency and as the editor of *Wisden* for 1934 and 1935. A sense of grievance crept into some of Jimmy Southerton's observations on the management of the bowling throughout the 1876–77 tour. Alfred Shaw, he felt, was put on too frequently and kept on too long without relief, while he himself stood idly by, awaiting a spell with the ball which sometimes never came. There can be no doubt, however, that by now Alfred was the better bowler.

On his return from Australia in 1877, Southerton resumed his familiar niche in English cricket. No longer so effective as of old with his "peculiar twisters," he still managed to mark a sterling performance for Surrey against Middlesex, at The Oval, on August 9, 10, and 11, with match figures of 14 wickets for 92 runs (7–38 and 7–54). An additional cause for satisfaction was the dismissal for low scores in both innings of his old bugbear, Mr C.I. Thornton, though unfortunately for old time's sake Ted Pooley was not involved in either instance. Owing to the visit of D.W. Gregory's Australians in 1878, the veteran's benefit match was deferred until the following season. He was allocated the North *v* South contest, at The Oval, beginning on July 17, but the match lasted only two days, and the beneficiary cleared the modest sum of around £275. At Cirencester, on August 28, 29, and 30, 1879, he made his exit from first-class cricket. Pooley was in the Surrey team, and the three Grace brothers were assisting Gloucestershire. The trio made only 25 runs between them (W.G. 10, E.M. 7, G.F. 8), but the Champion atoned for his batting failure with match figures of 15 for 116. Southerton, alas, had little success, taking only 1 wicket—not one of the Graces and not with the assistance of Ted Pooley.

Between C.W. Alcock, the Surrey secretary, and Jimmy Southerton there existed a cordial relationship based on friendship and mutual respect. One day not long after Jimmy had returned from one of his tours to Australia, he was talking to the secretary, and during the conversation the latter mentioned that he was suffering from an upset liver. Southerton made no comment at the time, but saw this as an excellent opportunity for expressing his gratitude and esteem by

Alfred Shaw
"The Emperor of Bowlers"

stealth, and the next morning he approached his friend, saying he had a box of pills which would cure him. Alcock laughed, slipped the box into his pocket and forgot all about it until the evening, when he suddenly remembered Southerton's special panacea. Opening the box, he found it contained no bitter pills but a much more pleasant physic in the shape of a gold fob for a watch-chain, engraved with Alcock's initials "from J.S." On the following day, Alcock strove to hide his emotion and embarrassment by chiding Jimmy for throwing his money about, but the veteran smiled at the success of his little stratagem, saying, "I knew you would never accept the locket unless I got you to take it by some dodge." This treasured gift was still in Alcock's possession some thirty years later.

Although his playing days ended in 1879, Jimmy Southerton still maintained his connection with The Oval, where he continued to be employed as superintendent of the ground bowlers. His stern sense of duty never faltered, and when his friend Mr Alcock begged him to spare himself and give up bowling so much in the nets, his old familiar failing of obstinancy re-asserted itself, and he refused, saying, "they liked it." Doubtless "they" did, and doubtless so did Southerton, but his conscientious insistence on giving a fair day's work for a fair day's pay proved to be his undoing. While carrying out his duties, he contracted a severe chill, which developed into a fatal congestion of the lungs, and he died at Mitcham, on June 16, 1880. His dependants, happily, were more adequately provided for than the families of some other cricketers, since he left an estate of £1,500.

With his death at the early age of fifty-two, "The Evergreen" established another kind of personal record, albeit a melancholy one. Of all that long line of Test cricketers, who have passed beyond the green fields, he was the first to shuffle off this mortal coil.

CHAPTER THREE

Roger Iddison *"The Old-fashioned Yorkshireman"*

BOTH before and during W.G. Grace's long and uninterrupted reign over the cricket fields of England, the majority of the Yorkshire Eleven came from the towns, cities, and villages of the old West Riding—from the districts of Sheffield, Leeds, Huddersfield, Bradford, and Halifax. The professionals, occasionally leavened with a sparse sprinkling of amateurs, whose origins lay in that sector of the county, dominated the scene, often to the virtual exclusion of contenders from the other quarters of the shire. Not always, though. Much good cricket was played with enthusiasm elsewhere, in the York district, for instance, where there were many accomplished gentlemen whose skills were not to be despised, and in Hull and the remainder of the East Riding. Rich in cricketing talents also were various areas in the old North Riding, few more so around the 1850's and 1860's than Bedale. Midway between a small town and a large village, Bedale is situated slightly west of the Great North Road. Near by, a few miles roughly towards the north-west, stands Richmond, and beyond, to the north-east lie the County of Durham and Stockton-on-Tees. All were famous centres for the summer game in the last century, and Bedale, losing nothing in comparison with the others, produced some cricketers of considerable merit. Take, for example, the Morton brothers, George and John, strapping six-footers of gargantuan build, who enjoyed a high reputation in the north, particularly the former, an excellent wicket-keeper, who turned out occasionally for the All England Eleven in the 1850's, and who was cut off in his prime at the age of thirty-two. Equal in height to George Morton, but towering head and shoulders above him in fame and cricketing prowess, was another George, surnamed Anderson. The latter, known to some of his associates as "The Old Scotchman," was a splendid forcing batsman, a pillar of the All England Eleven for well over a decade and more, and a regular member of the Yorkshire side for several years. Inferior to Anderson and the Mortons in stature, but their superior when it came to all-round ability, was Roger Iddison, perhaps the greatest cricketer produced by Bedale, though some would award that title to George Anderson, on the grounds of his forceful and punishing batsmanship.

Born on September 15, 1834, Roger Iddison was junior in years to the two Georges of Bedale, nor could he match them in the matter of inches, being only 5 foot 8 inches in height. As regards bulk, however, he was not far behind them, especially Morton, since Roger weighed around 12 stone or more in the earlier portion of his career, and considerably in excess of this with the passage of time. As befitted a man originally employed in the occupation of butcher, the word "beefy" would best describe his appearance. An ideal advertisement for the rapid and ready sale of his wares, he was portrayed by one of his eminent and knowledgeable contemporaries as a "strong, stout, red-faced, healthy-looking man—a true type of the old-fashioned Yorkshireman." His stalwart figure, broad in the shoulders and beam, was one to arouse admiration and envy in those more poverty-stricken days—the end product, one would say, of a liberal consumption of quantities of good, fresh meat, loaves of wheaten bread, and strong, bitter beer. To be fair to Roger, though, he was possibly no more addicted to the pleasures of the well laden table or the foaming tankard of ale than many of his fellow players. Doubtless, over-indulgence at times may have contributed its moiety to the relentless process, but he seems to have been endowed with the type of physique which, in the natural order of things, succumbs easily and rapidly to the acquisition of superfluous fat. Portly, dapper, wearing handsome side-whiskers that thickened into increasing luxuriance, Roger presented an imposing presence to the outside world, instantly recognizable on and off the cricket field to most of the public, with whom he enjoyed a generous measure of popularity.

In his salad days, Roger was probably as active as any man standing at some distance from the pitch and dashing about to cut off the twos and the threes with ease and aplomb. He was, however, hardly noteworthy for performing brilliantly in that role, and the problem created by the inexorable augmentation of weight and bulk inevitably forced upon him the compelling necessity of seeking a less physically demanding position in the field. In *Jerks in from Short-leg,* a semi-comic treatise on cricket published during Iddison's heyday, the author was at pains to advise all captains to choose the stoutest man in the team to carry out the duties of point. Such an individual would of a certainty find it well nigh impossible "to get away from the warm ones, and what his hands miss his body will frequently embrace and hold fast." On a slightly more serious note, the writer added that alertness was an essential attribute for the fielder at point ("He mustn't be a

Rodger Iddison and George Anderson
Courtesy Roger Mann

sleepy chap"). It might, perhaps, be libellous to maintain that the mild satirist definitely had the Yorkshireman in mind when penning these lines. True enough, Roger eventually presented a massive figure virtually impenetrable to any batsman who fancied the cut. To characterise him as "sleepy," however, would be woefully wide of the mark. Point was one of the most important posts on the cricket field at that period of the game's history, and Roger's expertise was surpassed by few of his contemporaries. In all first-class contests, at point and elsewhere on occasions, he held 133 catches, averaging almost exactly one victim per match.

At the outset of his playing days, Iddison was a fast, round-arm bowler, who was good enough to achieve results in minor matches, first as a change and later as one of the principal trundlers of the many teams he assisted in the north of England. The Law, enacted in 1864, permitting a bowler to deliver the ball over-arm above the level of the shoulder, was of no personal concern to Roger when it came into effect. Possibly the same motive that induced him to abandon the out-field in favour of the more sedate duties of point was partly instrumental in persuading him to relinquish any ambition of achieving success as a first-rate fast bowler. A few years before the over-arm action became legal, he had changed his methods entirely by adopting the more crafty art of "the slows," and he attained some renown as a lob bowler. His delivery was calculated to perplex all but the most experienced batsmen. Hiding the ball from sight until the very last possible moment, he made a habit of suddenly producing it as though from a concealed side-pocket just underneath his arm-pit and tossing it up with perfidious nonchalance towards his opponent, "just as one would chuck a penny to a beggar." The amount of break he could achieve from leg to off was enormous, sometimes as much as two feet or more, causing unhappy batsmen to flounder helplessly or dash wildly down the pitch into the jaws of impending destruction. Either they failed to connect and fell easy victims to the expectant stumper or, equally deceived by the extravagant bias applied to the ball, they gave a simple catch.

Roger's lobs often proved to be of immense value to his side in minor affairs against what was often somewhat mediocre opposition, and he achieved a fair amount of success in first-class contests, when he came on as a change or even, as sometimes happened, as an opening bowler. There was one famous occasion, however, when he met his Waterloo in a match at Lord's towards the end of his career. His conqueror was William Yardley, of Cambridge University, Kent, and MCC, who scored the first ever century in the varsity match in 1870 and set the seal on his performance by recording the second two years later.

Yardley, an excellent amateur batsman who was lost to the first-class game all too soon, passed on his recollections of the incident to a journalist and cricket writer over twenty years later. He took great delight in murdering slow, under-arm bowling, though Roger seems to have been unaware of this or to have forgotten it, since he was eager to try his luck. There was some good-natured banter between batsman and bowler as the latter was preparing to send down the first delivery of the (four-ball) over, with Yardley saying, "Roger, I'll bet you half-a-sovereign that I'll make more runs than you will bowl me balls." The bluff, burly Yorkshireman accepted the proposed wager without a moment's hesitation, and one of the umpires was soon persuaded to take temporary possession of the two coins and act as the stakeholder.

Roger's first delivery was one of his special, high-tossed teasers. It created no problem for Yardley, who stepped out of his ground and calmly dismissed the ball into the distance for four runs. Some more banter followed, during which Roger turned down his adversary's offer of another bet that he wouldn't manage to get Yardley's wicket in that particular over. It was just as well that the spirit of hard-headed northern prudence prevailed, otherwise Roger would have wasted his "brass." The second and third deliveries were worth two runs each to the batsman, who refused to go for a three and lose the strike, while the fourth yielded another four, making a grand total of 12 runs off the four balls. As soon as "over" had been called, Roger went and retrieved the two half-sovereigns from the umpire and presented them immediately to the surprised winner. The latter told the chastened but honest lobster that he could keep his own stake, provided he would expend it in standing treat to the other professionals in his team. A second condition exacted was Roger's willingness to refrain from bowling any more of his "slows" to Yardley, "for his own reputation's sake." Presumably, Roger agreed to these stipulations to a certain extent, but he was adamant in his refusal to accept the wicked suggestion to try another over for the same stakes on Yardley's partner, who had nearly run himself out in his eagerness to steal the strike. This incident may have taken place in the meeting between MCC and Yorkshire, at the end of May 1872, when Roger experienced the satisfaction—for the only time in important matches—of capturing W.G.'s wicket. Perhaps the Champion's luncheon disagreed with him on this occasion, seeing that Roger's third delivery after the resumption of play clean bowled him "neck and heels."

Throughout his first-class career, beginning in 1853 and ending in 1876, though playing little after 1872, Iddison took 209 wickets at an average of 16.73, plus 2 more for which the column of runs conceded is not available. His best performance in an innings occurred in the fixture between Yorkshire and Nottinghamshire, at Bradford, on June 22, 23, and 24, 1863, when he was by far the most successful bowler for either side, taking 7 wickets for only 30 runs. His best match figures were obtained while he was assisting a combined eleven of Yorkshire, with Stockton-on-Tees (or Durham County) against Cambridgeshire, at Stockton, on July 25, 26, and 27, 1861. Bowling unchanged with the same partner throughout both the visitors' innings, he dismissed 10 batsmen at the low cost of only 67 runs (5–19 and 5–48). Only 9 wickets fell in each innings, with Cambridgeshire being a man short.

Of little repute as a batsman at the beginning of his career, Roger was not very much more than proverbial "cross-batted village-greener," but batting, as it turned out, was the department of the game in which he eventually made his mark. Teaching himself to play with a more orthodox straightness—though not, at first, as straight as some of the critics wished—he developed a confident technique of solid defence. He had no perceptible aspirations to be recognized as a pretty stylist, but, like any Yorkshireman worth his salt then and in subsequent ages, he was adept at meeting any crisis with grim determination. Time and time again, he showed himself capable of remaining at the wickets for long periods, coping successfully with hostile pace bowling and the vagaries of sub-standard pitches. His stance was somewhat unusual for those days: his feet were not splayed out at right angles but positioned parallel to the popping crease with both toes aligned in the direction of point. While waiting to receive the ball, he used to make a strange movement with his left leg, either a nervous twitch of anticipation or nothing more than an involuntary reflex action of which he may not have been aware. The development of his defensive powers was not the be-all and end-all of his batting. Exploiting the natural advantages of his sturdy thews and limbs, he excelled at the drive, especially to the off, and was famous for the impressive might of his hitting to leg. There were, of course, one or two flaws in the overall technique of his batting. Impeded by his bulk from taking many sharp singles helter-skelter down the pitch or abruptly halting his progress and scrambling back to safety, he was always liable to be run out, and his tendency to leave his ground could often prove fatal to the preservation of his wicket. Another failing, probably arising out of a desire to establish his confidence, was his notorious idiosyncrasy of always playing forward to the first ball he received. Once, when he was almost forty years old, and his foibles were well known, he was taking part in a minor match at Dudley. Aware that his batting no longer justified a claim to a high position in the order, Roger, as captain, had put himself down at number 9. He was not, perhaps, too pleased at the feeble performance of the earlier batsmen, but he kept his pecker up by chatting to Alf

Smith, one of his team-mates. Treating Smith as his personal confidant, Roger launched himself into a lengthy monologue, saying how fit and well he was feeling, and how certain he was of making a good score. When the time came for the portly captain to go in, another member of the batting side who had overheard Iddison's oration nudged Smith and said, "Come, Alf, let's see Roger run the first one down." Automatically and unwisely playing forward as usual to the first delivery he faced from a wily bowler, he spooned up a simple return catch and departed crestfallen to the dressing-tent. Alf Smith was totally incapable of concealing his mirth, and his woebegone skipper hurled down his cap in disgust, turned sharply on his laughing friend and exclaimed angrily, "Oh, hang it, Smith, *I was too fit!*" I have serious doubts about the comparative mildness of the language as reported, since Roger was renowned for his colourful, uninhibited vocabulary.

In spite of his ups and downs, "the Old-fashioned Yorkshireman" was one of the most successful batsmen for several years. He never scored 1000 runs in a season—very few, indeed, did in Roger's time—and his highest aggregate, in 10 matches, was 460 at an average of 32.85 in 1867. From that year to 1870, he appeared in the top twenty of the national batting averages, occupying the third place in 1867 and 1869. His final average for his career was 18.76, and he scored 2 centuries, the best being 112 for Yorkshire against Cambridgeshire, at Hunslet, on July 12 and 13, 1869, when he kept up his wicket for over five hours, a feat which was acknowledged by the presentation of £5. In the following season, when Yorkshire encountered Surrey, at The Oval, at the end of August, another award came his way, when he scored 11 and 77. The next highest contributions on his side was 20 and on his opponents' 26. Although two of the Yorkshire bowlers shared 19 of the Surrey wickets between them, Roger was selected to receive "A silver cup offered by a Yorkshire Gentleman to the best all-round performance of one of the Yorkshire Eleven."

Such performances lay far away in the future, when Roger Iddison, at the age of only fifteen, began playing for his native place. Nor were his activities confined merely to Bedale matches, for in 1852 he began to branch out by appearing for Stockton-on-Tees, whom he assisted on a professional basis several times in subsequent seasons. Although Bedale continued to claim his services throughout much of the 1850s, Roger was signed up on special engagements to assist local teams in Yorkshire in their encounters with the All England and United All England Elevens. There was, of course, nothing particularly unusual in this: many professionals, whose careers coincided with the period when the itinerant elevens were travelling through the length and breadth of the country, were only too glad to seize the opportunity to earn extra match fees, regardless of the fact that they had little or more often absolutely no genuine connection with the clubs seeking their services on a temporary basis. It was a question of exploiting those natural gifts and going "where t' money is," and Roger betrayed no aversion to casting his net over an ever increasing compass, accepting engagements in neighbouring counties, such as Durham, Lancashire, and Lincolnshire.

"The Old-fashioned Yorkshireman," however, was not content to rub along with merely a succession of three-day contracts necessitating laborious journeys by rail to different localities in the north of England. However lucrative they may have been by the accepted standards of the time, a certain amount of wear and tear on the human frame—especially one as considerable as Roger's—was the inevitable consequence of racketing about the countryside. Far less arduous, since much of the travelling was eliminated, was employment as a coach or as a club professional. Of the latter, the scope was not limited solely to batting and bowling in matches, but also often involved some of the duties required of a coach as well as the care and maintenance of the club ground. As a coach, employed throughout a period of several weeks, Roger served some time at three of the leading public schools, namely, Marlborough, Uppingham, and Harrow. In such appointments, his equable temperament as much as his cricketing abilities stood him in good stead, prompting one of his pupils at Uppingham to remember him many years later as "a genial, thick-set man, and a slow bowler." I don't suppose that the quality of Roger's batting made much of a lasting impression on many of those he was called upon to instruct, since a school coach was required to spend most of his time bowling to budding batsmen.

Much more numerous were the engagements Iddison obtained with various clubs. Several of these in the early years were within striking distance of Bedale, and although the details are rather imprecise, it is likely that they were of comparatively short duration. In order to secure a more permanent billet, he found it necessary to uproot himself from his native county and migrate with bag and baggage over the Pennines to the Manchester district, where cricket was a more lucrative and thriving concern. In 1859 and the next two seasons, he was engaged by the Broughton Club, one of the most flourishing organizations in the area. Highly esteemed by his employers, he played regularly in the club matches, achieving a fair amount of local fame as one of the leading professionals in the neighbourhood. He was also shrewd enough to exploit his popularity and reputation by forming a business partnership with his younger brother, William Holdsworth Iddison, and opening a shop for the sale of sporting goods at Manchester. Not long afterwards, around 1864, he spent some three seasons with the Whalley Club, also in Lancashire, and during this time Roger was the immediate and unwitting cause of precipitating a far-reaching crisis, which created a profound disturbance in the world of English cricket throughout the remainder of the 1860s.

Roger made his debut in first-class cricket at the age of eighteen, when he assisted 14 of Yorkshire against the United All England Eleven, at Sheffield, on June 6 and 7, 1853. Batting low in the order, he made 4 and 0 not out, and held one catch, but he was not called upon to take a turn with the ball. On the basis of the sparse details of his previous form available to us, it is difficult to justify his selection for such an important match except on the grounds of expediency. From 1854 to 1856, he appeared in one first-class contest per season without distinguishing himself particularly, apart from holding six catches on one occasion. The most interesting of these three fixtures, though hardly from Roger's point of view, was the encounter between Yorkshire and Sussex, at Bramall Lane, Sheffield, on August 27, 28, and 29, 1855. An easy victory by an innings and 117 runs to the visitors owed much to their number one batsman, John Wisden, who marked 148, recording his highest score in the first-class game. Roger's own contribution was much more modest. In 1861, he appeared in four important matches, and in the following season the number rose to ten. The bulk of his career, in fact, lay in the period 1862 to 1872, when he notched up 115 of his total 134 appearances in first-class cricket and achieved a batting average slightly in excess of 20 runs per innings—a praiseworthy record for those days, when batsmen had to cope with bumpy, well grassed pitches and a succession of rearing bouncers and wicked shooters.

A regular member of the Yorkshire Eleven for most of the time in the 1860s and as far on as 1872, Roger's role in the team was not limited to batting, fielding, and operating as a bowler when a change was required. He soon developed an excellent knowledge of all the ins and outs of the game, exhibiting a flair for leadership, and as early as 1861 he was the Yorkshire captain, even though one or two of the side were his seniors. Shrewd and pragmatic in his approach, he had an infinite capacity for weighing up the situation and dealing with all eventualities. His obvious talent for managing affairs both on and off the field extended far beyond his service with Yorkshire, and he carried out the duties of skipper in other spheres. One of the best professional captains of his time, Roger could usually be relied upon to control the course of events with an air of solid, unflappable confidence, though if things went awry he occasionally became irritable and expressed his feelings in no uncertain terms, becoming very "effusive in his vernacular." Once, when an absolute sitter of a slip-catch eluded the butterfingers of a tall, dozy, gangling individual called Bill Bosomworth, Roger was totally unable to contain his pent-up feelings and yelled out,"Why don't you keep your eyes open, you bloody great ostrich?" The somnolent Bosomworth's rejoinder, if any, to this colourful invective, does not seem to have been preserved.

In Roger's time, when county matches were by no means frequent events, little attention was paid to the demands of stringent qualifications until shortly before his days on the cricket field came to an end. A few individuals, as we have seen in the case of James Southerton, suffered no misgivings about assisting more than one county in the same season. Should any conflict of interests arise, birth usually exerted a priority over residence, and Yorkshire always had the first call on Roger's services. By virtue of his engagements as a professional with the Broughton and Whalley Clubs and his business operations at Manchester, he established a residential qualification, and when not required by the White Rose he had no compunction about assisting the Red Rose and pocketing a match fee. In the intervals between playing for Yorkshire and other teams, he found the time to turn out for Lancashire in sixteen matches between 1865 and 1870. His batting average for his adopted shire, at 23.88, was better than his record for Yorkshire. Against Surrey, at The Oval, on July 19, 20, and 21, 1866, he opened the batting, scoring 49 at his first attempt and 106 at his second. This fixture marked the first encounter between these two teams as well as the first century for Lancashire in a county match.

An event with far-reaching consequences came off in the winter of 1861–62. Messrs Spiers and Pond, an Australian firm of caterers, dispatched a representative back to the old country to arrange for a team of English cricketers to undertake a tour down under. There were some thorny problems to be overcome, since some of the leading players were far from satisfied with the terms offered (quoted at £150 and all expenses paid), and they refused to make the trip. At his wits' end, but determined not to return empty-handed, the Melbourne caterers' agent resolved to seek aid from the authorities at The Oval and eventually twelve professionals signed contracts to take part in the first ever tour of Australia. Less than half of them could make any sort of claim to a place among the best in England, and some were not far removed from being virtually novices in the matter of representative cricket. One of two Yorkshiremen in the party, Roger had still to make his name to all intents and purposes. In fact, his performance on the tour was distinctly advantageous in advancing his prospects, since his first-class career in England began to blossom in the following season.

Under the captaincy of H.H. Stephenson, the Surrey all-rounder, the

English team, less one member who had gone on ahead, set sail from Liverpool on October 21 and arrived at Melbourne on Christmas Eve. The programme, which began on January 1, 1862, and ended on March 22, consisted of twelve fixtures against "odds," usually 22 opponents, and two extra eleven-a-side contests, one of which has been accredited as first-class. Roger, who did not miss a single match, had a very satisfactory tour in all departments of the game. He came fifth in the order of the batsmen with an average of 13.55, was the most successful fielder with 27 catches, and was employed more frequently as a bowler than any other member of the team. The leading wicket-taker, he accounted for 109 victims at an average of 6.79, plus 3 more for which the analysis was not reported. His best performance was reserved for the final match at Melbourne. Stephenson's men were contending against 22 of Victoria, and Roger far outstripped his team-mates by achieving match figures of 22 wickets for 105 runs (9–37 and 13–68).

Enjoying the supreme advantage of being a novelty in those distant parts, the members of the English team were fêted, wined and dined, and showered with presents. Roger had his share of all this largesse and wrote home, saying, "We are made a great fuss of; the Queen herself could not have been treated better." Although the Englishmen were twice defeated by teams of twenty-two opponents, Roger was apparently not particularly enthusiastic about the opposition's standard of play. On the other hand, he was profoundly impressed by the drinking capacity of some of the local inhabitants he encountered *(Plus ça change . . .)*.

Roger made his debut for the Players against the Gentlemen, at Lord's, on July 14 and 15, 1862. Opening the batting, he scored 11 in his first innings and followed this in his second with an excellent knock of 62, the highest individual figure of the match. He also appeared in the fixtures at The Oval in 1863 and 1864. But for unfortunate circumstances, he would have stood a good chance for further selection in the next few years. His aggregate in the three matches was 169 runs at an average of 33.80, but his bowling was attended by precious little success—only 1 wicket at a cost of 120 runs. Other "grand matches" in which he participated from time to time were a perennial favourite of the 1860s and 1870s, North *v* South, and England *v* a county or a combined team drawn from two. Some of the contests pitting North against South were rather dubious affairs, with many of the best players, both amateur and professional, unable for a variety of reasons to put in an appearance, and the deceptive grandiloquence of the title given to the match was largely a means of justifying a financial speculation on the part of the promoters. On one or two occasions, however, an aura of respectability was conferred upon these contests outside of the London grounds, when they were specifically designated as benefit matches in recognition of the services rendered to the cause of cricket by some deserving professional, either while he was still playing or after his retirement.

Some idea of "The Old-fashioned Yorkshireman's" popularity in many circles may be deduced from the fact that at least three matches were arranged in which he figured as the sole or partial beneficiary. The first of these occurred on September 22 and 23, 1865, at Whalley, in Lancashire, arising out of his engagement as the club professional. In an eleven-a-side match between two teams containing some reputable names, the Gentlemen of Lancashire beat the Players of Lancashire by 6 runs. I do not believe that the convention of according "the complimentary one" to the beneficiary had already been firmly established in those days. At any rate, it was certainly not observed in this match, since Roger failed to trouble the scorers in his first innings. He was more fortunate in the second, when he was the most successful batsman for the professional eleven with an undefeated 31. Immediately afterwards, he was one of five Yorkshire players who shared the proceeds of a match got up on the old Hyde Park Ground, Sheffield, between 18 Gentlemen of the North and the All England Eleven, though it is possible that this affair was not very profitable.

Of much greater importance was the benefit awarded by Yorkshire to Roger, who was characterized in a leading cricket annual as "one of the most sterling professionals of the day." W.G. Grace, then at the height of his youthful fame, was much in demand as a gilt-edged guarantee to swell the attendance on any ground in the country, and Roger could count himself fortunate that, as his complimentary match, he was given the first appearance of Gloucestershire at Bramall Lane, Sheffield, on July 29, 30, and 31, 1872. Yorkshire were, unfortunately, unable to command their full strength, although fast bowler George Freeman, as a token of friendship, consented to come out of semi-retirement in honour of the occasion. The visitors won the toss and elected to bat, and when play was brought to an end at five o'clock, they had scored 208 without losing a wicket, the Champion having made 132. Luke Greenwood, one of the Yorkshire bowlers condemned to toil fruitlessly throughout the 29th, received a telegram from an acquaintance requesting him to wire back the state of the game. "We have not got a wicket yet," was Luke's reply, "but are hoping to get one every day." It was the current practice at Bramall Lane to give a shilling to any member of the public who returned a lost ball, and when W.G. had lofted one of the perspiring Luke's deliveries over square-leg and out of the ground, an old lady appeared after a short interval clutching her prize. Approaching Luke, she demanded the customary payment, but the unfortunate bowler rose to the occasion, saying, "Nah, yon's him that hit it; yo mun go to him for t'brass." Nothing daunted, the old lady walked down the pitch and succeeded in persuading the highly amused Champion to hand over her fee.

The first Gloucestershire wicket fell with the total at 238, when W.G. surrendered his wicket to the long-suffering Luke Greenwood for 150. In reply to the visitors' eventual score of 294, the home side could manage only 66 runs in their first innings and were bundled out for 116 in their second attempt. The victory belonged largely to W.G., after pulverising the Yorkshire attack with such merciless severity, he went on to achieve match figures of 15 wickets for 79 runs (8–33 and 7–46). One of his victims in both innings was the beneficiary, who made 4 and a back-to-the-wall 34. Roger, one imagines, was able to swallow the humiliation of defeat with his face wreathed in smiles. His benefit turned out to be a "bumper," since the attendance throughout the three days was well over 16,000.

It will be remembered that, in the 1850s and thereafter, Roger was one of those professionals who were quite often engaged to assist local twenty-twos against the itinerant elevens. He was not, however, always to be found in the ranks of the opposition. As a sort of prototype of the average paid cricketer, he was only too willing to earn his wages when and wherever the opportunity presented itself, and in his time he assisted all the principal travelling teams, with the not unnatural exception of the United South of England Eleven. In 1854, he made his debut and solitary appearance for the season with the All England Eleven. Two years later, he had a more extended trial but failed to establish himself in the side. His service with the AEE continued on an intermittent basis up to 1869, but he was far from being a regular member of the team. Appearing in only 21 matches, he achieved little in the way of batting and not much more as a bowler, but he played his part in the field.

Although Roger fell short of making his mark with the All Englanders, he was far more successful with their principal rivals, the United All England Eleven, who had provided the opposition when he made his debut in important matches with 14 of Yorkshire in 1853. As a Given Man, assisting local teams of "odds," he encountered the United Eleven several times in the next few years. His best performance in this role occurred at Hovingham Hall Park, in September 1853, when he starred as easily the top scorer (20 and 55) for 22 of the Hovingham Club in an unfinished match, in which he also took 5 wickets. At Langton Wold, in Yorkshire, two years later, he atoned for a mediocre display of batting by recording match figures of 10 for 49 (5–19 and 5–30). In his other meetings with the United, however, his achievements were evidently considered insufficient to warrant an invitation to join the Eleven. His performance while on tour in Australia in the English winter of 1861–62 no doubt served as a reminder to John Wisden, the United captain, and his emergence as a recognized first-class cricketer coincided with the beginning of his service with Wisden's men. Playing in eleven of the fifteen United fixtures in 1862, his appearances in the next two seasons were probably limited by other duties, such as those of club professional, but from 1865 to 1869 he was a regular and established member of the UAEE, missing only ten matches. In all, he assisted the United 64 times, attaining a batting average of just over 17—a solid and satisfactory achievement, considering that all but eight of the fixtures were contests against "odds." He held some 65 catches and proved his mettle as a bowler with 57 wickets at an average of 9.73. This, however, is not the whole story, because he claimed 305 more victims when the analysis was not recorded. His best performance in one innings was 15 wickets, and in a match 25.

Roger made his debut for the United in the annual fixture with the All England Eleven, at Lord's on June 9, 10, and 11, 1862, and was ever present for the remainder of the series of encounters between the Two Elevens of England, which came to an end in 1869. He was soon recognized as one of the mainstays of the UAEE in these hard-fought, first-class contests, coming second in the final batting table with the high average of 23, which surpassed the figure attained by the best All England man. Only 6 catches came his way, probably because a more senior member of the team exercised the privilege of occupying the post of point. As an occasional bowler in four of the matches, he took 12 wickets at 10.08 each with his lobs.

Trouble was brewing between north and south in the early 1860s, and matters came to a head in 1864. An innocent victim of circumstances, Roger was the final cause of a rupture between the two sections of the country. A North *v* South match had been arranged to take place at Islington, in the first week in September, and he was commissioned to get up the northern side. His task turned out to be virtually impossible, since most of the northern professionals had previous commitments to appear in fixtures against teams of "odds," while the club employing him exerted a prior claim on his services. He succeeded in scraping together a scratch side to represent the North and nominated his brother, W.H., to be his deputy. The latter, unfortunately, failed to turn up, and the absence of Roger and most of the leading northern "cracks" was treated as a deliberate insult by the southern professionals, many of them Surrey men. They issued a tit-for-tat statement, declaring their refusal to take part in another

North *v* South contest, and in the autumn they cancelled their membership in the All England and United All England Elevens and formed a new body call the United South of England Eleven. The northerners, in their turn, interpreted these manœuvres as a blatant attempt to break up the two older elevens with the dire threat of a loss of summer wages. This schism between north and south, which lasted up to 1869, had other consequences, as far as Roger was concerned. Banding together with four of his county team-mates, he became embroiled with the powerful Sheffield committee, and all five were suspended for refusing to play in an encounter with Surrey in 1865. There was some sympathy for the culprits in other circles, hence the two benefit matches of the same year previously mentioned. Roger and all but one of the group made their peace at different times with the committee and returned to the fold, but "the Old-fashioned Yorkshireman" was never again selected to assist the Players against the Gentlemen.

Undismayed by these experiences and mindful, perhaps, of the fact that he would not be able to continue playing after a few more years because of his weight problem, Roger decided to channel some of his energy into managerial activities by becoming one of the leading cricket entrepreneurs in the north. When the old United All England Eleven ceased to exist in 1869, he endeavoured to fill the gap by forming, in collaboration with his friend George Freeman, the United North of England Eleven, whose operations began in 1870. During the first three seasons of the United North's existence, he appeared in all but two of the matches, but it soon became obvious that public interest in the activities of itinerant teams was on the wane, unless W. G. Grace was playing. Before the final collapse of the United North, Roger played his part in the foundation of yet another body called the Yorkshire United County Cricket Club. The original aims of this organization were to spread and maintain an interest in cricket throughout the county and "to give to rising players opportunities for distinguishing themselves." Yorkshire United did not enjoy universal popularity in the shire and, as influence of such individuals as Roger declined, this Eleven became virtually identical with an itinerant team, seeing that its principal object seemed to be the provision of wages for the regular professionals in the interval between bona fide county matches.

As the very model of a confirmed getter-up and manager of a variety of matches, Roger was immortalized in an amusing chapter in W. E. W. Collins' book, *Leaves from . . . An old Country Cricketer's Diary*. Thinly disguised—though "thinly" is hardly an appropriate epithet in this context—he appears as "Roger Itchinson," captain and manager of the All England Eleven, a position which the original, of course, never held, but that is only a minor matter in this instance. Speaking in a literary and occasionally eccentric Yorkshire dialect with a smattering of Mummerset, he is described as pulling down "the scale at seventeen stone." Collins may not have been guilty of too much exaggeration in this delineation of Roger's dimensions. As early as 1873, another writer observed that the burly Yorkshireman appeared "to be going the way of all flesh, or to be failing proportionately as the accumulation of flesh becomes more decided," while the 1876 edition of one of the cricket annuals records Roger's weight as 15 stone.

As one of the secretaries of the United North of England Eleven and later Yorkshire United, Roger was associated with Lord Londesborough, one of the most munificent patrons of cricket in Yorkshire and elsewhere, one of the founders of the Scarborough Cricket Festival, and President of MCC in 1876. From time to time, the generous peer employed Roger as his cricket agent to get up matches and engage players. Their relationship was cordial, with no bargaining and quibbling about expenses. A cheque for the required amount was always handed over to the agent without demur, inducing Roger to declare, " 'Is Lordship just 'angs 'is purse on the gate and lets anyone 'elp 'issen as likes."

Apart from the occasional Yorkshire fixture, most of the matches got up by Roger for his employer were minor affairs. Several took place near the Londesborough residence at Lyndhurst, Hampshire, and in 1876 Yorkshire United contended against the New Forest Rangers and subsequently 16 of the New Forest. One of several well known amateurs assisting the local sides was R. G. Hargreaves, who never reached the first rank as a cricketer but achieved a more durable sort of fame by marrying Miss Alice Liddell, the original inspiration of Lewis Carrol's *Alice in Wonderland.* At luncheon one day during the course of one of these matches, Roger was tucking in at the professionals' table. Selecting a succulent plum for dessert, he found himself disputing its possession with a tenacious wasp and, according to an ominous rumour, had the misfortune to swallow both. A high ecclesiastical dignitary is said to have swallowed a bumble-bee with fatal consequences. Roger was more fortunate, since, said a reporter, "a strong emetic administered by a friendly hand unhoused the arch traitor in the Yorkshire camp, and [it] now lies embalmed in Roger's curiosity chest, as an emblem of his third visit to Lyndhurst." One cannot help feeling that the Victorian craze for collecting curios was taken to extremes on this occasion.

For about twenty years, Roger was one of the most popular residents of York, where he lived a full life, getting up matches, selling sporting goods, and working as an auctioneer and commission agent. According to one of his cricketing contemporaries, he "looked the picture of health" in the mid-1880s, but his hale and hearty appearance eventually succumbed to the inroads of a fatal malady. Like Alfred Mynn, another cricketer of massive proportions, he fell victim to diabetes. This incurable disease was complicated by the onset of consumption, and after several months' suffering Roger died on March 19, 1890, at the age of 55. A host of mourners and "sympathising friends"—among them his brother, W. H. Iddison, and George Freeman, his team-mate in many a cricket match—attended the funeral. There would have been many more but for the inconvenience of the time and date (Saturday afternoon) arranged for the interment in York Cemetery. Among the many floral tributes was a reminder of the deceased's original occupation in the shape of "a handsome wreath . . . sent in a glass case by the butchers of the Shambles"—the narrow, picturesque, little street destined in the fullness of time to be converted into one of the major tourist attractions in the city of York.

CHAPTER FOUR

R. P. Carpenter "The Old Gardener"

In the eyes of the older generation at one time, there was no finer batsman among the professionals than George Parr, "The Lion of the North." Widely acknowledged as the successor to Fuller Pilch, George bore his honours with dignity and composure, sublimely confident for several years that there was nobody of sufficient merit to wrest from his grip the coveted title of premier batsman of England. By about 1860, however, when George was approaching his middle thirties, younger rivals had arisen to pose a threat to his hitherto undisputed right to the crown. From his own county of Nottinghamshire came his friend and protégé Richard Daft, a graceful, stylish player with a solid defence and a developing array in scoring strokes. Daft was not the only challenger in the lists. Two more contestants bidding fair to supplant "The Lion of the North" had also appeared to stake their claims in the persons of Thomas Hayward and Robert Carpenter, both of them Cambridgeshire men. Since these two aspirants came from the same county, the debate was side-tracked from the question of Parr's supremacy to a prolonged argument over *their* comparative merits. Suffice it to say, for the time being that Hayward could be regarded as the more brilliant and Carpenter the more durable.

Born at Cambridge, on November 18, 1830, Robert Pearson Carpenter began his working life by following the trade of bootcloser. This occupation, however worthy it may be, evidently aroused very little enthusiasm in him as a permanent means of earning his daily bread. Like several of his fellow townsmen, who went on to make a name for themselves on the cricket field, he fell under the spell of the more enthralling atmosphere pervading Parker's Piece in his native town. Opportunities for perfecting his innate talents on that famous ground were not neglected, and gradually he resolved to adopt cricket as a full-time career—a decision from which, in one way or another, he never wavered for the remainder of his active life, which, as far as Bob Carpenter was concerned, lasted until shortly before his death. A

TDG—C

modest beginning as a club professional at Godmanchester in 1854 led on to a three-year engagement at Ipswich, a brief but profitable stint at Birkenhead, and a temporary position coaching the boys at Marlborough College in 1859 and 1860. By then, however, he had already ascended rapidly to the highest ranks as a professional cricketer with a national reputation, secure in the knowledge of being able to earn regular wages throughout the summer months.

Fairish of complexion, with short, smoothly brushed hair and a carefully nurtured growth of whiskers encircling his face and meeting eventually under his chin, Bob Carpenter was of medium height and weighed between 11 and 12 stone in his heyday, though he put on more flesh in the twilight of his career as a player. A strong, sturdy man, robust in both body and mind, he was fortunate enough to possess an excellent constitution, and his infrequent absences from the cricket field arose from temporary injuries rather than recurring bouts of ill-health. In this he was an exception among some of his team-mates, since more than one of his Cambridge contemporaries succumbed early in life to the onset of debilitating diseases and were carried off when barely past their prime. Not so Bob Carpenter, who was rarely missing from the action, and who continued to play until he finally withdrew into honourable retirement.

As a bowler, Carpenter was not much to speak of against anything beyond rather fragile opposition. Delivering at varying pace with an under-arm action, he enjoyed some success early in his career in minor contests, but he was rarely given a spell with the ball in first-class matches. But if the quality of his bowling against experienced opponents was not much more than negligible, by no stretch of the imagination could the same be said of his fielding. He began by taking the post of long-stop, and it is worth recording in this connection that, in the absence of a regular stumper, he stepped into the breach on several occasions and kept the wickets without giving much away. Though obsolete for many years now, long-stop was a key post in the field-setting in Carpenter's time, requiring courage, keen eyesight, and a safe pair of hands. Of even greater importance, perhaps, than long-stop was point, a position which, in addition to the same skills, demanded instantaneous reflexes and the ability to stop or catch the ball with either hand. Carpenter possessed all those qualities and, graduating from his original place as the wicket-keeper's back-up, he soon became and remained one of the most expert points in the game. There was some variety in the methods employed by the specialists in the position at that time. E. M. Grace, an expert practitioner in the arts of gamesmanship and a holy terror to timid and indecisive batsmen with a fatal penchant for the uncertain prod, stood not far from the wicket as a rule and operated a system of intimidating his opponents by stealing nearer with every delivery to gobble up a catch within a foot or so of the bat. Carpenter preferred to take up his stance at a greater distance from the crease—at least, to begin with—but frequently adopted the same tactics as E.M. by closing in on his victim in anticipation of an easy dismissal. Another of his favourite ploys, reserved usually for the discomfiture of some of thc inexperienced batsmen encountered in minor contests, was to miss the ball deliberately and let it go past him to the fielder at cover-point. The latter, being in the know, would then throw down the wicket of the unwary striker attempting a risky run. In all matches throughout his career, both first-class and minor, Carpenter held over 800 catches, many of them at point.

Having had ample opportunities to observe Bob Carpenter in action, W. G. Grace had no reservations about the superior quality of his batting and went on record with the opinion that "He may be safely placed as one of the finest of our great batsmen." Standing erect at the crease and comfortably balanced on his feet, he developed a technique capable of overcoming the hazards presented by the surface of the rough, untrustworthy pitches he encountered on many grounds. The strain of the agonised stretch forward was anathema to him, and his defence, widely acknowledged to be one of the most difficult in England to penetrate, was based exclusively on back play. His patience and vigilance were legendary, and he never played by guess but always watched the ball coming on to the bat, dealing with each individual delivery strictly on its merits. Bumpers and shooters were a constant threat to any batsman's wicket in those days, but Carpenter was rarely found wanting, and his incredible skill and split-second reactions in coming down hard on a viciously shooting delivery were frequently rewarded with a prolonged round of applause from discerning spectators. It would be an error, however, to think of him as a mere stonewaller, for he was never a dull batsman to watch, and merely sitting on the splice was an abomination in his eyes. His scoring strokes ranged wide over most of the entire playing area, with full-blooded cuts steered in front of rather than behind point, massive drives both off and on, and enormous leg-hits usually sailing clear of the heads and hands of the out-field. Driving, in fact, was his method of dealing with a slow or slow-medium bowler trying to tempt him into unfamiliar forward defensive play. At such a moment, Carpenter would leave his ground and "hit the ball like a horse kicking, often getting to it before it could pitch," and if, by any chance, he advanced from the crease and found he had misjudged the flight, he would check the ball with a backward defensive block. Slow bowling was meat and drink to him, but he always carefully refrained from scoring too many runs in one over, lest the bowler should be taken off.

The names of Robert Carpenter and Thomas Hayward were frequently treated as almost inseparable in the minds of the public, and there was some justice in this automatic association of two of the greatest cricketers of their time. They were photographed together, wearing spotted shirts and billycock hats, and they were regular team-mates in the Cambridgeshire Eleven and other sides. Both were considered to be excellent batsmen—Hayward was a good medium-pace, round-arm bowler as well, who once performed the hat-trick for the Players against the Gentlemen—but there was a marked difference in their approach. Richard Daft, their contemporary and arguably as great a batsman as they, exercised commendable tact in stating that he didn't think there was anything to choose between them. As a model of free-scoring, wristy elegance, Hayward was undeniably superior to Carpenter, and for this reason was probably considered to be the more attractive batsman from the spectators' point of view. He employed the forward defensive stroke and was generally at his best when playing against fast bowling on ground that was hard and true, but Carpenter was more of a fighter, capable of coping with the varying conditions of pitch and weather and dealing with all kinds of bowling. Hayward's record as a batsman in first-class cricket was slightly better than Carpenter's, averaging nearly one run more per innings, but he played in fewer matches. Handicapped by indifferent health, he once fell down in the throes of a fit while batting in a minor contest, at Oxford, in 1874. With his constitution impaired, he suffered a tragic loss of form, and he died of consumption at the early age of forty-one, when his Cambridge twin, an older man, was still as sound as a bell and only just thinking of hanging up his bat. Fortunate was the captain who could have both of them in his team, but if you could only choose one and you had a couple of trustworthy change bowlers, you would probably have plumped for the more reliable Carpenter.

Tom Hayward had a good knowledge of the game, but Bob Carpenter's was probably better. Skilled at reading the play and judicious in the management of his bowlers and fieldsmen, he was one of the best professional captains of the period, though he liked to have his own way in all things. Among many of his friends and acquaintances at Cambridge he was known as "The Old Gardener," a nickname whose origin is obscure. Perhaps it arose from a confirmed habit of frequently dealing with imperfections in the turf of the pitch between overs or even deliveries, or, possibly, from his famous reputation for digging out the shooters.

Bob Carpenter made his first appearance in an important match at Fenner's Ground, Cambridge, on April 30 and May 1, 1855, when he assisted the Cambridge Town Club against the University team. Batting at number seven in his only innings, he made 15 runs, the

Thomas Hayward and Robert Carpenter
Courtesy Hulton Picture Library

second top score on his side. In the equivalent fixture of 1856, transferred from Fenner's to Parker's Piece, he marked 4 and, in the second innings, was equal top scorer with 16, but he missed the match in 1857. The following season, however, presented "The Old Gardener" with a golden opportunity to advance his status. Engaged by John Wisden to assist The United All England Eleven against 18 of Christ Church, at Oxford, on May 27, 28, and 29, he contributed 34 to the total. On the strength of this highly promising performance, he was picked to play for the United against the All England Eleven, at Lord's, on June 7 and 8. This was his first match at headquarters, where he was virtually unknown, but the "colt"—a misnomer, in a sense, seeing that he was already twenty-seven years old—soon made the spectators sit up and take notice. All England, batting first, were dismissed for 111 shortly after the interval for dinner. The United then made an inauspicious beginning, losing one of their opening batsmnen off the last ball of the first over. Enter Bob Carpenter, at first wicket down, to face the intimidating shock tactics of John Jackson (very fast right) at one end and Edgar Willsher (fast left) at the other. Wasting no time in opening his account, he proceeded to play a brilliant innings, which "quite astonished the beholders," scoring all round the wicket and displaying his soon to be celebrated expertise in coolly fending off the high-flying bouncers and dauntlessly killing the frequent shooters. His treatment of Jackson was particularly severe, but the latter's thirst for revenge was eventually assuaged. He softened up Carpenter, as it were, by hitting him in the back when throwing in the ball, and the shaken batsman was clean bowled by Jackson almost immediately afterwards. Carpenter made 45, one of the most famous performances in the series of contests between the Two Elevens, and at the conclusion of his innings he was presented with a new bat as a token of MCC's appreciation of his achievement. He made six more first-class appearances in 1858, losing his form for a time until he assisted The Married against The Single, at The Oval, and was easily top scorer of the match with a splendid knock of 84, his highest of the season. Thirteen years later, in 1871, this unusual fixture was resurrected at Lord's, with Carpenter and Richard Daft the only survivors from the previous contest at The Oval.

With his performance in 1858, Bob Carpenter had "arrived" without a shadow of doubt, and for the next few seasons up to the end of 1864 he had no difficulty in commanding a regular place in representative matches. As a result of the schism between north and south, which hamstrung first-class cricket for several years, Carpenter appeared in few grand matches until matters were adjusted between the warring factions, but, from 1870 until he gave up regular active participation in the game, he resumed his natural place in big-time cricket. "The Old Gardener," it is only fair to say, was one of the most ardent members of the clique of northern professionals, who contributed to the regrettable boycotting of southern counties and grounds.

There was no official county championship in the 1860s, but occasional fixtures between a handful of the counties deemed to be first-class formed part of the complete programme for the season. From 1857 to 1871, Cambridgeshire played 39 matches, contending against Kent, Middlesex, Nottinghamshire, Surrey, and Yorkshire. Two other opponents were Cambridge University and MCC. Carpenter made a very satisfactory debut for his County in 1861 by scoring 57 against Surrey, at Fenner's, on May 20 and 21. In the return fixture, at The Oval, five weeks later—the same match which saw the departure from first-class cricket of Billy Buttress—Carpenter reached exactly three figures, his most spectacular scoring stroke being a magnificent drive, for which he was awarded 6 runs in accordance with the then Law XXVIII (lost ball). He shared a long stand with Tom Hayward and, subsequently, a purse of £18 raised by a collection from the appreciative crown. There were evidently plenty of affluent spectators at The Oval for this match. Having reached 50 in his first innings, for which he was awarded "a talent sovereign," Surrey's Julius Caesar more than doubled this in his second by ominously making 111. Yet this was one of those occasions when "the dreaded Nelson" brought nothing but good luck, seeing that a collection for Caesar also realized an extremely generous sum of money. Tom Hayward, incidentally, went one better than his partner by marking a century in *both* matches against Surrey in 1861.

"The Old Gardener" flayed the southern county's bowling at Fenner's once again the next season with a hard-hitting innings of 80. Other notable exploits included 77 against the University, at Fenner's, in 1865, and 97 not out against the expert bowling of the Yorkshiremen, at Bradford, in 1866. Remarkable also was his performance against Kent, at Gravesend, in 1868. The visitors, requiring only 34 to win, collapsed and lost 7 wickets before obtaining the required number. With Tom Hayward gone for 0, "The Old Gardener" kept his head when it came to the crunch. In at number 4, he carried out his bat for 9, prompting one of the cricket annuals to observe that "Cambridgeshire owes its victory mainly to the wonderfully steady play of Carpenter."

Unfortunately, Cambridgeshire, who relied heavily on a body of talented professionals headed by Bob Carpenter, Tom Hayward, and George Tarrant, the fast bowler, were doomed to a short-lived and precarious existence at the top. By 1870, that all-important nucleus of the team had virtually vanished, and of the great ones only Carpenter remained as a potent force. Cambridgeshire played only three matches in 1868, one in 1869, and none in 1870. One final fixture came off on June 22, 23, and 24, 1871, after which the County relinquished the cherished status of first-class. The opponents were Surrey, and the venue The Oval, where Carpenter and Hayward had not appeared for several seasons. The latter played two graceful innings of 33 and 40, but he was outshone by "The Old Gardener," who provided a perfect illustration of his combination of almost invulnerable defence and punishing attack by emerging unscathed twice, with unbeaten scores of [illegible] and [illegible]. He played 32 times for his County Eleven, sometimes acting as captain, and attained a batting average of 31.42, which was extremely high for the time.

Bob Carpenter assisted the North more often than his County, appearing regularly from 1858 up to 1865 and again from 1870 to 1873. The opponents were the South throughout both periods, Surrey in the early years, and Nottinghamshire once during the time of the great schism. To begin with, he made little impact, but later marked some good scores. His best effort was 91 not out, compiled in five hours and a-quarter, against Surrey, at The Oval, on August 4 and 5, 1862, with only two other batsmen making worthwhile scores. During the course of a long partnership with George Anderson, the tall, powerful, aggressive batsman from Yorkshire, "The Old Gardener" was involved as the non-striker in an unusual and exhausting experience. There were no lines marking boundaries in those days, and almost all hits had to be run out. Anderson unleashed one enormous drive, which went soaring over the heads of the ring of spectators. The fielder, who eventually retrieved the ball far beyond them, misjudged his return and failed to clear the ring at his first attempt. When the ball finally arrived back on the pitch, Anderson had added no less than 8 runs to his score. The mystery of the obstacle that impeded the fielder's throw-in was revealed many years later, when one of the spectators, a Mr H. C. Troughton, wrote a letter to *The Times* in 1919, explaining that the ball had struck him in the middle of his back!

Other representative matches in which Carpenter appeared were fixtures involving a team entitled "England" against such opponents as Surrey, and Gentlemen *v* Players. He played 18 times against the Gentlemen, making his debut at The Oval, in 1859, when he opened the innings, scoring 44, and his final appearance at Prince's Ground, in 1873. His figures for the series were good—an aggregate of 725 runs at an average of 26.85—and he holds the record for having marked the first two centuries scored against the Gentlemen at The Oval. In 1861, he made 106, adding 139 runs for the third wicket with Tom Hayward, but this was less than his exploit of the previous season. His contribution, from number 1, to the total of 328, was 119, and during his innings he smashed one ball clean out of the ground and sent another to the top of the pavilion.

There was a period of several years when Carpenter and Hayward "were spoken of with awe and reverence." Contributing so much to the biannual steamrollering of the Gentlemen, they came to regard themselves with pride as the mainstay of the professional team. At The Oval, in 1862, however, the amateurs threatened to turn the tables, and the Players had a real dogfight on their hands. Hayward and Carpenter were dismissed for 31 and 43 respectively in their second and the final innings of the match and were observed leaving the ground while play was still in progress and many runs still required. A startled member of the Surrey Club accosted Carpenter, saying, "You are not going before seeing the result?" "Yes, we are," replied Bob, "We've lost the match—me and Tom are out!" In fact, "The Old Gardener" was wrong. The Players succeeded in staving off defeat by playing out the time, one of the not out batsmen being George Anderson, the hero of the mighty hit for 8 some weeks later on the same ground.

In the early 1860s, Carpenter and Hayward occasionally joined forces to play in single-wicket matches. They made a good team together, particularly in the batting department, though most of the bowling had to be done by Hayward. Their first important venture came off at the old Hyde Park Ground, at Sheffield, on September 26, 27, 28, and 30, 1861, when their opponents, designated as 3 of Stockton-on-Tees, were T. Robinson, T. Darnton, and T. W. Hornby, all of whom appeared in first-class cricket. The Cambridge pair were backed by Mr John Jackson—not the famous fast bowler of Nottinghamshire but a gentleman from Catterick, well known in racing circles—while the Stockton trio were sponsored by Dr Richardson, a fellow townsman, and the *raison d'être* for the contest was the opportunity it presented for some heavy betting (£200 a side). To the intense satisfacion of the Catterick punter, Carpenter and Hayward emerged as easy victors. Subsequently, they issued a challenge to play against any two men in England, and abortive attempts were made at one time to match them against William Caffyn and George Griffith, two top all-rounders from Surrey, who might well have beaten the Cambridge men.

At the conclusion of the county match between Nottinghamshire and Cambridgeshire, at Trent Bridge, on July 3 and 4, 1862, Carpenter and Hayward teamed up with George Tarrant to contend against 3 of Nottinghamshire (Alfred Clarke, Richard Daft, and John Jackson, the fast bowler). The time available allowed only one innings to each team, the visitors being dismissed for a single scored by Hayward, and the home side being put out for 12.

The most famous of the series of single-wicket contests originated in a meeting at Stockton races, when the two backers of the Sheffield match renewed their rivalry. Mr Jackson, known as "the northern betting leviathan," offered to lay £200 that Carpenter, Hayward, and Tarrant would take on and beat a team of five men representing Stockton. The challenge was accepted by Dr Richardson, and, according to one account, the stakes were doubled. Arrangements were made to promote the match at Stockton-on-Tees, on September 25, 26, and 27, 1862, and the home team was made up of the three who had played at Sheffield, augmented by the addition of William Halton, a batsman/wicket-keeper with first-class experience and well known in the district, and George Atkinson, who played regularly for Yorkshire in the 1860s.

In the presence of a large and raucous crowd, 3 of Cambridgeshire totalled 13 runs and their opponents 14 in the first innings. During his second spell at the crease, Carpenter was looking well set, when he was suddenly run out for 5. The uproar from the on-lookers that greeted the fall of this prized wicket was so tumultuous that it startled the team of a horse-drawn omnibus parked on the ground, and the driverless vehicle made a wild double-circuit of the enclosure, knocking down some of the spectators. In a scene reminiscent of that favourite motif of Western films, the runaway stage-coach, Halton and Fred Lillywhite, the scorer, managed to climb on to the omnibus. Fred, unfortunately, was soon pitched off to land with a bump on the grass, but Halton clung on desperately, succeeded in securing the reins, and pulled up the stampeding horses, "for which plucky feat he was liberally rewarded."

Once order had been restored, the visitors took their total to 28. At intervals throughout the match, Mr Jackson could be heard offering to wager "£1,000 to £500 on the Three," and at one time "£1,000 to £1 that neither of the Five gets 100 runs." Only those in the most legless state of inebriation could have been sufficiently lame-brained to accept the second bet. There were evidently plenty of takers for some of his other proposals, however, since 3 of Cambridgeshire romped home to defeat the Five by 22 runs, and "the northern betting leviathan" is said to have gone home with heavily laden pockets.

Knowledge of "The Old Gardener's" prowess on the cricket field was not confined solely to the shores of Great Britain. He was a member of the doughty band of twelve professionals taking part in the first ever tour abroad. The party, consisting of 6 from the All England Eleven and 6 from the United All England Eleven, with George Parr as captain and John Wisden to assist him, set sail from Liverpool on the *Nova Scotia* on September 7, 1859, and arrived at Quebec on the 22nd. Between September 24 and the same date in the following month,

Parr's men were engaged in five matches against teams of twenty-two players in Canada and the USA. In addition, three supplementary, eleven-a-side contests were got up, the tourists being divided between the two teams, and the numbers completed by local cricketers. Tom Hayward, who played in all eight fixtures, had the highest aggregate (265), the highest individual score (60), and an average in all matches of 22.08. Carpenter, who stood as umpire in the first encounter, scored 196 runs at an average of 24.50, and was ahead in the eleven-a-side matches, whereas Hayward outstripped his rival in the contests against "odds." Neither did much bowling, but "The Old Gardener" proved his worth in the field by holding 27 catches—far more than anybody else in the team. He was involved in a curious incident, when the English side were contending against 22 of Philadelphia, towards the end of the second week in October. While he was batting, one of the local bowlers, who would have won few prizes for consistent accuracy and length, sent down a wide delivery, which was called by the umpire. Carpenter, however, yielding to a rare rush of blood to the head, swung wildly with his bat, connected with the ball, and gave a catch. After some discussion, it was ruled that the umpire's original decision should stand, and the batsman was allowed to continue his innings.

In all but the roughest weather, Bob Carpenter turned out to be a good sailor, and in those days, when passengers at sea were largely thrown back upon their own resources in the matter of entertainment, he was worth his weight in gold as the possessor of "the largest amount of vocal talent among the cricketers." As a singer of popular sentimental ditties, he was much in demand, particularly when he could be persuaded—and Bob needed little persuasion on this score—to give yet another rendering of an oft-repeated song, entitled "The Sweet Little Cherub That Sits Up Aloft." In addition, he was an equable companion, easy to get on with, not given to excess in the consumption of strong liquors, and always willing to take a hand in a game of cards, especially cribbage, which was one of his favourite pastimes.

With such a wealth of off-field talents to augment his wizardry as a batsman and a fielder, it was not surprising to find Carpenter engaged for another tour abroad, when George Parr took a party of twelve to play in Australia and New Zealand in 1863-64. An ambitious programme was arranged, consisting of sixteen fixtures with teams of twenty-two opponents, three supplementary eleven-a-side matches, one of which is rated as first-class, and several single-wicket contests. "The Old Gardener" played in all nineteen of the regular matches, but had evidently no desire to try his hand again at the single-wicket version of the game. William Caffyn, who remained in Australia for several years at the conclusion of the tour, was the most prolific batsman with an aggregate of 475 runs at an average of 19.00 and a highest score of 43. Next came Carpenter, who totalled 447 runs at 18.62 per innings. He was not quite so consistent as Caffyn, and his aggregate was boosted in the penultimate match of the tour, against 22 of Ballarat, on April 18, 19, and 20, 1864. In a mind-boggling feat of endurance, remaining at the wickets for about nine hours (!), he made 121, the only century scored by a member of Parr's team down under. His fielding record was again stupendous. He held no less than eight catches twice in the matches against "odds," and his final tally—just exceeding twice as many as the next man's (the wicket-keeper)—was 67.

When Bob Carpenter accepted John Wisden's invitation to assist the United All England Eleven on 1858 and played his historic innings of 45 against the All Englanders, at Lord's, he established an association, which lasted for more than a decade. The series between the Two Elevens of England, beginning in the season before "The Old Gardener's" debut and ending in 1869, consisted of nineteen matches. Two had already been played when he made his first appearance and, thereafter, he was absent from the United side only once—in 1864, the encounter taking place before Parr's team had arrived back in England from the tour of Australia and New Zealand. Starting as an ordinary member of the United Eleven, he eventually became the most important and influential individual in the team, succeeding John Wisden as captain and taking over some of the latter's secretarial responsibilities. The schism between north and south, which brought about the wholesale secession of the southern professionals from the Two Elevens, resulted in more serious consequences for the United Eleven, who were in grave danger of extinction. Thanks to "The Old Gardener's" enthusiasm and administrative abilities, combined with his leadership, batting, and fielding, the existence of the UAEE was prolonged for a few more years.

In the contests against the All England Eleven, Carpenter was by far the most successful United batsman, amassing 611 runs for an average of 24.44, an excellent record, considering the condition of the pitches and the terrifying fast bowling he encountered. George Parr, the top man for All England, had more innings and, in the first thirteen fixtures, faced bowlers of more moderate pace. He scored slightly more runs (622), but his average, at 21.44, was less. By way of further comparison, it may be observed that Richard Daft's aggregate for the AEE was 529 (average 20.34) and Tom Hayward only 469 (average 17.37). Like Parr, neither Daft nor Hayward had to face the bowling of Jackson, Tarrant, or Willsher. In six innings, including two in one match, Carpenter was the top scorer for the United. His best contribution occurred on July 4, 5, and 6, 1859, when the Two Elevens met in a contest arranged for the benefit of Mr J. H. Dark, the proprietor of Lord's. Opening the innings for the United, "The Old Gardener" administered a severe mauling to the All England bowling. After a stay of four hours and a-half at the wickets, he just missed his century, being bowled for 97. He left the pitch to the accompaniment of vociferous applause, "the assembled thousands literally rising at him," and the grateful beneficiary, Mr Dark, ceremoniously presented him with a new bat "for exhibiting such a masterly display of cricket." The United humiliated their opponents in 1859, winning easily by 9 wickets. Not so at Lord's three years later, when All England made a disastrous beginning to their second innings before staging a recovery. Their victory would have been a foregone conclusion but for the capital efforts of Bob Carpenter. Going in at first wicket down, he was still undefeated at the fall of the last wicket with 63 runs to his credit. The splendour of his performance stands out in sharp relief, seeing that the only other score in double figures was 21 and the total 126! Once again, "The Old Gardener" was the recipient of a new bat, and, for good measure, he was top scorer on second hands, marking 39 out of a total of 129. Nor did his immense value to the United in the series rest solely on his batting. He held 25 catches—more than any other fielder in either Eleven.

In 1861, when there were three contests between the Two Elevens, Carpenter participated in seventeen first-class matches, the maximum in his whole career. From 1863 onwards, apart from one season (1872), his appearances at the highest level were restricted each year to single figures. Nevertheless, he was rarely unemployed during the summer months, earning his bread and butter by playing regularly for an itinerant eleven against local twenty-twos. Throughout his permanent engagement with the United All England Eleven, he played in at least 144 matches, all of them against "odds," apart from the encounters with the All England Eleven. He was missing from few of the United fixtures for a period of twelve years, during several of which he played in *all* of the contests arranged. As a striking example of his gluttony for work and wages, one need only cite the season of 1861. In addition to the seventeen first-class matches, he appeared in all ten of the United's engagements against local teams, and in the next two years he was absent from only three games out of a maximum of thirty-five.

In conditions normally militating against the scoring of many runs by an individual, Carpenter was more successful than many of his contemporaries in adapting his technique to overcome the problems posed by the opposition, whose teams of twenty-two often included one or more excellent professional bowlers. His tendency to loft the ball when hitting in the direction of square-leg occasionally brought about his downfall, but his overall performance for the United yielded a batting average of almost 20 runs per innings—outstanding in this form of cricket, when double figures were considered to be commendable. Centuries were extremely rare, but "The Old Gardener" managed to attain three figures twice, both in the same season. Against 22 of East Hampshire, at Southsea, on May 22, 23, and 24, 1862, he marked 122—beating the previous record in an "odds" match—and early in September, against 22 of Odiham, he reached 108. In these contests, many of his runs were scored off the same two bowlers, both of them county men, albeit not of the very best. As a fielder, he missed little, taking 273 catches, and although his performance with the bat in 1860 was, by his standards, only mediocre, he ended the season as easily the most successful United bowler. His under-hands, a type of delivery often fatal against "odds," yielded 155 wickets at less than 5 runs apiece in only 14 matches. When the United contended against 22 of West Bromwich, on July 12 and 13, they were assisted by three first-rate bowlers, but their efforts paled into insignificance compared with the devastating form of "The Old Gardener," who returned the astonishing match figures of 25 wickets for 103 runs (11-42 and 14–61)!

The United All England Eleven went into a decline in the late 1860s and ceased to exist after a solitary fixture in 1869, depriving some of the players of a much needed source of income. With the additional collapse of Cambridgeshire as a first-class county. Carpenter might have found himself in straitened circumstances, especially as he was the father of nine children. His first loyalty had always been given without stint to the United Eleven, and he maintained this bond throughout the series of contests against the All Englanders. When not required by the United, however, he had no qualms about turning out for the AEE, making his first appearance in 1859 and his last in 1876. During this period, in fact, he logged more matches for All England than he did for the United, recording a slightly higher batting average and many more catches, but he was rarely put on to bowl. He marked one century in "odds" matches, reaching the colossal figure of 174 against 18 of Radcliffe-on-Trent, on July 21, 22, and 23, 1870. Three times he played for the AEE in first-class matches, his most spectacular performance occurring in the fixture with Yorkshire, at Bramall Lane, Sheffield, on July 17, 18, and 19, 1865. Batting at number 5, "The Old Gardener" was involved in a stand that advanced the total from 117 to 301, and he was not dismissed until he had reached 134. This was his highest score in first-class cricket, and the highest by any batsman in first-class matches for the All England Eleven. It was only fitting that, when Carpenter made his two hundreds for the AEE, he shared long partnerships with Tom Hayward, who also scored a century in each match.

As far as the weather was concerned, the cricket season of 1872 was an almost unmitigated disaster. The lowering skies and torrential rainfall of April were succeeded by late frosts and showers of sleet in May, which in their turn gave way to frequent thunderstorms for the next six weeks. A period of fine, hot weather brought a temporary respite in the second half of July, but August was another month of perpetual gloom and rain-sodden grounds. For Carpenter, now turned forty-one and feeling the occasional twinge, there was little pleasure to be derived from standing for long periods on the damp grass, even though his thickening figure gave him some insulation against the icy blast of the bleak, bone-chilling winds. The dreary weather was not his only affliction. He played in ten first-class fixtures, and in more than half of these he was haunted by the prospect of a living nightmare, in which he was condemned to be eternally fielding out in the presence of W. G. Grace—a run-scoring machine in perpetual motion. The crisis reached its zenith in the first week of July, when the Gentlemen met the Players at Lord's and The Oval. At headquarters, the Champion scored 77 in just under two hours and 112 in two hours and a-quarter. Proceeding immediately to the Surrey ground, W.G. gave a repeat performance by harvesting 117 runs in three hours, but mercifully for Carpenter and his team-mates, this was the Champion's only innings. After the conclusion of these dismal proceedings—dismal, that is, for the Players and their supporters—Carpenter was heard to express a feeling of grim satisfaction, saying, "I have had about enough of fielding out to Mr. Grace this week; but thank goodness I shall be on *his* side the next match." In a special fixture, beginning at Lord's on the following Monday, Carpenter and W.G. were assisting England against a combined eleven of Nottinghamshire and Yorkshire. England won the toss and took first knock with W.G. opening the innings, as usual. Carpenter came in when the total stood at 77 for the loss of 2 wickets. Did he, perhaps, wish he had bitten his tongue out rather than boasting with glee about being on the same side as the Champion? With the latter scoring twice as rapidly and with most hits having to be run out, "The Old Gardener" suffered one of the most prostrating periods of his whole career. By 2.30 p.m., the total had risen to 150, and when play was resumed after the luncheon interval 27 more runs were added. At this point, Carpenter, almost collapsing from sheer exhaustion, gave a catch at the wicket. His contribution to the stand of exactly 100 runs was a well played 36, and W.G. proceeded to carry out his bat for 170. Retiring a wiser if sadder man, Carpenter realized that it was much harder to be batting with the Champion, as you did get an occasional rest when you were fielding against him. Asked how he felt about his chastening experience, he observed that it was "not so much of a catch after all to play on the same side with Mr. Grace, as most of your time is spent in running *his* runs."

At their next encounter, at The Oval, towards the end of the month, the Champion rubbed salt into the wounds. On opposite sides once more, in a North *v* South match, Carpenter made a pair (caught by W.G. in his first innings), whereas his redoubtable adversary scored 114 in two hours and a-half. It might be argued, however, that the ageing professional had the last laugh. At Canterbury, a fortnight later, in yet another contest between North and South, W.G.'s mind was probably absorbed by other matters. He made only 15 at his first attempt, took no wickets, and was compelled to miss his second innings through the necessity of having to dash to Liverpool to embark on a ship taking him on a tour of North America. Encouraged, possibly, by the impending departure of his tormentor, "The Old Gardener" celebrated by scoring a hard-hit 57.

Bob Carpenter played in seven matches in 1873, with indifferent success, and then virtually retired from first-class cricket, though he turned out twice the next year and once, finally, in 1876, when he assisted the Players of North against the Gentlemen of the South, at Prince's Ground, on May 18 and 19. W.G., who made 6 and 72(!), caught Carpenter in the first innings and claimed his wicket as the bowler in the second.

And so, as a player, "The Old Gardener" called it a day. As one of the most accomplished batsmen of the period which included the sanctioning of the over-arm delivery and the advent of W. G. Grace, he could look back with pride on the achievements of his career. In first-class matches, he scored 5,220 runs, with four centuries, at an average of 24.39, and held 190 catches—a record excelled by few of his contemporaries.

In the unusually hard winter towards the end of 1878, a stretch of grassland near Grantchester was flooded to create a skating rink, and this area was used a week before Christmas as the venue for a cricket match on ice between twelve townsmen of Cambridge and a team from the University. Cambridge Town, skippered by Bob Carpenter, took first innings and ran up a total of 326. Top scorer, with 89, was their captain, now aged forty-eight. The surname of his partner in a quick-scoring stand of 132 runs was Hayward—not, alas, Tom, who had already passed away, but Tom's elder brother Daniel, formerly a member of the old Cambridgeshire Eleven.

Carpenter's association with cricket was not severed by the end of his playing days in the first-class game. For many years, he was a familiar figure on most of the principal grounds in the country, standing as umpire in county matches and other important fixtures, until a deterioration in his eyesight in the 1890s compelled him gradually to relinquish this occupation. Carrying rather less weight than he did when batting with W.G., at Lord's, in 1872, he remained hale and hearty until within a few days of his death, which occurred at his residence in Mill Road, Cambridge, on July 14, 1901.

"The Old Gardener's" skill was handed down to the next generation. One of his sons, Herbert Arthur, began a career with Essex and MCC ground staff while his father was still umpiring, and played for his county as late as 1920. With an impeccably straight bat, Herbert was inevitably famous for the strength of his back play in defence or forcing the ball away for runs. Herbert's nephew was Jack O'Connor, also of Essex fame between the two World Wars, who won an England cap against South Africa in 1929 and three against West Indies in the following winter.

CHAPTER FIVE

G. F. Tarrant
"Tear'em"

WHEN Cambridgeshire enjoyed first-class status in the world of cricket for an all too brief period in the 1860s, one of the leading lights of the County Eleven was George Tarrant. The strength of the side lay in its professionals, particularly those in the upper echelons of fame, and, together with Thomas Hayward and Robert Carpenter, Tarrant formed a mighty triumvirate of such surpassing excellence that more than one other county would have been glad of their services. Born at Cambridge, "of humble parents" in the words of one journalist, he first saw the light of day on December 7, 1838. His given names were George Frederick, and, according to the birth certificate, his father was an innkeeper called James Tarrant. The latter had evidently not progressed very far through the stages of elementary education, since, on registering the birth, he endorsed the documents not with a signature but with a X as his mark. In passing, one wonders how an individual incapable of even signing his name managed to keep the accounts and check the sales connected with the inn at which he was "mine host." The other "humble" parent is shown on the birth certificate in the space for the name, surname and maiden surname of the mother as Eliza Tarrant, formerly Wood.

While still in his youth, George Tarrant "exhibited a strong passion for cricket," according to one of his obituarists, and his obvious all-round talents soon manifested themselves on Parker's Piece and Fenner's Ground, at Cambridge, where he found, like Billy Buttress and Bob Carpenter, that there were ample opportunities and to spare for a budding cricketer to make his way. At an early age, he followed the path trodden by many of his contemporaries by seeking employment as a club professional. His first engagement was at Botesdale, in Suffolk, as the successor to Fred Reynolds, another Cambridgeshire player, who became associated with Old Trafford as a bowler, ground manager, and administrator for many years. By 1859, Tarrant had left Suffolk for a post at the Manchester Broughton Club, and during this season he assisted the Players of Lancashire against the Gentlemen of the County. It is unlikely that he clung much longer to the vocation of professional to a club. In the following year, he made his first-class debut, and he was regularly employed as a professional cricketer in matches of varying importance throughout the 1860s.

George Tarrant—he seems to have largely ignored the Frederick—was an excellent man to have on any side. Keen and active, he was a splendid fielder, able and willing to take any position, but outstanding at short-slip, long-stop, or cover-point. As a batsman, he had no great pretensions to style and elegance, and he was of little repute to begin with, being regarded as a natural number eleven. With this state of affairs he was evidently far from satisfied, and, having worked assiduously at his batting, he converted himself into a very useful performer, capable even of opening the innings. Patient, cast-iron defence was not his forte: by natural inclination he was an adherent of the creed of putting the bat vigorously against the ball and, when well set, he could be counted on to force the rate of scoring as well as any man.

Preserved in the Pavilion at Lord's is an oil painting, painted on a photograph, of Tarrant wearing the contemporary cricketing costume of a spotted shirt and flannel trousers, complete with a heavy belt. Judging by the features, the subject is probably portrayed as he appeared fairly late in the 1860s. An earlier likeness also exists, a wood engraving copied from a photograph, which was published in an illustrated sporting journal in 1863. With his sparsely whiskered face and arched eyebrows surmounted by a dark, slightly baggy cap of the pattern popular at that period—he also favoured a billycock hat from time to time, witness the painting at Lord's—Tarrant stands eternally frozen in the attitude of delivery. He is wearing a striped shirt with a white collar and a short tie, white trousers girdled by a narrow belt at the waist, and drab foot-wear. The left sleeve is buttoned at the wrist, the right rolled up to the elbow—this also appears in the portrait at Lord's—the right arm is extended level with, even slightly below the shoulder, the index finger and thumb applying the main purchase to the ball. Unfortunately, the exact secret of his grip is not revealed, since the position of the seam is not clearly visible. Tarrant, with his round-arm action, is delivering literally over the wicket, and if both feet are well forward of the bowling crease, this may be merely an instance of artistic licence on the part of either the photographer or the engraver, or both.*

Specially posed pictures of nineteenth-century bowlers are not always entirely trustworthy—there are, for example, some rather

*This portrait is reproduced in G. Derek West, *The Elevens of England* (London: Darf Publishers Limited, 1988), p. 63.

G. F. Tarrant
"Tear'em"

Courtesy Roger Mann

odd-looking photographs of Tom Emmett and Bobby Peel with patently bent wrists. Nevertheless, this engraving of Tarrant possibly gives a fairly accurate representation of how he might have looked at the split second of releasing the ball. No "still," however, can create any conception of his ferocious pace, and herein lies the enigma of Tarrant's bowling. Two of his eminent contemporaries in the art of speed were John Jackson of Nottinghamshire and handsome George Freeman of Yorkshire. They were 6 foot tall or thereabouts, weighed around 14 stone, and were both powerful men endowed with the sort of physique that makes fast bowlers. Not so Tarrant, who was only 5 foot 7 inches in height and weighed around 10 stone. Pale, slight, and almost delicate in appearance, he possessed an indomitable will that imposed excessive demands upon his wiry, slender frame, and his superhuman exertions may well have taken their toll and contributed to the shortening of his career on the cricket field. Lord Harris, who occasionally betrayed a liking for the sensational, repeated a rumour that, after Tarrant's death, an autopsy revealed the astonishing fact that "his heart was much misplaced, being far to the right of its proper position."

Several of those who watched Tarrant bowling or faced up to his thunderbolts have left their impressions of this awesome experience, thereby making it possible to form some idea of his methods. Imbued with the perpetual desire to bowl down the batsman's wickets—for he preferred the role of sole executioner and placed little reliance on the assistance of his fielders in the eternal quest for victims—he worked out a system that would compensate for his modest physique and help him to achieve that speed for which his restless spirit craved. Equally at home either over or round the wicket, Tarrant took a long run, longer than some of his contemporaries, and tore up to the crease. "He was all over the place like a flash of lightning, never sparing himself, and frightening timid batsmen," said W. G. Grace. Yet there was method in this seeming madness. Tarrant conformed to the technique employed in the round-arm period by smaller men, whose declared aim was fast bowling. His approach to the wicket was usually somewhat sideways-on, with the object of getting his left leg more across his right in order to swing round his body in the act of delivery. Bowling level with the shoulder, he was adept at mixing bumpers with deadly straight balls or occasional break-backs from the off. The hapless batsman was frequently beaten by sheer speed, and sometimes the ball would cannon off the pads on its way to the stumps.

George Tarrant's habitual nickname was "Tear'em," or occasionally "Tear-away," and this was indicative not only of his bowling, but in part also of his character, for, wrote one journalist with masterly understatement, "in manners he was not the most urbane of men." To begin with, he was very pugnacious and, having some skill as a boxer, was always ready to use his fists. Obstinate, moody, and excitable by nature, he succumbed easily to sudden fits of ill-temper and was apt to lose his head in a moment of crisis. There was no mock modesty about Tarrant, who, while fully aware of his own excellence, was sometimes intolerant of the shortcomings of others and bluntly outspoken almost to the point of rudeness. That same journalist, who deplored what he considered to be "Tear'em's" woeful deficiency in the matter of polished behaviour, declared that "the consciousness of his own power as a cricketer made him perhaps more free in his address than he had any right to be." The distinctions in the class system in those days were, of course, more rigid than they are now, as appears even in the more sympathetic judgement penned by another obituarist, who seems to have had a better understanding of "Tear'em's" personality than his more censorious colleague:

> By many he was thought to be conceited, but such was not the case; and if abrupt expressions escaped his lips, they proceeded from channels that were not fathomed by any one. To other than men as ignorant as himself he was seldom overbearing; having devoted a lifetime and his heart and soul to the game, he was simply conscious of his own power.

Notwithstanding these more temperate words from his apologist, "Tear'em" was not, you would say, a particularly likeable man, but his character was rather more complex than it seemed. However unpredictable he may have been, there were also times when he revealed a more generous and even tender streak in his make-up. W. G. Grace remembered how, at the age of fifteen, he was chosen to assist 22 of Bristol and district in their match with the All England Eleven, at Clifton, in 1863. This was the future Champion's initial encounter with genuine first-class bowling, and he spared no pains in preparing himself for the coming ordeal. "I practised for a little during the luncheon hour," he recollected, "and Tarrant was kind enough to bowl to me for five or ten minutes, a kindness which turned out very useful." This welcome practice gave the youngster the confidence not only to cope with the pace of John Jackson and Tarrant himself but also to start hitting out, with the result that "Tarrant was shunted, and Tinley took his place and bowled lobs." W.G. went on to make 32 before he lashed out and was bowled by one of Tinley's twisters. Another player to benefit from some free batting practice to Tarrant's bowling during the luncheon interval at another match was Johnny Mullagh, a leading member of the Aboriginal cricketers' team touring England in 1868.

Between 1861 and 1868, Tarrant assisted Cambridgeshire in 31 matches and was by far and away the most successful bowler in the history of that short-lived organization, as far as first-class games are concerned. He seems to have had a particular liking for contests against Yorkshire: in 8 matches between 1861 and 1867, he claimed 69 wickets at an average of 8.46, plus 5 more wickets for which the analysis has not been preserved. His tally included the feat of taking 5 wickets in an innings 9 times (best 7–33) and 10 wickets in a match 5 times (best 13–60). It was against Kent, however, rather than Yorkshire, that he recorded his best figures in inter-county fixtures. The two sides met at Chatham, on June 12, 13, and 14, 1862, when "Tear'em" returned match figures of 15 wickets for 56 runs (7–40 and 8–16), and all but three of his victims were clean bowled.

In all important and first-class matches during his career (1860–1869), Tarrant obtained 410 wickets—plus 11 for which the analysis is not available—at an average of 11.70. He took 5 wickets in an innings 41 times and 10 in a match on 16 occasions. His best performance in a single innings (10–40) was achieved when he was playing for England against 13 of Kent, at Lord's, on July 6 and 7, 1863. In the same contest, he recorded his finest figures in a match (16–98), and 11 of his dismissals were clean bowled. His most successful season was 1862, when he appeared in 15 matches and took 96 wickets at an average of 10.07. This was the same year in which he proved so destructive against Kent, at Chatham, but another notable feat occurred in North *v* South, at Lord's, on July 21 and 22. Operating unchanged throughout the South's first innings, "Tear'em" clean bowled 8 batsmen for only 26 runs. And, as if to show that his merits were not restricted exclusively to his bowling, he accomplished a good all-round performance for the All England Eleven against 14 of Yorkshire, at Barnsley, on August 25, 26, and 27, in the same season, by scoring 6 and 60 and taking 3 wickets for 41 runs and 7 for 26.

"Tear'em" obtained his only century in first-class cricket when playing for Cambridgeshire against Cambridge University, at Fenner's Ground, on May 28 and 29, 1866—and, incidentally, there were merely 15 hundreds all told in the whole season. He had a couple of off-days as regards bowling, but in his second innings he scored 108. After commenting on praiseworthy performances by four other batsmen, one of the cricket annuals adds ". . . but *the* innings for severity of hitting and rapidity of accumulation was that 108 of George Tarrant's—off a single [4-ball] over of Mr. S. G. Lyttelton's he made 13!" By 1866, he was, of course, one of the leading stars of cricket, but this match is also worthy of note, since it marked the only first-class appearance of Edward Tarrant, "Tear'em's" younger brother or half-brother. There was evidently an element of hero-worship and an obvious desire for emulation in Edward's attitude towards the most celebrated member of the family. A local reporter attending the match was moved to observe that "Some amusement was created by the appearance of the younger Tarrant, who very much resembles his world-known brother."

Oddly enough, "Tear'em's" debut in first-class cricket occurred at the age of twenty-one before his initial appearance for Cambridgeshire. He was engaged to represent the All England Eleven in the needle match against the United All England Eleven, at Lord's, on May 28, 29 and 30, 1860. This low-scoring contest—only one of the four innings reached three figures—which resulted in an All England victory by 21 runs, was remarkable for the performance of three participants. For the United, William Caffyn achieved match figures of 10 wickets for 95 runs, but he suffered the mortification of seeing one of his deliveries savagely punished by George Parr, who dispatched the ball far away into the garden beside the Tavern with a mighty leg-hit for six runs. "This ball," Caffyn remembered, "pitched outside his leg-stump and did not break in at all as I meant it to do, and it was promptly hit out of the ground." The United medium-pacer accounted for Parr in both innings, but not until the latter had scored 55 in his second knock.

The third notable performance was Tarrant's. When the United Eleven took their first innings, their opening pair faced the bowling of John Jackson and Edgar Willsher. "Tear'em" had a hand in the fall of the first wicket, snapping up a catch in the slips off Jackson. Willsher bowled fairly economically but failed to achieve any penetration, and after fourteen overs he surrendered the ball to the newcomer. The latter, "short in stature, light framed, but as active as a cat," displayed an action which reminded several veteran spectators of Sam Redgate, the legendary fast bowler of an earlier generation. According to one reporter, "his balls are so difficult to hit away that they required a totally new arrangement of the fielders." Another journalist noted, rather ominously, that the tyro betrayed "a very great tendency to over-bowl himself." Be that as it may, "Tear'em" soon struck, obtaining a wicket in his second over ("which is always encouraging to a colt at Lord's"). In partnership with Jackson, he wrapped up the innings, the two fast right-handers dismissing the United for 89 runs. Tarrant recorded a splendid analysis: he delivered 26 overs, of which 16 were maidens, and captured 6 wickets for only 28 runs. Five of these dismissals were achieved without the intervention of the fielders, and among the four clean bowled was his fellow townsman, Bob Carpenter, who was sent to the right-about for only 6. Unfortunately, the debutant was unable to reproduce this devastating form in the second innings. He assisted the All England Eleven against the United in nine more matches in the 1860s and took 5 wickets in an innings on two future occasions, but 6-28 remained his best analysis in one innings in the series.

Other first-class fixtures in which "Tear'em" participated, especially in the early 1860s, were matches in which one of the sides was entitled "England," contests between the North and the South, and Gentlemen *v* Players. He assisted the professionals against the amateurs four times, at The Oval in 1862, where he was not particularly successful, and at Lord's in 1862, 1863, and 1864. In his first appearance of the series at St John's Wood, where, as an experiment, all those taking part in the contest were under thirty years of age, he had an excellent match with both bat and ball. Top scorer, with 27, in the Players' first innings, he made 39 in the second, a figure exceeded by only two of his team-mates, who were better known for their batting than their bowling (this was the match in which Roger Iddison made his 62). The Gentlemen appeared to have gained the upper hand at the start of their first innings, thanks, in part, to E. M. Grace, and the first three bowlers for the professionals accounted for only one wicket between them. Any hope for a prolongation of the Gentlemen's promising beginning was dashed by the advent of "Tear'em." In the space of 17 overs, including no less than 10 maidens, he gave away only 17 runs in exchange for 7 wickets (5 clean bowled, 1 lbw)—his best performance in an innings in his four appearances in the series. He was unchanged, in partnership with James Lillywhite, junior, in the second innings and added two more scalps to his tally, one of them E. M. Grace's, clean bowled for 7. His return at Lord's the following year was rather more expensive by his standards: 5–61 and 3–54, but on each occasion he took a wicket, he bowled down the stumps, including those of E.M., who went cheaply again. "Tear'em's" finest overall performance was reserved for the encounter in 1864, his final appearance in the series. Suffering the martyrdom of an overwhelming defeat by an innings and 68 runs, the Gentlemen were restricted to only 60 at their first attempt and one less at their second. The Players enjoyed the unusual luxury of not having to call upon the services of two of their crack bowlers, John Jackson and R. C. Tinley, since the destruction of the amateurs was achieved by the partnership of Edgar Willsher and George Tarrant, who were unchanged throughout *both* innings. "Tear'em's" match figures were 11 wickets for 49 runs (6–25 and 5–24, including 9 clean bowled and 1 lbw). His complete record was outstanding. Bowling in 8 innings, he took 30 wickets at an average of 9.80 each, and the quality of his powers of penetration is graphically revealed by the details of how he dismissed his victims—clean bowled 24, lbw 2, caught 4!

In a first-class career beginning in 1860 and ending shortly after the start of the season of 1869, Tarrant appeared in only 71 matches. By the end of 1864, he had already played in 47 of these, the remaining 24 being spread sparsely over the period 1865–1869. The principal reason for this was undoubtedly the regrettable schism between north and south, master-minded on the northern side by George Parr, captain of Nottinghamshire and captain and secretary of the All England Eleven. "Tear'em," influenced by his two Cambridgeshire team-mates, Bob Carpenter and Tom Hayward, followed Parr's lead in refusing to turn out for the Players against the Gentlemen, the North against the South, and other representative teams. At the same time, there was a decrease in the number of fixtures between northern and southern counties. When the rift was repaired, Tarrant was no longer in the reckoning.

The diminution in the number of first-class appearances did not have the automatic effect of depriving "Tear'em" of a regular income in the summer months. He played plenty of cricket from 1865 onwards, just as he had done in the previous seasons of the 1860s, appearing for the two most famous itinerant elevens. By turning out a few times for the United All England Eleven, he earned some extra match fees, but the United, as far as "Tear'em" was concerned, were in reality the opposition. His principal affiliation lay with George Parr's All England Eleven, whom he first assisted at Lord's, in 1860, on the occasion of his debut in first-class cricket. He played six times for the AEE that year, but from 1861 to 1868 he was a regular full-time member of the organization, missing very few matches in the extensive programme arranged annually by Parr. Full details of these fixtures are not always available, but it seems that Tarrant assisted the AEE in almost two hundred matches. Apart from the first-class contests against the United All England Eleven and two others during the period, the AEE spent their time travelling round the country, fulfilling engagements with local teams.

Tarrant's role in these contests against "odds" was that of an all-rounder rather than exclusively a bowler, and it was not unusual for him to occupy a high place in the batting order, sometimes even opening the innings. The average of a batsman playing in this type of cricket, restricted in his stroke-play by the gaggle of fielders and the roughness of the grounds, was in many instances rather low. In all matches for the All England Eleven, Tarrant averaged over 11 runs per innings, which was by no means a failure. As a bowler, of course, he was featured prominently, frequently sweeping aside the frail batting of his opponents. The details on the score-sheets, it will be remembered, are not always complete, and sometimes the name of a bowler taking a wicket or a fielder holding a catch has been omitted. As far as it is possible to tell on the evidence now available, "Tear'em's" aggregate of wickets in all matches for the All England Eleven totalled somewhere in the region of 1,275, and for about three-quarters of these the analysis is lacking. One of his best performances, possibly *the* best, occurred when the AEE encountered 22 of Hull, assisted by three first-class bowlers, on September 7, 8, and 9, 1863. The home side went in first, and during the time they were at the wickets, a wind of hurricane proportions swept across the forlorn ground. Perhaps this climatic phenomenon lent some assistance to Tarrant in his annihilation of the opposition. He took 17 wickets—possibly 18, for in one instance the bowler's name is omitted from the mode of dismissal—while Willsher took 2, and one batsman was absent. In the second innings, "Tear'em" accounted for 6 batsmen, with a match return of at least 23 wickets. Twenty-two of Hull, in their two attempts, scored 131 runs off the bat, and since All England employed at least three other bowlers (Willsher, Jackson, and Tinley), Tarrant's wickets would not have cost many runs each. That same propensity for hitting the stumps was well in evidence again. In Hull's first innings, his 17 dismissals were brought about in the following manner: clean bowled 11, lbw 2, caught and bowled 1, caught 3. The six in the second innings were all bowled, so "Tear'em" was solely responsible for getting rid of 20 out of the 23 batsmen whose wickets he took!

Tarrant's duties with the All England Eleven were not confined to batting, bowling and fielding. He was, it will be remembered, an accomplished and courageous pugilist, and on this account he was often assigned the role of bodyguard to George Parr, being always ready to protect his chief and employer from harm. On one occasion, the All England captain was suddenly confronted by a belligerent drunk, who assailed him with a volley of insults and challenged him to put up his dukes. Now, fisticuffs were not Parr's strong point, but on glancing round and seeing Tarrant at his elbow, he threw one punch at his opponent before stepping neatly to one side and shouted, "Go at him, "Tear'em!" Obedient to his master's command, the faithful "minder" went swiftly into action and hammered the offender into the ground.

In 1863-64, Tarrant was engaged to be a member of George Parr's team touring Australia and New Zealand, the party consisting of eleven professionals and E. M. Grace, elder brother of W.G., one of the most accomplished amateurs of the day. Like most travellers in those days, "Tear'em" was not the best of sailors, nor was he entirely happy at sea. On one occasion, the team were sailing from Sydney to Melbourne, and the steamer was involved in a collision with a smaller ship, which foundered at once. Pandemonium ensued, during which Tarrant "quite lost his head". Dashing down to his cabin, he hastily assembled a much prized collection of presents and curios acquired in various places on the tour. Emerging on deck once more, he tried to get into a boat, which, in fact, was being lowered to rescue the crew of the sinking vessel, not the passengers on the bigger ship, who were in no danger. The sailors roughly ordered him to get out of the way "in no very choice language," and, for once "Tear'em" was cowed into submission and compelled to knuckle under. His panic-stricken behaviour at this critical moment was in stark contrast to that of the team's other fast man, John Jackson. The latter, having taken full advantage of an excellent luncheon served to Parr's men before the departure from Sydney, was found fast asleep in his berth, oblivious to all the excitement caused by the collision!

On dry land, however, "Tear'em" was in his element. A bundle of nervous energy, he missed little on the field of play, taking part in all, or possibly all but one of the various matches played (against "odds," eleven-a-side, and single-wicket contests). Throughout the tour, he was employed more as an all-rounder rather than as a specialist bowler. His performance with the bat was generally more than adequate, and he fielded with his usual keenness and efficiency, holding 19 catches. With the ball, however, he was used rather sparingly. Most of the bowling was allocated to John Jackson and R. C. Tinley, the lobster, who was well on the way to a grand total of 300 wickets by the end of the tour. The medium pace of Tom Hayward, of Cambridgeshire, was more in evidence than the thunderbolts of "Tear'em." In several matches, the latter spent his time fielding out, while Tinley, in particular, was casting his spells and bamboozling the jittery opposition with his insidious under-hands. When the opportunity came his way, however, "Tear'em" was not found wanting, and he took 72 wickets in all. His best performance statistically occurred in the final match of the tour, a drawn game with 22 of Victoria, at Melbourne, on April 21, 22, and 23, 1864. In the first innings, he took 5 wickets, adding 12 in the second, and he hit the stumps 13 times. Earlier, at the beginning of the same month, in a contest against 22 of New South Wales, at Sydney, he was the fifth England bowler to be put on in the first innings. Did Parr, one wonders, have any regrets over his decision to keep Tarrant out of the attack for so long, especially since his team scraped home by only one wicket? In only thirty-five deliveries, "Tear'em" plundered 7 wickets without conceding a single run!

Whatever he may have felt about the preference given to others in the bowling department, "Tear'em" could have had no grounds for complaining about the number of turns he was given with the bat. He had twenty-seven innings; only one other team-mate had the same number, and all the others had less. Employed as an opening batsman in thirteen of the matches, at least in the first innings, he established a regular partnership with E. M. Grace, who accompanied him to the wickets on no less than eleven occasions. Ostensibly an amateur, though doubtless well paid for his services, E.M. found himself in an anomalous position. Obliged to tread carefully at the beginning of the tour, he was aware of some resentment among one or two of the party, who seemed to be looking for any excuse to start a quarrel, though the situation improved as the weeks went by. With Tarrant, however—"not," one remembers, "the most urbane of men"—E.M. seems to have struck up an enduring friendly relationship, which went beyond the regular matches. They continued their partnership in three of the six single-wicket contests arranged during the tour, and in another, when E.M. played with John Jackson, Tarrant was selected to field for the pair. Each played one match on his own, and when "Tear'em" took on 11 of Ararat, he produced a typical performance. Although he had two of his team-mates to field for him (Alfred Clarke and Tom Hayward), he was solely responsible for the dismissal of the opposition for only 4 runs—9 bowled, 1 lbw, 1 caught and bowled. E.M. decided to remain some time longer in Australia after the tour was over. He presented Tarrant with a brooch for his wife, but, beyond a small gift to Hayward for his daughter, he gave the others nothing "except my good wishes." When the moment for the departure of the team arrived, E.M. remembered that "two or three shook hands with me with tears glittering in their eyes." One of them, no doubt, was the formidable "Tear'em."

In almost every past age of cricket, there have been players whose names have gone down in the history of the game with the reputation of being real "characters." One has only to call to mind W. G. Grace himself, his contemporary Tom Emmett, and, in much later times, F. S. Trueman. They are featured in countless anecdotes, some of which may have been refurbished with the passage of time, and their drolleries have been treasured with loving care. George Tarrant must be excluded from this category. Perhaps he was too absorbed in life's daily struggle—for cricketers were not well paid at that time—or thought of little beyond his perpetual onslaught on the batsmen facing up to him. One anecdote has, however, survived in one of the books by Richard Daft. The latter had the story from Tarrant himself, and we might infer that the grim fast man was not entirely lacking in a vestige of wry humour. Daft's version gives a vivid picture of "Tear'em," not only the pace of his bowling, but also the impatience and irascibility of the man. Once, it appears, he was playing in a match—probably for the All England Eleven against a local twenty-two—and one of the umpires was grievously afflicted with a speech impediment. This, as was only to be expected, became more marked in moments of nervous stress, as the story illustrates:

> Tarrant was bowling and cried "How's that?" for leg before wicket. The umpire being appealed to so sharply could not for some time speak a word, although it was plain to be seen he was endeavouring to give his decision; but Tarrant, who was very impatient, took up the ball, saying, "Oh, I can't wait any longer;" bowled another ball which knocked the batsman's middle stump down just as the umpire called out, "N-n-not out!" "Not out?" roared Tarrant; "why, look at his middle stump!" It was a long time before the poor umpire was able to make him understand that the decision referred to his appeal for the leg before of the previous ball.

Once he had got over his fit of ill-temper, "Tear'em" was evidently able to appreciate the humorous side of the situation and showed no reluctance in telling the story as much against himself as the unfortunate official. Sad to relate, he was involved in another event, which was totally devoid of any humour, and which took place before his home crowd in a first-class match. This lamentable incident showed Tarrant at his worst, and it probably contributed much to the unflattering portrayal of his character that has been handed down to us. It occurred, moreover, at the time when, as a result of the great schism between north and south in 1864, many of the leading northern professionals were in bad odour because of their refusal to appear in matches on some of the southern grounds.

On June 4 and 5, 1866, Middlesex played on their home ground at Islington against Cambridgeshire and were crushingly defeated by an innings and 48 runs. Tarrant was the top scorer of the match—it was his best season with the bat—amassing 64, largely with drives and leg-hits, though his innings was described as "rather flukey." With Tom Hayward at the other end, he bowled unchanged, taking 7 wickets for 55 runs and 5 for 29. In the return match, at Fenner's, on August 16 and 17, Middlesex won the toss and took first innings again, and this time the positions were reversed. Although their opening pair had gone cheaply by the time the total was barely in double figures, the next four batsmen dominated the Cambridgeshire bowling with scores of 64, 48, 33, and 59. Fielding at point for the home side, as usual, was Bob Carpenter. He ought, perhaps, to have been in another position, since he had recently suffered an injury to one of his fingers, which had not quite healed. When the total had reached 170, one of the Middlesex batsmen made a fierce cut, and the ball struck Carpenter on the injured finger with such force, that he was compelled to leave the field. Middlesex were eventually dismissed for 248, and Cambridgeshire lost one wicket before stumps were drawn. Tarrant, it is reasonable to imagine, was not in the best of moods that night, suffering a severe case of wounded pride: his bowling had received an unaccustomed trouncing to the tune of 4 expensive wickets at a cost of 120 runs.

Carpenter's injury prevented him from taking any further part in the match, and an arrangement was made which was comparatively rare but not unique at that time. Since he had not batted, it was mutually agreed that another player should replace him in the home side. This deputy was Charles Newman, a cricketer of no outstanding merit, who had turned out twice for Cambridgeshire that season. One person, however, jibbed at the arrangement. Was there bad blood between Tarrant and Newman, or was it "Tear'em's" obstinate and, let us face it, entirely justified opinion that Newman was no real substitute for a crack batsman like Carpenter? We shall never know the working of Tarrant's mind, but he "refused to play further in the match, assigning as his reason that he had previously told those in authority that 'he would not play if Newman did,' and he would keep his word." Reduced to ten men, Cambridgeshire were defeated in only two days by an innings and 4 runs.

Tarrant's withdrawal from the match was recorded with little further comment in some of the journals, apart from referring to his objection to the substitution of Newman for Carpenter. Others were more severely critical, condemning his behaviour as "perfectly unjustifiable" and "another specimen of 'professional' intolerance, not much longer to be borne by the real supporters of cricket." It was especially maladroit of "Tear'em" to drop such a monumental clanger in his home town. At a special dinner in 1864, he, Carpenter, and Hayward had each been presented with a silver goblet, "in testimony of the credit that their cricket abilities and honourable conduct have brought upon their native place." Two years later, a local newspaper expressed the view that Tarrant "was much to blame for not sacrificing private feeling to the public good," which implies that he was not on the best of terms with Newman.

Many years later, a member of the Middlesex team retained a rancorous recollection of the incident, dubbing the offender "that spoilt child of fortune" and asserting that he had deliberately done his best to ruin the match. In fact, long before the end of play, "Tear'em" was already regretting the consequences of his impulsive obstinacy, particularly the inevitable forfeiture of his match fee. He offered to take his turn with the bat in the second innings, but those in authority were adamant and "very properly refused to allow him."

In the score-sheet of the match reproduced in newspapers and books, Tarrant's name appears sometimes in the middle of the batting order, sometimes at the end, and even not at all. The word "absent" is given in place of the mode of dismissal, but one version has "refused to go in," and another "shamefully absent." The compiler of *Scores and Biographies*, who rarely neglected an opportunity to castigate the northern professionals for the part they played in the schism between north and south, combined the language of those two more emphatic comments, with the result that "Tear'em" will always be remembered as the man who "'shamefully' refused to go in."

Tarrant made a formal apology for his conduct at a meeting of the Cambridgeshire CCC in February 1867, but he had already taken steps to rehabilitate himself publicly in connection with a business venture, on which he embarked in December 1866, but a few months after the Middlesex match: he became the landlord of *The Birdbolt Inn*, Newmarket Road, Cambridge. This was announced in one of the sporting newspapers, which assured its readers that Tarrant regretted his recent behaviour and attributed his refusal to play on certain grounds "to the counsel of men who ought to have given him better advice." The givers of bad advice were probably George Parr, Bob Carpenter, and Tom Hayward, three of the hardest "hard-liners" in perpetuating the hostility between north and south.

During the next three seasons, Tarrant participated in nine first-class matches, all on northern grounds, but in one of them the opponents were Kent, and his willingness to associate with southern professionals was displayed two years after the tragic incident in the encounter with Middlesex.

Australia and New Zealand were not the only countries visited by Tarrant. At the beginning of September 1868, a team consisting of seven southern and five northern professionals set sail for North America. The captain was Edgar Willsher of Kent, and "Tear'em" was one of the party. Six matches, all against twenty-twos, were played in Canada and the USA, with Willsher's men undefeated (five victories, one draw). By now, it might be argued, "Tear'em's" powers were on the wane. Although he had rendered sterling service to the All England Eleven, his record in three first-class games in 1868 was mediocre, apart from an analysis of 6 for 76 in the AEE's annual fixture with the United Eleven. His experience of the tour of North America might have created a feeling of *déjà vu*. Employed as not much more than a change bowler down under in 1863–64, he found himself cast in the same role in 1868. His erstwhile team-mate, John Jackson, was no longer on the scene, but since "Tear'em's" first visit overseas a new crack fast man had come to the fore in the person of Yorkshire's George Freeman. The latter, on at one end in every innings, was usually supported at the other by the captain, Ned Willsher. Freeman took 106 wickets at the astonishing average of 2.00, while Willsher's tally of 62 cost only 2.35 runs apiece. Three other first-rate bowlers—George Griffith, James Lillywhite, junior, and Alfred Shaw—were put on in only seven innings between them and shared 22 wickets. As for "Tear'em," he too was frequently unemployed. His name appears only four times in the details of the bowlers' doings. He had one good analysis (12–16), and he obtained 20 wickets at an average of 3.65. Only nine of these were clean bowled, a possible indication that the pristine sharpness of his cutting edge was becoming slightly dulled, considering that the opposition encountered in Canada and the USA was modest in the extreme.

In addition to the annual contest with the United All England Eleven in 1869, "Tear'em" assisted the AEE in ten matches against "odds." After playing against 22 of Sunderland, on July 1, 2, and 3—he scored 21 and did not bowl, or, at any rate, took no wickets—he went on to stand as umpire against 22 of Hull, but he was taken ill and returned to his home at Cambridge. He lingered there in adverse circumstances for a year, suffering from a prolonged attack of pleurisy which brought on phthisis, and during his last few days he was delirious and almost blind. Tarrant, aged thirty-one, died at 5.00 p.m., on Saturday, July 2, 1870, exactly twelve months after his final appearance for the All England Eleven.

The biographical sketch of "Tear'em" in *Scores and Biographies*, while declaring he was "commonly known as George Tarrant under which appellation he appears in these pages," records his full name as "George Tarrant Wood." The last is not entirely accurate. His birth certificate, it will be recalled, gives his christian names as George Frederick, registering his parents as James Tarrant and Eliza Tarrant formerly Wood, but "Tear 'em's" death certificate is made out in the name of George Frederick Wood. And Wood, it seems, is the name perpetuated among the descendants of this great bowler, for the portrait at Lord's was presented to MCC on August 1, 1951, by his grandson, Mr W. M. Wood, residing in London.

CHAPTER SIX

Edward Pooley
"A Rare Genius for the Game"

RICHMOND Green in Surrey was one of Ted Pooley's favourite stamping-grounds. As a teenager, contending against other schoolboys in single-wicket matches and backing himself for small sums, he was soon acknowledged as cock of the walk. Though the game provided him with a steady source of pocket-money, he entertained no idea at that time of adopting cricket as a profession. A career in commerce beckoned, and he obtained a five-year apprenticeship in the office of a soap-merchant. There is no evidence that Ted Pooley was a particularly godly youth. Nor, seemingly, did he set much store by an ostentatious parade of cleanliness. Allergic to the prospect of a prolonged association with the manufacture of soap, he decided to forfeit his indentures after serving three of the five years. His thoughts were turning to cricket again, and the opportunity to escape and exploit his natural talents came in May 1861 with an invitation to play at The Oval for a team of 12 Surrey Colts against 12 Gentlemen of the Surrey Club. Pooley was over twenty-three at the time—a little mature on paper to be regarded as a colt—but his father intervened, saying he would look more like a colt if he knocked five years off his age. Accordingly, Ted reported his date of birth as February 13, 1843, and soon severed all connection with the soap-merchant. Pooley was not a stickler for the proprieties. His inclination for betting, nurtured in those single-wicket contests on the Green of his native Richmond, and his willingness to cheat over the matter of his age, were indications of certain flaws in his character destined to surface throughout the progression of his life both on and off the cricket field.

Short of stature and weighing less than 10 stone in his early twenties, Pooley was endowed with rather flashy good looks, wavy hair, incipient fluffy side-whiskers, and an almost cherubic countenance that made him look younger than his actual age—hence the unquestioning acceptance of 1843, rather than 1838, as the year of his birth. His features coarsened slightly as he grew older, and his whiskers matured in size and thickness, but he never put on much weight and, barring injuries, was rarely unfit to take the field in a first-class career lasting over twenty years. Like many of his fellow professionals, he was fond enough of alcoholic beverages, though there is no record that this ever interfered with his performance during a match. He displayed at times a disturbing inability to control a violent and ugly temper, and what was in those days termed "filthy language" was no stranger to his lips. On the credit side, he never lacked courage and, as an early version of London's "cheeky chappie," his genial nature and earthy optimism enabled him to survive when beset by adverse conditions that would have crushed a weaker soul.

Ted Pooley was not markedly successful in his outing with the Colts, but nevertheless he was called up to assist Surrey twice that season, making his first-class debut against Kent, at The Oval, on August 19 and 20, 1861. The following season, he turned out eight times for the County and, without achieving anything remarkable, gave some sign of future promise as a hard-hitting batsman, while already distinguishing himself as an excellent run-saver at long-leg. Whenever it suited his purpose in those early days, he gave others to understand that he could bowl slow lobs, "but with that he does not excel," according to the compiler of *Scores and Biographies*—which should surely receive an award as one of the most striking examples of magisterial understatement, seeing that Ted took no more than 6 wickets in a first-class career beginning in 1861 and not ending until 1883.

In 1863, Ted Pooley played twice for Surrey and once for the Players of Surrey, but the season marked a watershed in his advancement to lasting fame. This momentous event occurred at The Oval, on July 16, 17, and 18, in the match between Surrey and Kent, and many years later he still retained a vivid recollection of the circumstances:

> Old Tom Lockyer's hands were bad, and the ground being fiery he could not take his usual place behind the sticks. Mr F. P. Miller, the Surrey captain, was in a quandary as to who should relieve him, so I, saucy-like, as usual, went up to him and said, 'Mr Miller, let me have a try.' 'You? What do you know about wicket-keeping? Have you ever kept wicket at all? was Mr Miller's remark. 'No, never, but I should like to try,' I replied. 'Nonsense,' he said, when just at that moment H. H. Stephenson came up and remarked, 'Let the young 'un have a go, sir.' Mr Miller thereupon relented. I donned the gloves, quickly got two or three wickets, and seemed so much at home that Tom Lockyer was delighted, and said I was born to keep wicket and would have to be his successor in the Surrey team. What he said came true.

Edward Pooley

Courtesy Roger Mann

For the record, Pooley made his debut as a wicket-keeper in Kent's second innings with one catch and one stumping off a slow, under-hand bowler, and he conceded only one bye. Stephenson's recommendation was, perhaps, not so disinterested as one might suppose. Generally regarded as the second-best professional stumper in England, H.H. would have been the natural choice to deputize for Lockyer, but he might not have been relishing the possibility of having *his* hands knocked about by the ball flying off a pitch "as hard as a turnpike road!" The scene gives an indication of other aspects of Pooley's character—an engaging personality and an abundance of self-confidence possessed by this "saucy-like" youngster.

The veteran wicket-keeper, Tom Lockyer, recovered and continued to assist Surrey up to 1866, so, for the time being, Pooley remained on the fringe of the County side. Uncertain, perhaps, of his future at The Oval, he drifted away to set up in business with a cricket and cigar depot at Islington, near the ground then used by the newly formed Middlesex County Cricket Club. In the same year (1864), he acted as secretary for a minor itinerant team entitled the New All England Eleven, which expired not long after its foundation. As we have already seen, there was nothing in the Laws of Cricket in those days to prevent an individual from turning out for more than one county in the same season, and although Pooley played three times for Surrey and twice for the South, he assisted Middlesex in six matches. In the autumn of the same year, he was one of the founder-members of the United South of England Eleven. One of the most famous of the travelling teams, the United South began operations in 1865 and, thanks to the presence of W. G. Grace as a star attraction, lasted until about 1880. Throughout much of this Eleven's existence, Pooley played side by side with the Champion on a regular basis whenever he was available.

Pooley appeared for Middlesex in their first match of 1865, but was soon claimed by his native Surrey, with whom he then remained permanently until his retirement, initially sharing the wicket-keeping with Tom Lockyer, and becoming the first choice for the post from 1867 onwards. With Old Tom devoting himself exclusively to his role as the landlord of *The Sheldon Arms* at Croydon, Ted Pooley rapidly assumed his predecessor's mantle as the premier professional wicket-keeper in England, an unofficial title he held against all contenders for many years. Gifted with keen eyesight, finely tuned instincts, and an exceptionally safe pair of hands, he performed his duties with a somewhat theatrical brilliance that delighted the Oval crowd. His principal rivals also bore surnames beginning with the letter P—bearded, short-tongued Henry Phillips of Sussex; bluff, burly George Pinder of Yorkshire; and the quietly efficient Tom Plumb of

Buckinghamshire, whose first-class appearances were largely limited to such contests as North *v* South. It was generally acknowledged that Pinder and Plumb probably had the edge on Pooley when it was a question of keeping to fast bowling—they had, it must be admitted, more practice—but Ted had no superior when the slower bowlers were on, as they usually were throughout much of the time he was performing at The Oval.

Between the two World Wars, Kent could boast with pride of the deadly partnership of "Tich" Freeman, the leg-break and googly bowler, and Leslie Ames behind the stumps. Equally illustrious and no less lethal in the 1860s and 1870s was the duo of foxy James Southerton, with his slow off breaks, and Ted Pooley. Formed in 1866, this combination did not become complete until 1873, when Southerton had ceased playing for his native Sussex and cast his lot permanently with Surrey. Throughout their long and fruitful association, Southerton and Pooley accounted for 275 wickets (127 caught, 148 stumped) in first-class matches, and they were eminently successful as well when playing together for the United South of England Eleven in minor contests against "odds." The modes of dismissal "caught/stumped Pooley, bowled Southerton" appeared with almost monotonous regularity in the score cards of the time, though Ted was also no mean performer when supporting other members of the Surrey attack. Even as late as 1878, in the encounter with Kent, at The Oval, on August 19, 20, and 21, he proved that he could still hold his place at the top as the supreme master by claiming 10 victims off the bowling of the slow, left-arm trundler, E. Barratt (6 stumped), and Southerton (2 caught, 2 stumped).

Pooley's most remarkable achievement as a wicket-keeper undoubtedly occurred in the period July 6 to July 22, 1868, in five matches for Surrey, when his tally of dismissals amounted to 36 (18 caught, 18 stumped). This total included 1 catch and 12 stumpings from Jimmy Southerton's bowling, including 5 stumped in one innings, but Surrey's opponents in two of the contests were Sussex, who at that time were still exerting a prior claim on Southerton's services. In the first match of his "purple period," Pooley disposed of no less than 12 wickets (8 caught, 4 stumped)! In fairness to the batsmen, it must be added that the pitch favoured the bowlers, but nevertheless, according to one of the cricket annuals, Pooley achieved "a feat of rare occurrence." It was more than that: 12 victims to a wicket-keeper in one match in first-class cricket still stands as a record, surpassed by none and equalled only by two Australians, H. B. Taber and D. Tallon. Alas for the fame of the Southerton-Pooley partnership! The off-breaker, through assisting Sussex in that memorable encounter, was denied the opportunity of sharing in Ted's triumph, apart from being one of the stumpings.

Pooley made his debut for the Players against the Gentlemen, at Lord's, in 1866, and his final appearance at The Oval, in 1879—a total of twenty-five matches. Apart from the seasons of 1873 and 1877, when extraordinary circumstances accounted for his absence, he missed only two matches throughout the period. One reason for his well nigh permanent occupation of the wicket-keeper's slot for the professionals was his affiliation with a southern county with headquarters situated in the capital—an immense advantage over Phillips, Pinder, and Plumb. Another reason, in addition to his excellence with the gloves, was that Ted Pooley was undeniably the best batsman of the Four Ps. His overall record in the contests with the Gentlemen was, in fact, only moderate, even by the accepted standards of the day, with an average of 15.73. He played, however, some very useful innings at times, with a top score of 85, as well as obtaining 40 dismissals (29 caught, 11 stumped).

Once he had established himself in the Surrey Eleven, Ted Pooley began to make his mark as a batsman, being particularly successful around 1870. Brimming over with exuberant self-confidence, he was a rapid run-getter, forcing the pace with high-powered drives and brilliant cuts, being especially strong in his off-side play. He was known, at times, to have scored at the rate of around a run a minute, and his occasional adoption of more circumspect tactics would give rise to such comments as "an unusually careful innings." Living dangerously at the crease, he was often dismissed by catches in the deep. One of the most famous instances occurred in the first ever encounter between Gloucestershire and Surrey, on Durdham Downs, on June 2, 3, and 4, 1870. W.G. was bowling some tempting deliveries on the leg side, and Pooley was indulging in some vigorous leg-hitting, which was, however, being largely nullified by the presence of some of the crowd encroaching on the playing area. Ted, not unnaturally, objected to this obstruction, and the offending spectators were with some difficulty persuaded to withdraw behind the boundary marked only by a ring of flags. This, in fact, worked to his disadvantage, because C. R. Filgate, the fielder at long-leg, was able to go to a deeper position, where he soon held on to a catch from one of Ted's hefty leg-hits.

Although he took five catches by way of compensation, Pooley had to be content with modest scores in that match with Gloucestershire. The season of 1870, however, was his most successful with the bat. In all first-class contests, he marked a total of 1,084 runs (average 23.06, highest score 94)—only the fourth batsman to attain a four-figure aggregate since 1864—and he came tenth in the national averages. The following season, his tally was 926 runs, which included the only first-class century of his career—125 for the Players of the South against the Gentlemen of the South, at The Oval, on June 29, 30, and July 1. His innings, which lasted about 165 minutes, included 3 fives and 9 fours.

From 1872 onwards, the quality of Pooley's batting steadily declined. His seasonal total never approached the thousand mark again, for two very good reasons. Now in his thirties, he was beginning to find that the demands made on him by his wicket-keeping duties were taking their toll, and although he retained his free style of play, his powers of concentration at the crease were on the wane. Added to this was the matter of injuries. Appearing in such representative teams as the Players, the South, and the Players of the South, he came up against bowlers whose pace and ferocity eclipsed the more gentle deliveries he was accustomed to taking at The Oval. Once, in a match at Lord's, a ball bounded off the rough, cracked pitch, struck him in the mouth, and knocked out three of his teeth. Back in the dressing-room, Ted was gingerly inspecting the damage and washing the blood out of his mouth, when he was told that somebody wished to be introduced to him. The visitor turned out to be Jem Mace, the pugilist, hero of many a bloody bone-crushing bout with bare knuckles in the prize ring, and an authority on the subject of giving and receiving a violent blow in the mouth. It was Mace rather than Ted who was filled with awe. "Pooley," said Jem, "I would rather stand up against any man in England for an hour than take your place behind the wicket for five minutes. I heard that ball strike you as if it had hit a brick wall."

On another occasion, when playing for the United South of England Eleven in a minor match in Jersey, Pooley was the victim of an equally sanguinary accident. One of the batsmen lashed out at a deliberately tempting leg-side delivery, but failed to connect with the ball. The bat, continuing in its rapidly swinging arc, smashed the unfortunate wicket-keeper on the nose and pole-axed him to the ground. Happily, these facial injuries were isolated incidents, which yielded to medical treatment, but the damage to his hands was more serious and of much longer duration. An occupational hazard for any wicket-keeper at the best of times, the condition was most marked in Pooley's case. Every finger and the thumb on each hand was fractured at one time or another during his long career. According to one writer, these crippling injuries, exacerbated by the later onset of rheumatism, had transformed Pooley's hands into "mere lumps of deformity," suggestive of the tortures of the thumbscrew. Another writer was equally appalled at the gruesome sight, saying he had never seen "such unhappy wrecks."

The season of 1871 was particularly bad for Pooley, and more than once he was compelled to surrender the gloves to a team-mate or stand out of a match. While this gave him the chance to concentrate on his batting if the injury were not too severe, it also restricted his opportunities for scoring and possibly prevented him from reaching 1000 runs for the second time. Selected to assist the South against the North in the Canterbury Festival, on August 7, 8, and 9, he was suffering from a badly broken forefinger at the time and sent a wire to say he could not play. Back came the reply, telling him to attend at the ground on promise of payment whether or not he played. Such an invitation required few second thoughts, and Pooley accordingly travelled down to Canterbury and reported to his captain, who told him that some members of the South team had not yet arrived. This piece of news made no impression on Ted, who was, rather ominously, "enjoying a comfortable pint," when suddenly he was ordered to go in at number 4. Hastily he went to the wickets, padless and with boots unlaced. He made 93—with a broken finger!—against J. C. Shaw and Martin McIntyre, two of the leading pace bowlers of the day, and he was rewarded with the proceeds of a collection taken on the ground. Doubtless, he celebrated the occasion with one or two more "comfortable pints."

As the condition of his hands gradually grew worse, Pooley became increasingly and not unnaturally reluctant to keep to fast bowling. When not engaged in first-class fixtures, he earned extra wages by playing for the United South of England Eleven, mainly against twenty-twos, with W. G. Grace as one of his regular team-mates. The Champion was amused by the transparent subterfuge adopted by Ted to protect his hands. After inspecting the condition of the pitch, he would return and announce to W.G., or possibly his brother G.F., one of the managers of the team, "First-rate wicket, sir; slow bowling is sure to come off to-day." The solemn observance of this comic ritual was repeated two or three times without deceiving anybody, and after a while it became a standing joke with the members of the United South to forestall their wicket-keeper by hastily inspecting the pitch and remarking with perfectly straight faces, "A slow bowler's wicket to-day, Pooley."

Considering the numerous occasions over the years when W.G. and Pooley appeared in the same match, either as team-mates or members of the opposing sides, the Champion had ample opportunities for observing Ted's various foibles and his outlook on the game. In the conclusion to his pen-portrait of the great stumper, W.G. dilates on one aspect of Ted's character:

> Once or twice he was thought to have been too eager in appealing to the umpire for a decision, and was accused of trying to entrap the

batsman. My experience of him never showed that; and if he had exceeded the laws I should have certainly put it down more to keenness to win than a desire to overreach. He was always on the alert to stump or run out a batsman if he moved his foot before the ball was dead, but the batsman had only himself to blame if it came off; and if a mistake had been made, the umpire was more to blame than Pooley.

A piece of very special pleading, one might say, since W.G. was after all one of the leading authorities on the art of gamesmanship and could not have failed to recognize a kindred spirit in Pooley. Certainly, throughout his career, the latter was involved as one of the principal actors in more than one incident savouring of sharp practice. Take, for instance, the match between Surrey and Cambridge University, at The Oval, on June 18, 19, and 20, 1868. Towards the end of the Cambridge second innings, C. A. Absolom, a flailing, unorthodox type of batsman with a good eye, set about the Surrey bowling, but, with victory in sight, his promising innings was abruptly terminated in an unusual manner. He drove the ball into the deep to score six—all run out—and went for a seventh on an overthrow, but while he was running, the ball was returned and struck his bat. Seeing his chance immediately, Pooley appealed, and the somewhat inexperienced umpire (a member of the Surrey staff), "believing that the bat was purposely placed in the way of the ball," gave the batsman out for "Obstructing the Field." The harshness of this decision was recognized instantly by the Surrey captain, who offered Absolom another innings, which he refused. Surrey won the match by 14 runs.

It was Oxford University's turn two years later, at The Oval, on June 30 and July 1 and 2, 1870, and once more the over-zealous attitude of Ted Pooley created difficulties for the Surrey Committee. On the second day of the match, during the visitors' first innings, C. E. B. Nepean was batting and had scored 9, when the ball struck his leg, and there was an appeal. The umpire said "not out," but the unfortunate batsman heard only the second word. Believing that he had been adjudged lbw, he left his crease, whereupon Pooley broke the wicket and appealed successfully for "run out." This time, Surrey derived no advantage from Pooley's manœuvre, since Oxford eventually won the match by 3 wickets, but the umpire's decision, which "merited the public censure it received," caused so much hostility that the fixture was not played again for over ten years.

Another incident occurred in the match between Sussex and Surrey, at Hove, on August 19, 20, and 21, 1872. Sussex took first innings, and their crack batsman, Henry Charlwood ("there is scarcely a more dashing hitter in England") had made 73 and looked well set for a century. Stepping out of his crease, he played the ball but mistimed it, and, thinking it was rolling back towards the stumps, hit it a second time, while the non-striker was still in the act of backing up in anticipation of a run. Pooley (who else, after all?) instantly appealed to the umpire, who gave Charlwood his dismissal for "Hit the Ball Twice." Unfortunate it was for the sake of amicable relations that the official giving the dubious decision was the Surrey appointee, Julius Caesar. Once a prime favourite as a player with the Oval crowd, Caesar, curiously enough, was also one of the umpires in the two previously mentioned matches against Cambridge and Oxford in 1868 and 1870 respectively. Opinions at Hove differed as to whether Caesar was right or wrong in his decision, but his ruling "caused much unpleasant excitement." Surrey won this match by 2 wickets.

The contest between Gloucestershire and Surrey, at Clifton, on August 26, 27, and 28, 1875, provided W. G. Grace with firsthand evidence of Ted Pooley's "keenness to win," and at the time he showed no very great appreciation of it. Surrey were dismissed for 181 on the first day, and at close of play Gloucestershire, amid a tense atmosphere of turmoil and strife, had reached 38 for the loss of 2 wickets. Going in first for the home side, the Champion chose to open the batting with R. E. Bush rather than his brother and usual partner, E. M. Grace. Bush, a promising youngster and captain of the Clifton College Eleven, was only nineteen at the time. This was his sixth appearance in first-class cricket, but his first encounter with Surrey, and he was rather green in the ways of the world. Having scored 21 in only ten minutes, W.G. fell victim to the Southerton-Pooley combination and was succeeded by F. Townsend. Shortly afterwards, the latter made a single, both batsmen gained their ground, and the ball was returned to the bowler. Evidently believing that it was dead, Bush stepped outside his crease, perhaps to do some gardening—a fatal move. The opportunity was too good to miss, and Pooley signalled to the bowler to throw over the ball. No sooner was it in his hands than he broke the wicket and appealed for "run out." The umpire, an old Surrey professional called William Mortlock, ruled in Pooley's favour, much to the vociferous anger of the all-amateur Gloucestershire team and their supporters ("Some most hideous noises were then made by a few of the spectators"). Members of the Grace family openly disputed Mortlock's decision, particularly Alfred, who was not playing but, in spite of this, "was allowed to give vent to his feelings in no uncertain terms," adding that he would make it his business to see that none of his brothers took part in benefit matches got up in the future for any of the offenders. While these threats were being delivered, W.G. strode out on to the field to argue with the Surrey team. All was in vain, however, since Mortlock peremptorily refused to rescind his decision, and Bush had no option but to make his way to the dressing-room. Pooley's gamesmanship received its just deserts. G. F. Grace conducted a remorseless massacre of the Surrey bowling, scoring 180 not out, with 3 fives and 20 fours. The visitors were overwhelmed by an innings and 84 runs: in their second knock, only Pooley (!), with 29, showed any resistance to E. M. Grace, whose lobs took 7 wickets for 46 runs. W.G. was obviously seething with rage at the time, but perhaps the passing years appeased his wrath, and he came to regard the incident as merely an example of Ted Pooley's "keenness to win." One, moreover, worthy of imitation, it seems: in the Test Match at The Oval, on August 28 and 29, 1882, while fielding close to the wicket, the Champion ran out an Australian batsman in identical circumstances.

An acutely developed taste for gamesmanship was, on the whole, an almost minor shortcoming in Pooley's make-up. Other failings of a more serious nature manifested themselves in certain situations. Antagonistic and even belligerent at times, he was extremely sensitive to adverse comments on his professional skills, especially his batting, and more than once he found himself at loggerheads with members of the sporting press. On one occasion, in 1869, he took exception to the remarks of one reporter, who had committed the cardinal error—in Pooley's eyes—of expressing his preference for the talents of two other professional batsmen. Burning with resentment at this apparent slur on his expertise and learning that the unfortunate journalist was in the Tavern at The Oval, Pooley assailed the culprit with a volley of bad language, challenged him to put up his fists and, at the same time, offering to back himself for a stake of £1—an interesting reminiscence, perhaps, of those boyhood contests on Richmond Green. Pooley, as we shall see, continued being addicted to betting for some time to come. The impending punch-up was averted, but on this occasion the matter did not end there. Pooley was hauled before the court, where he was compelled to apologize for his behaviour and was bound over to keep the peace.

Pooley's weakness for betting was to surface again four years later, with dire consequences. In the first few weeks of the season of 1873, he was occupied in dividing his time between first-class matches and games with the United South of England Eleven. He was completely out of form with the bat, but maintained his reputation with the gloves, and in the United South's opening fixture he snapped up 10 victims (3 caught, 7 stumped). After appearing for the South against the North, and Surrey Club against MCC, he assisted the United South in two more "odds" matches towards the end of May, and in the first fortnight of June he played three times for Surrey at The Oval. The next county fixture, against Yorkshire, took place at Bramall Lane, on June 16 and 17, and for neither the first nor the last time Pooley failed to resist the temptation to indulge in some betting. According to *his* story, he made several wagers for small sums on the number of runs scored by different players on both sides. Some twenty-odd years later, in his recollection, the stakes involved had been transformed into something rather more innocuous—two bottles of champagne, with no money involved! The rumour of his activities evidently caused some sort of altercation before the match at Bramall Lane had ended, perhaps because it was being alleged that he had laid £50 against a Surrey victory and had contributed to his side's defeat by deliberately giving away his wicket in the second innings. This, or something like it, was the version accepted by the Surrey Committee, and Pooley was forthwith suspended from playing any more for the County in 1873. The result was a sizeable reduction in his income, since he was also automatically banned from participating in all other first-class matches—hence his absence from the three contests between Gentlemen and Players, as well as other representative fixtures in 1873. There still remained, however, his wages from the United South of England Eleven, whom Pooley assisted twice in June and twice in the first half of July. Then his head was placed on the chopping block. At a meeting at The Oval (under the influence of the Surrey Committee?), a motion was carried unopposed that "Pooley be suspended from playing with the United South of England Eleven until he is reinstated in the Surrey Eleven." By what means Pooley and his family survived throughout the next few months is not known, since there was no unemployment benefit in those days. Maybe he managed to secure a few engagements as either a player or an umpire in minor affairs, and once, out of charity perhaps, he was given the opportunity of earning a match fee by playing for the United North of England Eleven against 18 of Scarborough towards the end of August, which rather surprised one journalist ("What right Pooley had to play as a member of the U.N.E.E. is not clear"). This reaction is quoted in *Scores and Biographies*, but one wonders if either the compiler or the reporter had any opinion on the presence in the United North team of Mr W. R. Gilbert. A Londoner by birth, and the best known cousin of the Grace brothers, Gilbert played four times for Middlesex and nine times for the United South in 1873, so what right *he* had to assist the UNEE is not clear either.

Once the season was over, Pooley presented his case in writing to the Surrey Committee. While admitting that he had—once again!—been guilty of using "coarse language", he insisted that illness rather than intentional lack of effort was the cause of his failure with the bat against

Yorkshire, at Bramall Lane, and he gave a detailed explanation to the Committee of the bets he had laid on the performance of several players in the Yorkshire and Surrey teams. His plea for reinstatement, supported by six of his professional team-mates, was accepted by the Committee, and Pooley resumed his place in the Surrey side and the United South Eleven in 1874. It seems a pity not to mention the two bottles of champagne that constituted the wager in the later version of the incident: Pooley and Henry Jupp had them for breakfast the next day!

The first team ever to tour Australia (1861–62) was in no way representative of anything remotely resembling England's real strength. Dissatisfied with the terms offered, several crack professionals turned down the opportunity to join the party, and it will also be recollected that the promoters had recourse to the aid of the Oval authorities. In the end, half the side consisted of Surrey men, not all of the best by any means. Pooley, according to his own statement, was asked to make up the numbers, although at that time he had played only twice for the County, but he declined the invitation, as he had other things on his mind ("To tell the truth, I was doing a bit of sweethearting at that time"). He was not so reluctant to go abroad at the end of the season of 1868, when he took part in the brief tour of Canada and the USA as a member of an all-professional team, who played six matches against twenty-twos in September and October.

A second chance for Pooley to tour down under arose in 1876, when the team of twelve professionals, under the leadership of James Lillywhite, junior, set sail for the Antipodes. Ted accepted the invitation, and during the course of his travels he cultivated a moustache to go with his side-whiskers and took to wearing a sort of bush-hat, which gave him a decidedly raffish and devil-may-care appearance. After playing nine matches in Australia, the party went on to New Zealand. Pooley's old partner, James Southerton, who kept a diary of some of the events, recorded one interesting item of information concerning some of the financial arrangements. On the voyage to New Zealand, Lillywhite announced that he would pay an allowance of four shillings a day for drinks to each member of the team during this leg of the tour. Only one individual felt that this offer was not sufficiently generous—Pooley, "whose inside," observed Southerton, "must be lined with some imperishable material!"

After eight fixtures against "odds" in New Zealand, Lillywhite's men returned to Australia for six more games, including the two which inaugurated the series of Test Matches between England and Australia. By rights, Ted Pooley ought to hold the unassailable record of being the first wicket-keeper to play for England in an eleven-a-side international contest. Unfortunately, through his own folly, he deprived himself of that honour. Drink and lack of self-control undoubtedly contributed their part, but, apparently heedless of the events that led to his suspension in 1873, he became involved in another disastrous episode of betting. Towards the end of February 1877, Lillywhite's team were playing against 18 of Canterbury, at Christchurch (NZ). While refreshing himself in an hotel bar, Pooley made a wager, offering £1 to 1 shilling that he could name the individual score of each member of the home team. The bet was accepted by a local man called Ralph Donkin, whereupon Ted craftily declared that each of the opponents would score a duck.

From his vast experience of playing against teams of "odds," and the mediocre batting usually exhibited in such matches against first-class opposition, Pooley was on safe ground in perpetrating this all too familiar trick upon the gullible Donkin. A satisfactory number of ducks appeared on the score-sheet, and Pooley demanded £1 for each of them, at the same time offering to pay 1 shilling for every score obtained by the more fortunate members of the Canterbury side. Realizing that he had been conned, Donkin refused to pay up. A heated argument led to flying fists, and a violent brawl ensued, with consequences that were to bring "Pooley's services with the team to an unpleasant end."

Shortly after this regrettable shindy, Pooley was arrested and charged with assaulting Donkin and damaging property exceeding the value of £5. On the charge of assault, he was fined with costs; on the second indictment, he was remanded to appear together with the team's baggageman—also involved in the fracas at the hotel—before the Supreme Court at Christchurch early in April, where he was found not guilty and discharged. Out of sympathy, the local populace raised a subscription and presented him with 50 guineas and a watch and chain. Pooley travelled back alone to England via America, arriving on July 9, and making his first appearance of the season for Surrey against Nottinghamshire, at Trent Bridge, on July 12. As in 1873, he was missing from the three contests between Gentlemen and Players, which had just finished.

Perhaps Pooley had at last realized the dangers of betting, since nothing else on that score has been recorded against him. He assisted the Players three more times, making his last appearance at The Oval, on July 3, 4, and 5, 1879, since by then another stumper whose name began with P—Richard Pilling of Lancashire and MCC—was coming to the fore. Throughout the next few years, Ted continued playing for Surrey, and although his batting powers had largely ebbed away, he occasionally made some useful scores. His form with the gloves did not desert him, and, in the eyes of one writer, he remained "a relic of past ages of excellence." Recognition of his long service and impending retirement came in his benefit match, North *v* South, at The Oval, on June 21, 22, and 23, 1883, which was a success in both the cricketing and financial sense. W.G. played but failed to make a big score for the occasion, and the wicket-keeper for the South was one of the Ps—Henry Phillips of Sussex. Pooley's final appearance for Surrey, rather appropriately against his other county, Middlesex, occurred at Lord's, on July 16 and 17, when, surprisingly, he made no dismissals. He made his exit from first-class cricket when assisting Eleven of the South *v* Eleven of the North, at Tunbridge Wells, on August 30 and 31, 1883. W.G. made a better showing this time, and Pooley, at number 10, made 8 not out and 1, and held 2 catches in the North's only innings.

For several years after he had ceased playing in first-class cricket, Ted Pooley obtained some employment as an umpire. He stood in the Gentlemen *v* Players match, at The Oval, in 1884, but he probably officiated more in games of lesser importance. There is a tale, however, that on one famous occasion—date and place unspecified—he had the temerity to give W.G. out lbw, much to the Champion's disgust and indignation. Advancing down the pitch in a menacing manner, W.G. demanded in his high-pitched voice, "Which leg did it hit, Pooley, which leg did it hit?" Equal to the occasion, Ted had his answer pat, retorting, "Never mind which leg it hit; I've given you out and out you've got to go!"

In addition to umpiring, Pooley had a series of other jobs, some outside of cricket, but in the 1890s his health began to fail, and he was attacked by rheumatic fever. Improvident in his playing days like some other contemporary professionals, and now deprived of a small pension from Surrey CCC on the grounds of persistent intemperance, he was reduced to living in straitened circumstances and became a denizen of various workhouses. At one time, a premature report of his death appeared in the press, and he was granted the rare but somewhat dubious privilege of reading his own obituary. He died in Lambeth Infirmary, on July 18, 1907, after years of soul-destroying penury and ill-health, which he bore with the same indomitable courage and cheerfulness shown by a later generation of Londoners during the Blitz in World War II.

Even allowing for the condition of many of the grounds on which he played and the attacking style he usually adopted, Pooley's record as a batsman in first-class matches was comparatively modest—a final average of 15.86. After 1871, his batting deteriorated, and he never again attained an average of 20 runs or more in a season. The superb quality of his wicket-keeping, however, endured with little falling-off up to the end of his career. In matches for the United South of England Eleven, mainly against teams of "odds," he performed some wondrous feats. In first-class contests, his achievements were little short of sublime. In addition to his still unbeaten record of 12 dismissals in a match and his tally of 36 victims in five consecutive games, he was a model of consistency, enjoying considerable success in most seasons, his most prolific being 1868 (23 matches, 42 caught, 39 stumped) and 1870 (27 matches, 43 caught, 36 stumped). Throughout his first-class career, extending from 1861 to 1883 (370 matches), his aggregate of dismissals amounted to 854 (496 caught, 358 stumped), making him the most successful wicket-keeper in the nineteenth century. After he had made his final bow, and first-class cricket knew him no more, Ted was honoured with a glowing valediction in one of the cricket annuals:

> The last season has witnessed the retirement of POOLEY, and a rare genius for the game is gone with him. A wonderful wicket-keeper to the end of his day to slow bowling—in his prime to fast also—and a bat conspicuous for pluck in an up-hill match, and for very rapid run-getting, he was the sort of cricketer that the South does not produce now, as it did of yore.

CHAPTER SEVEN

Henry Jupp *"Young Stonewall"*

A SUMMER holiday in the peace and tranquillity of the Surrey countryside was Frederick Gale's idea of heaven. With plenty of woods and meadows where the children could play and run wild in the sunshine of the livelong days, their father luxuriated in the opportunity to forget the cares of authorship and journalism and indulge in his favourite pastimes of cricket and fishing. Village cricket, in fact, was Mr Gale's passion, and when he rented a cottage on Brockham Green one summer, he soon took the necessary steps to join the local team. There was nothing much parochial about the so-called "Brockham Eleven": membership was not restricted to the actual boundaries of the village, and the club officials never hesitated to seek out promising cricketers within a radius of several miles. Shortly before an important fixture with a powerful Horsham team, one of the Brockham cricketers approached Mr Gale and had no difficulty in persuading him to provide some pecuniary assistance in acquiring the services of a promising youngster for the forthcoming contest. The terms were a match fee of five shillings, dinner money, and the price of a railway ticket. Mr Gale's investment was repaid with interest. A veritable host in himself, the recruit was largely responsible for Brockham's easy victory, making a big score, bowling at one end, and long-stopping at the other without letting a single bye. This "infant prodigy," who was under twenty at the time, was retained for the next match, at home, against Epsom. Excited at the prospects of his discovery, Mr Gale wrote a letter to William Burrup, the Surrey secretary, asking him to come down to Brockham. Burrup accepted the invitation, bringing a knowledgeable companion with him. Both were favourably impressed, and some two years later the youngster appeared in the Surrey Eleven. The name of Mr Gale's *protégé* was Henry Jupp.

Born at Dorking, in Surrey, on November 19, 1841, Harry Jupp was a little below rather than above medium height. Of muscular build, sturdy, and broad across the shoulders, he possessed unplumbed depths of stamina, and his powerful physique more than compensated for his comparative lack of inches. His hair, which showed a tendency to curl and later to thin, was parted in the centre. After several years, he cultivated a thick moustache, which, in conjunction with his heavy eyebrows, lent an almost forbidding air of brooding masculinity to his features. By temperament he was somewhat taciturn and to strangers seemed rather sullen and sulky in his manner, but he was an excellent cricketer, a good team-mate, and a sheet-anchor to any eleven.

Harry Jupp's connection with The Oval began in 1861, when he was employed there as a part-time cricketer and part-time bricklayer. Surrey, at that time, had one of the strongest county sides in the country, capable of holding their own against the Rest of England and the North. The Eleven consisted mainly of hard-bitten professionals, who were celebrated for the mastery of their craft, but some were no longer in the first flush of youth. Although he showed obvious potential as a first-rate cricketer, Jupp found himself confronted by the jealousy of some of his seniors, who, naturally, showed little inclination to surrender their places and wages to any johnny-come-lately. He made his mark before the public in an unusual manner in the match between Surrey and Cambridgeshire, on July 24 and 25, 1862. Two of the visiting team were late in arriving at The Oval, and Jupp fielded as a substitute in the deep where, running from long-off to long-on, he distinguished himself by holding a marvellous catch. Shortly afterwards, he was selected to play for Surrey in a home fixture against the North, on August 4 and 5, and he appeared in two other important matches that season. To begin with, it was the same story in 1863—no place for Jupp until the middle of July, when he turned out against Kent, at The Oval. Batting at number 10 in the first innings, he made 17 not out and fully justified his promotion to number 2 in the second by scoring 74 not out. Selected for all but one of the remaining Surrey fixtures, he ended with an average of 31.00.

Although Harry Jupp could play his part with the ball in minor matches, he did little bowling in first-class cricket. In the other departments of the game, however, he was undeniably far out of the ordinary. An excellent fielder, particularly at long-stop or in the deep, he was also quite a good wicket-keeper in an emergency, but it was his batting, above all, that brought him lasting fame. Solid and reliable rather than graceful and elegant would be the best way to describe his style. He was certainly one of the most correct batsmen of his time, and it was alleged that he used to draw a chalk line on the floor in front of a full-length mirror and practise daily to make sure he would play with a straight bat. From 1864 until his retirement in 1881, he was a regular member of the Surrey team. In his early days, and occasionally later, he

Henry Jupp
"Young Stonewall"

Courtesy Roger Mann

was known to employ his physical strength to the full by smiting the ball with laudable vigour, and he was always a masterly judge of the sharp single and a quick runner between the wickets. A natural anchor man by temperament and inclination, and later out of sheer necessity when the rest of the Surrey batting proved unreliable for much of his career, Harry Jupp was content to settle for this role. His defensive technique, based on firm back play, assumed an air of impregnability and soon earned him a nickname. William Mortlock, one of the senior Surrey men, renowned as an unbowlable batsman and an equally unbeatable long-stop, became known around 1863–64 as "The Surrey Stonewall" and "Stonewall Mortlock." The same epithet, which may have owed something to the fame of the Confederate general, "Stonewall" Jackson (died 1863), was soon applied to Harry Jupp as well, with Mortlock becoming "Old Stonewall" and Jupp "Young Stonewall"—an early usage of the term in connection with slow, defensive batting.

Jupp's methods proved unbearably irksome to unfortunate bowlers and fieldsmen alike on numerous occasions. One of the most celebrated instances quite early in his career occurred in a minor match, at Southampton, on September 25, 26, and 27, 1865, when Fourteen Gentlemen of the South were overwhelmingly defeated by Eleven Players of the South. The chief tormentor of the hapless amateurs was Harry Jupp, who occupied the crease for a whole day in scoring a chanceless 216, made up of 7 fours, 18 threes, 28 twos, and 78 singles. It says much for the reputation he had already acquired that one report credited him erroneously with 135 singles!

Immediately after this one-sided contest came a match at The Oval between Eighteen Gentlemen of the Surrey Club and the United South of England Eleven. Much stronger in cricketing ability as well as in numbers than the leather-hunting martyrs of Southampton, the Eighteen Gentlemen had obtained the services of E. M. Grace, who was their top scorer and most successful bowler. Faced by a virtually impossible deficit of runs, the United South began their second innings with a strenuous effort to stave off defeat. Jupp was displaying those barnacle-like qualities for which he was already becoming famous, and it was patently obvious that some desperate measures were needed to dislodge him from the crease. E.M., it might be said, held an even more advanced post-graduate degree in the arts of gamesmanship than his brother W.G. in future times, and on that day he set in motion a crafty scheme to dispose of his obdurate opponent. Abandoning his round-arm action, he opted for some high-tossed lobs. The first delivery of what was later referred to as his "shell practice" rose to a height of about fifteen yards and came down within reach of the astonished Jupp,

E. M. Grace

who nevertheless succeeded in hitting the ball away for two runs. To the accompaniment of loud barracking from the uninhibited Oval crowd, who disapproved of such unorthodox manœuvres, E.M. returned to the fray. His second delivery was even higher, and Jupp, thinking perhaps that the umpire would call a wide, offered no stroke. This was a grave error of judgement, since the ball fell with unerring aim or, more likely, good fortune "nicely on the top of the middle stump." The umpire gave Jupp out, a decision which he accepted with a bad grace—no pun intended—and some of the spectators invaded the pitch and converged on E.M., who prepared to defend himself by seizing and brandishing one of the stumps. Order was eventually restored, and the match ended in an easy victory for the Gentlemen. The fairness or otherwise of E.M.'s tactics was debated with pros and cons in the sporting press for several days by various correspondents adopting such pseudonyms as "Half Volley," "Bucephalus," and "Longus Stoppus"—which showed the benefits to be derived from a classical education, but did the ancient world play cricket? Young Harry Jupp, however, had been taught a salutary lesson: always be on your guard against the Graces!

After his big score against Kent in 1863, Jupp was recognized as an opening batsman, a role in which he was usually cast throughout much of his career. In the early days, his partner was "Old Stonewall" Mortlock on occasions, but more often he went in with Thomas Humphrey. The latter, already established in the Surrey eleven, was "an old-fashioned-looking chap," slightly shorter than Jupp and sometimes known as "The Pocket Hercules." An attractive, attacking batsman, scoring freely with splendid cuts for which he was famous, Tom Humphrey was the first man to make 1000 runs in a season in first-class matches, a feat he achieved in 1865. For several years, the partnership, a happy blend of Humphrey's eye-catching brilliance and Jupp's steady reliability, was unmatched in the world of cricket. Their mastery of judging the sharp single, based on complete mutual trust, was brought to perfection. They developed the habit of playing the ball a few feet down the pitch and stealing a run, "almost carrying the ball with them as they went," and always taking the first run quickly in the hope of going for a second one. By about 1870, Humphrey's neat elegance and run-getting powers had begun to desert him, and though he hung on for a few years in first-class and minor cricket, he was a mere shadow of his former greatness.

In 1869, when the Humphrey-Jupp partnership still retained a little of its splendid lustre, two gentlemen made a special journey from the west country for the sole purpose of seeing the Surrey twins in action. The United South of England Eleven were contending against a twenty-two at Swindon, on August 26, 27, and 28, and the opening pair for the visitors were W. G. Grace and Harry Jupp, with Tom Humphrey dropping down the order to number 6. W.G.'s father and one of his friends were the two travellers, and the "Surrey boys" were batting when they arrived. Jupp (135) and Humphrey (65) stayed in for a long time, scoring freely off the Swindon bowling, and they were still at the wickets when the time came for the elder Grace's departure. Such an uninterrupted feast of perpetual run-getting can evidently jade the palate of some choosey onlookers and leave the appetite still unsatisfied. "What do you think of them?" W.G. asked his father. "Wonderful!" he replied; "but, do you know, I should like to see someone else before I go."

From 1864 to 1874, apart from one year, Harry Jupp's name appeared in the top twenty of the national batting averages. His best position—second to W.G.—occurred in 1874, his most successful season, when he attained his highest aggregate of 1,275 runs (average 36.42), with three centuries. On seven other occasions, he passed 1000 runs and only rarely did he fail to reach a seasonal average of 20.00—a remarkable feat of consistency on pitches, which were by no means all of the shirt-front variety. He scored 12 centuries in all, a good record for the time, apart from W.G., of course. His highest, for Surrey against Lancashire, at The Oval, on July 19, 20, and 21, 1866, painstakingly compiled in 390 minutes, was 165, and it included 1 five, 4 fours, and 74 singles!

There were times, naturally, when Jupp could force the pace, but, on the whole, they were spaced out at infrequent intervals. Without doubt, the necessity for supplying some ballast and stability to the shaky batting of his Surrey team-mates governed his tactics for several years, until his methods became second nature to him. He strove unceasingly to eliminate as far as possible the risk of having to surrender his wicket cheaply. Ignoring the example of Tom Humphrey, he rarely employed the cut except latish in his career, and sometimes, "owing to excessive caution," he would make no attempt to play balls on the off side, even on a plumb wicket. He excelled at the drive, both off and on, but many of his runs came from deflections, and one of his favourite strokes—aesthetically ugly but generally highly effective—was performed by raising his left leg and playing the ball hard away under it. Such a manœuvre could be hazardous if the timing were faulty, but evidently Harry Jupp felt that this was one risk worth taking, seeing that he scored many runs by it. With his style of defensive play, blocking ball after ball, there was always the chance that a "head" bowler like W.G. could lure him to self-destruction with slight variations in length and pitch, and Jupp, to his ill-disguised disgust, would find point and short-leg crowding round him in anticipation of a cocked-up catch.

Like W.G., Harry Jupp was not the best of losers and had a rooted objection to abandoning the crease. It went against his nature to walk before an appeal, and he was known to express his displeasure when a decision went against him. On one ground, however, his word was law, overruling the fiat of any umpire. At Dorking, his home town, where he was extremely popular, "and did very much what he liked, in cricket at all events," it was the custom for several years to arrange a benefit match for him. The story tells that, in one of these affairs, Jupp was batting and, in playing back, he trod on his wicket, dislodging one of the bails. Completely unperturbed, the beneficiary retrieved the fallen bail, replaced it on the stumps, and resumed his guard. There was a pregnant pause. Then the captain of the fielding side ventured a mild expostulation, saying "Ain't you going out, Juppy?" "No, I ain't," replied Jupp, "not at Dorking!" As if to drive home the point, he went on to score a century.

Philip Mead, the famous Hampshire left-hander of a later generation, was regarded by some as a barn-door type of batsman. On hearing criticisms being levelled against the great Phil, a Hampshire member retorted acidly, "Of course, Mead was very slow: I once watched him stonewall all day against Notts for 280." There can be little question that Harry Jupp was far slower than Mead, and there is ample testimony of the Dorking hero's insatiable hunger for batting. As mentioned previously, he spent six hours and a-half over his highest score of 165, while his second hghest—154 against Sussex, at Hove, on July 20, 21, and 22, 1874—was spread over nearly six hours. Against Kent, at The Oval (1877), and Yorkshire, at Bramall Lane (1880), he was at the wickets for part of all three days. In 1867, he consumed over five hours in scoring 97 against Kent, at Gravesend, and 91 against Middlesex, at The Oval. He came to be regarded as the very model of a stonewaller, a yardstick for measuring the efforts of batsmen displaying the same technique. When R. G. Barlow, of Lancashire, scored 27 in two and a-quarter hours for the Players against the Gentlemen, at The Oval, in 1876, his performance, said one of the annuals, "put Jupp into the shade for steadiness," and it speaks volumes for "Young Stonewall's" fame that Dick Barlow was dubbed "the Jupp of the North."

Twelve times in his first-class career Jupp went in first and carried his bat throughout a completed innings—a figure exceeded by only three other batsmen. He was the first of only four players to perform the extremely rare feat of carrying his bat throughout *both* innings, when Surrey met Yorkshire, at The Oval, on August 17, 18, and 19,

1874. On first hands, he contributed 43 to a total of 95 in about two and a-quarter hours. Surrey were compelled to follow their innings, and this time Jupp remained undefeated for four hours, his share of the total of 193 being 109. His reward was a purse of £20 or more, collected from the admiring Oval crowd—but, alas for "Young Stonewall's" epic struggle, Yorkshire won by 4 wickets!

In two previous matches, Jupp had already come within a hair's breadth of anticipating this record by being the last man out in one innings and carrying his bat throughout the second—another exploit unequalled for many years to come. Against Hampshire, at The Oval, on July 9, 10, and 11, 1866 he made 31—run out, the tenth wicket to fall—and 94 not out. His complete tenure of the crease lasted about eight and a-half hours, and he ran all of Surrey's match total of 407, apart from 2 wides. The second instance occurred in the contest between Surrey and Nottinghamshire, at The Oval, on July 21, 22, and 23, 1873. "Young Stonewall" made 53 in the first innings (total 102), finally succumbing to a return catch to the bowler, while in the second he took out his bat for 51 (total 113). These two scores, said one of the cricket annuals, "stand forth Triton-like amongst the minnows with which they are surrounded" (the next highest in each innings were 17 and 14). As in the earlier fixture with Hampshire, he was on the field for the whole of the match, but in much more demanding circumstances. This was the season when Ted Pooley, the regular Surrey wicket-keeper, had been suspended on the grounds of alleged misconduct, and on this, as on several other occasions during the season, Pooley's duties were entrusted to Harry Jupp, who held 4 catches and let only 6 byes out of Nottinghamshire's combined total of 334 runs. During all three days, it may be added, the temperature reached the proportions of "tropical heat." This might well be set down as Jupp's most outstanding performance on the cricket field. As a remarkable instance of expertise, dedication, and stamina, it has few parallels in the history of the game.

In some ways, Harry Jupp bore the characteristics of a Yorkshireman. His dour, gritty style of batting, experienced in all its awe-inspiring splendour several times by the representatives of the broad acres, would have earned the critical approval of the Sheffield "grinders", whose knowledge and appreciation of cricket were matched by few other crowds in England. Like many of the Yorkshiremen of his time, too, Jupp practised a certain economy of words and cared little for the niceties of polished speech—all of which contributed to the impression of surliness he was apt to create in conversation with comparative strangers. On one occasion, when he was playing on the same side as W.G., somebody asked him if he knew who was going to

W. G. Grace and Henry Jupp
"Jupp and Grace. What more do you want?"
Courtesy Hulton Picture Library

open the batting. "Jupp and Grace," was the terse reply. Nettled by the brevity of the answer, the word order, and, perhaps, the omission of any title before the Champion's name, the questioner said, in mild disapproval, "Don't you think it would be more polite to say 'Grace and Jupp'?" "Well," retorted Jupp, apparently greatly surprised but possibly tongue in cheek, "that's just what I said—Jupp and Grace. What more do you want?"

The triumphant season of 1874 was followed by one, which was, by Jupp's high standards, rather poor from the statistical point of view. He began 1875 in good style, playing "with all his old science and stubbornness," but the death of his wife was a grievous blow, which affected his form throughout the remainder of the season. In all matches, he scored only 639 runs, with a highest figure of 60, and his average fell to 18.25. There was a partial recovery in 1876, when, for the eighth and last time, he attained his 1000 runs in the season, but the days were beginning to draw in for Jupp. With justice, he was still regarded as one of the best professional batsmen of his age, producing some sterling performances and maintaining a good average in 1877 and 1878, but he was no longer such a consistent and successful accumulator of runs.

Whenever he was well set throughout his long career, Harry Jupp frequently gave the impression that his interminable innings could be protracted into eternity. Cool and phlegmatic by nature for most of the time, with a supreme confidence in his ability to defend his wicket against all types of bowling, Jupp nevertheless was apt to reveal a fatal flaw in his technique and powers of concentration in moments of personal crisis. One may shed a tear for the fate of the Australian left-hander, Clem Hill, who scored 99, 98, and 97 in three successive Test innings, but Jupp's misfortunes call for more profuse lamentation. The "nervous nineties" gave him an attack of the jitters to a marked degree, since he fell short of the coveted three figures no less than fifteen times, though, in all fairness, he ran out of partners and was undefeated on four occasions. With the exception of 95, he marked every figure from 99 down to 90.

The contest between the Gentlemen and the Players, at The Oval, on July 3, 4, and 5, 1865, was notable for the debut in the series of Harry Jupp and W. G. Grace, as well as Alfred Shaw, "the Emperor of Bowlers." From then until his final appearance in 1880, "Young Stonewall" was virtually a permanent fixture for the professionals. He assisted the Players in 33 matches—only George Ulyett of his contemporaries and, of course, W.G., recorded a higher number—totalling 1,344 runs, with a highest score of 72. With no not outs to offset his 64 innings, he still played with sufficient consistency to achieve an average of 21.00, which, by the standards of the time, was quite a good record.

W.G. assisted the Gentlemen in all but one of the matches in which Harry Jupp represented the Players—the Champion, ill with scarlet fever, was compelled to miss the Oval fixture of 1867. They were adversaries, of course, in county matches between Gloucestershire and Surrey, but they were often team-mates in other first-class contests as well as in minor games for the United South of England Eleven. Grace and Jupp—or Jupp and Grace, according to "Young Stonewall's" way of thinking—were regular opening partners in one or both innings well over twenty times between 1868 and 1876, mainly in contests between North and South, of which there was a plethora in the first half of the 1870s. W.G. was impressed by Jupp's superb defence and patience, but felt that "if anything he was a little too steady," choosing to preserve his wicket at all costs and blatantly neglecting heaven-sent opportunities for attacking the bowling. The two were poles apart in their conception of batsmanship, but the Champion had no reservations over Jupp's excellence as a fielder. "He was," recollected W.G., "about the safest catch in the long field I ever saw . . . No catch seemed impossible to him."

Jupp took part in three tours abroad, the first in September and October 1868, when he was a member of Edgar Willsher's party of twelve professionals visiting Canada and the USA. "Young Stonewall" came a meritorious third in the batting averages, with 17.22, and produced some typical performances. The third contest, against 22 of Boston, was played in appalling conditions, the whole field being waterlogged by five days of incessant rain, and the rough turf of the actual pitch having "holes in it big enough to lose the ball." The tourists had never encountered anything like it before, not even in the most remote districts of rural England. Harry Jupp opened the batting in both innings. In his first outing, he made only 3, scoring his first run after he had been at the wickets for 40 minutes! In his second, he was easily the top scorer with 36 and was the last man out.

In 1873–74, W. G. Grace took out his team of five gentlemen—including his younger brother G.F. and his cousin W. R. Gilbert—and seven professionals to tour Australia. Among the second group were Harry Jupp and two of his Surrey team-mates, James Southerton and Richard Humphrey, younger brother of Jupp's erstwhile partner Tom. Like many of his contemporaries, Jupp was not the best of sailors, and to him was attributed the mournful observation "that he would have liked the Bay of Biscay *stiller*," which was evidently considered an appropriate witticism in those less sophisticated times. W.G.'s men were engaged in 15 matches, usually against 22 and never less than 15 opponents.

"Young Stonewall" played in all the matches of the tour and, apart from the last one, he opened the batting with his captain, at least in the first innings. This was a remarkable instance of resilience and staying power, considering the misfortunes that beset him at the Antipodes. He always had a great liking for a glass of champagne, particularly at breakfast time, and insisted that he preferred it neat rather than diluted with seltzer water, as was sometimes the custom in those days ("No, thank you, sir; I have always found champagne good enough by itself"). Whatever restraints he may have imposed upon himself in England—and, in justice to Jupp, there is no record that he was ever unfit to play—he seems to have opted for greater freedom when far from home, and on at least two occasions he suffered the penalty for over indulgence and possibly mixing his drinks. Much was made of the team after their arrival at Melbourne, and William Oscroft of Nottinghamshire, one of the seven professionals, recollected that they were "most hospitably treated." When, finally, they got back to their hotel at night, most of them were "slightly exhilarated" and were unsteady in their gait—because they had not yet recovered their land-legs! On reaching his room, Jupp passed out, rolled under the bed and lay there until broad daylight. With commendable charity, Oscroft suggest that Harry probably thought he was still at sea "and had to get into his berth as usual." By the time the first match of the tour was played, he was sufficiently acclimatized to bat well in the first innings, and the team's "fielding was brilliant, Jupp's especially." So, the effects of the ceremony of welcome wore off in a short time, but much worse was still to come, and at Melbourne once again.

After playing a drawn match with 18 of Victoria towards the end of the tour, the team moved on by sea to Adelaide. During the course of bidding farewell to Melbourne and Victoria, "the scene of much pleasure as well as pain," according to the anonymous chronicler of events, possibly G. F. Grace, the members of the English team were lavishly entertained. Jupp, like most of the others, "had been taking farewell nips," which had a most unfortunate outcome. Exactly how many "nips" he had imbibed is hard to say, but not long after they were at sea, "Young Stonewall" suddenly appeared on deck rather the worse for wear. He was, it seems, suffering from something approaching the throes of delirium tremens, seeing flashing blue lights and beacons—an interesting variant from pink elephants—and he claimed that he had been accused "of making himself in a mess" and of assaulting other passengers in the ship's saloon. The first accusation turned out to be false, and Jupp was with great difficulty put to bed. He spent, to put it mildly, a restless and disturbed night, frequently demanding reassurance as to the state of his cleanliness and complaining that people were dancing over his head and climbing on the ceiling. Unfortunately, he was no better once the ship had docked at Port Adelaide, and James Southerton had to remain by his bed-side throughout most of the day. Left alone for a short while, the sufferer suddenly jumped up from his bed and rushed out of the hotel into the street, screaming that he couldn't bear it any more and he was going to hospital. He was intercepted by Southerton and the physician who was treating him, taken back to the hotel, and quietened with a sedative.

The calming effect of the drug had worn off by the early hours of the morning, and "Young Stonewall," succumbing to a much worse attack, began to hallucinate once more, swearing and yelling and waking up the whole house. He became so violent and uncontrollable that the assistance of two policemen was required to tie him up, and so, trussed like a fowl for the table, he was conveyed in a cart to the hospital, where he was incarcerated in a padded cell. The rest of the team travelled by coach to Kadina to play against 22 of Yorke's Peninsula and, on the way, they received a telegram announcing that Jupp had escaped! Further messages were delivered to them at Kadina, saying that the invalid had recovered and was coming on to join them. And join them he did. On a pitch whose grasslessness was rendered still more dangerous by a "bushel" of pebbles—W.G. had them swept up and removed—the Englishmen made only 64, but this modest total was enough to secure a victory by an innings. So remarkable and rapid was Harry Jupp's recovery that he was able to open the batting with his usual partner. He made 10, which was five more than W.G., and only one batsman achieved a higher score. The home side, having reached 42 in their first innings, could manage only 13 runs in their second, prompting the comment that "There is a fine opening for a good coach at Kadina."

Harry Jupp's second visit down under and his final tour abroad occurred in 1876-77, when James Lillywhite, junior, took his party of twelve professionals to play matches in Australia and New Zealand. The team had more than enough bowlers but was a little thin on the ground in the batting department, throwing an extra burden on such members as "Young Stonewall." Twenty-three matches, it will be remembered, made up the programme, which began in the third week of November 1876 and ended in the middle of the following April. In the first leg of the tour, Lillywhite's men were engaged in eight "odds" matches against various teams in South Australia, New South Wales, and Victoria, and one eleven-a-side contest against New South Wales. Proceeding next to New Zealand, they took part in eight more fixtures against local twenty-twos and eighteens, after which they returned to Australia for the final six encounters, including the first two Tests in the series England *v* Australia.

"Young Stonewall" did not have the happiest of tours. It all began in Adelaide, with an episode curiously reminiscent of the events that befell him on his arrival with W.G.'s party. On the first night ashore, he returned to his bedroom in the hotel and, forgetting that he was now on dry land, he crawled under his bed as though getting into a ship's bunk and fell asleep. When he awoke the next morning, one of the first things he saw was a window. Flummoxed by the unfamiliar shape, he exclaimed in bewilderment, "That's a new port-hole, isn't it?" This temporary aberration, like the previous one, was charitably put down to a failure to regain his land-legs.

Jupp played in the first match of the tour—against 22 of South Australia, at Adelaide, on November 17, 18, and 19, 1876—and in his only innings was second top scorer with 35. He then fell victim to a severe and prolonged attack of "rheumatism, sciatica, or something of the kind" in his hips and loins. Unable to walk or get up and down without assistance, he was on the side-lines for several weeks. Before he had completely recovered from this excruciating ailment, he was stricken down by another one, which also rendered him helpless and unfit for cricket. On medical advice, he was compelled to remain in a dark room for a fortnight, suffering from a painful inflammation of the eyes. This condition, said one of his team-mates (Alfred Shaw) rather mysteriously, was "brought on in various ways." There was, in fact, nothing sinister in the cause of his illness, such as a punch-up. James Southerton, another member of the team, reported that, while travelling overland, Jupp contracted a cold in his eyes. This produced such alarming symptoms that, on arriving at Ballarat, he was obliged to seek treatment from a physician, who ordered the confinement in a dark room, "which," Southerton quaintly added, "troubled him much."

As a result of these maladies, Jupp missed all but the opening match of the first leg of the tour, and he was left behind when the party, reduced to eleven men, set sail for New Zealand. Some of them thought they would never see him again, but, to their amazement and relief, he joined them in time for the contest against 22 of Nelson in the middle of February. Absent for eleven of the first twelve matches—almost half the entire programme—he resumed his place in the side. This was just as well, because shortly after Jupp's arrival in New Zealand the team lost the services of their wicket-keeper, Ted Pooley, in those unhappy circumstances related in a previous chapter.

Alfred Shaw recollected that, on one occasion—he didn't say exactly when—"Jupp suffered from delusions that took him out into the country, and he was lost to us for a few days." This suggests a repeat performance of the onset of DTs on the earlier tour with W.G., followed by the added complication of straying off into the outback.

Whatever the truth or otherwise of this report, Harry Jupp was certainly in fine fettle for the opening match of the return to Australia, which was the first ever Test between the two countries. England batted second, with Jupp at number one, and he enjoyed a slice of luck at the beginning of his innings. In playing back, he trod on his wicket and knocked off one of the bails "but no one seeing it, of course, he could not be given out"—an interesting variant of "Not at Dorking!" "Young Stonewall" went on in his usual patient style to make 63, the top score of his side. In doing so, he established an unbeatable minor record, by scoring the first half-century for England in a Test Match.

Lillywhite's team did not arrive back in England until June 2, 1877—one member disembarked even later—and consequently they missed the early contests of the season. Harry Jupp made his first appearance for Surrey in the home fixture against Gloucestershire, on June 7 and 8. He was evidently short of practice and had not yet recovered his land-legs again, since his return to the fray was, by all standards, extremely inauspicious. In the first innings, he was lbw, first ball, and in the second, lbw again, for 4. The bowler on each occasion was W. G. Grace! He soon settled down, however, and "showed little falling off, his play being as steady, and at times as successful, as ever." Nevertheless, a decline in his powers became obvious in the first part of 1878, when his old, sure form deserted him completely, though he rallied later in the season and managed to attain an average of 20.84. It was, doubtless, his indifferent batting that brought about his omission from the Surrey eleven in the encounter with Gloucestershire, on June 20, 21, and 22, provoking one of the cricket annuals to exclaim, "Fancy the horror of the Oval *habitués* at finding Jupp omitted from the county team!"

"Young Stonewall's" exclusion from the ranks on that occasion might possibly have been construed as a sort of reprimand for what he did, or rather did not do, in the previous match against Cambridge University, when he was given the captaincy. Although he had a wealth of experience and a good knowledge of the game, Jupp fell far short of the requirements of a good captain. It was a twelve-a-side match, beginning at midday, and when rain brought the proceedings to a close at 5.20 p.m., Cambridge had reached 216 for the loss of 10 wickets. Their final total was 256, which, as it transpired, was plenty and to spare in defeating Surrey by an innings (Jupp 5 and 2). The Cambridge runs were scored off 166 overs, of which 158 were delivered by two bowlers, E. Barratt (slow left-arm) and F. Johnson (fast-medium left-arm), who operated unchanged throughout the whole of the first day's play! Jupp, it must be assumed, forgot that he was more than just a mere member of the team in this match.

In 1879, "Young Stonewall" experienced the worst season of his career since he began playing regularly for Surrey. The dying embers glowed brightly at times in 1880, when he scored his final century. The opponents were Yorkshire, the scene Bramall Lane, on June 14, 15, and 16, and the match, interrupted by rain on the second and third days, yielded the quintessence of a vintage Jupp performance. Surrey went in only once, and Jupp, at number two, carried his bat throughout the completed innings for the last time in his career. In scoring 117, which included 49 singles, he was at the wickets for part of all three days.

The following season, Harry Jupp turned out for Surrey in the early matches, but he gave ample evidence that his form had passed beyond the point of no return. Omitted from the side in June, he returned once in July and made his farewell appearance against Sussex, at The Oval, on August 1 and 2, 1881 (run out for 4 in his only innings). A fortnight earlier, a fixture between North and South was played there for his benefit, yielding a sum of well over £400. In his years of retirement, "Young Stonewall" could turn his thoughts to the contemplation of a successful first-class career of solid achievement unrivalled by many of his contemporaries—an aggregate of 15,319 runs at an average of 23.78, with 12 centuries, and 229 catches and 19 stumpings. From about 1867, he had combined his cricketing duties with the occupation of innkeeper at various places in Surrey and at Weston, near Southampton, where he had the misfortune to lose his second wife. In 1888, his health began to deteriorate and, suffering from various ailments, he expired at his sister's home in Bermondsey, on April 8, 1889.

In the period from his retirement as a player until less than a year before his death, Harry Jupp returned to the scenes of his former triumphs by standing as an umpire, officiating frequently in first-class matches, particularly from 1884 to 1888. It proved to be a chastening experience. Notorious in his playing days for his reluctance to leave the crease, he had rarely restrained himself from voicing his dissatisfaction with adverse decisions. Now, no longer a grumbler, the boot was on the other foot with a vengeance, when he found himself the perpetual target for the batsmen's displeasure. Jupp's conscience pricked him, and after an especially trying day of rejecting confident appeals, he unburdened himself to his fellow official, James Lillywhite, junior, his old captain on the last tour of Australia and New Zealand, and said, "Do you know, Jim, I should like to have all the umpires, who used to stand when I played, before me and apologize to 'em."

CHAPTER EIGHT

J. C. Shaw
"The Splendid Performer"

Of the youth and adolescence of W. G. Grace much is known. We are familiar with the details of the cricket-mad family, the private pitch in the orchard, the constant practice, the female members—no mere spectators, but very useful auxiliaries, supplementing the fielding expertise of Don, Ponto, and Noble, the three dogs trained to retrieve the ball—and, above all, the painstaking coaching by the boy's elders, particularly Uncle Pocock. Guided lovingly through the rudiments of cricket, carefully nurtured, and gradually introduced to competitive matches, W.G. was ready as a teenager to take his place in the first-class game and confront that long line of formidable adversaries—fast, medium, and slow—who yearned for the honour of capturing his wicket.

By way of contrast, comparatively little is known of the early life of James Coupe Shaw, one of the most redoubtable opponents encountered by the Champion at the outset of his triumphant career. They both made their first-class debut in the same season (1865), within a few days of each other, but there was a marked disparity in their ages. W.G., who failed to trouble the scorers on his first appearance but took 13 wickets, was only sixteen, whereas Shaw had reached the mature age of twenty-nine. As might be expected, his first-class career was nowhere near so long as W.G.'s.

A native of Sutton-in-Ashfield, a place long famous as a nursery of Nottinghamshire cricket, Jemmy Shaw was born on April 11, 1836. As to how he spent almost the first thirty years of his life the annals are largely silent. It is believed, however, that he obtained some professional engagements, and it is known that he was employed at Oxford in 1865, when he performed a remarkable feat of superb bowling. During the first three days of June, he played as a Given Man for 20 of Christ Church against the newly founded, itinerant United South of England Eleven, ten of whom on this occasion were crack professionals from Surrey and Kent. The Oxford men won the contest easily by an innings and 147 runs, with Jemmy taking 7 wickets in the first innings and 6 in the second. The news of his outstanding ability with what some of the journalists of those days called "the leathern sphere" filtered back to the Nottinghamshire Committee. Without even the customary formality of a trial with the colts, he was drafted into the County Eleven for the contest against Surrey, at Trent Bridge, on June 26, 27, and 28. Jemmy's contribution to the home team's victory by eight wickets was 9 as last man and match figures of 5 wickets at a cost of 55 runs. Quite a satisfactory debut for a somewhat elderly newcomer who would soon be recognized as the spearhead of the Nottinghamshire attack, until, in the fullness of time, he was finally left out of the side.

Jemmy's advent on the first-class scene could hardly have come at a more opportune moment. Worn out after years of yeoman service with Nottinghamshire and the All England Eleven, the stalwart John Jackson was approaching the end of his playing days in important matches. His famous, round-arm bowling action, once compared with the smooth and regular precision of a well lubricated piece of machinery, was starting to seize up, and the County Committee were urgently seeking a replacement. Jemmy Shaw was not alone in the contest. Senior to him in the side was George Wootton, a short, compact man, who often played alongside Jemmy in county matches in the later 1860s. A fast-medium left-hander, Wootton once captured all 10 wickets in an innings for the All England Eleven against a rather weak Yorkshire team, deprived by circumstances of some of the best players, but on the whole he was most successful on the rough, unreliable pitches at Lord's, where he was engaged as one of the ground bowlers from 1862 to 1873. A much more dangerous rival than Wootton was George Howitt, a very fast but not always accurate left-hander, who possessed the ability to cut the ball both ways. On uneven ground—the rule rather than the exception in those days—Howitt was regarded for several years as a potential threat to body and limb, if not life itself. He had, however, decided to take up his residence in London and was signed up by Middlesex, whom he assisted from 1865 to 1876. Although, in those days when qualifications were much more lax, he also turned out for Nottinghamshire in eight matches between 1866 and 1870, Howitt was identified more closely with his adopted county. It was during this period that he performed the extremely rare feat of dismissing W.G. for a pair in a minor match. With George Howitt largely out of the reckoning, however, the potential threat to Jemmy Shaw really failed to materialize, and he was not long in establishing himself as John Jackson's natural successor for both Nottinghamshire and the All England Eleven.

Jemmy stood rather above medium height, but he gave the impression of being taller, having a powerful physique, with an abundance of strength in his arms and shoulders, suggesting, perhaps, that he might have hardened and developed his muscles by arduous labour, such as toiling at the coal-face in his native district. He wore at times a moustache on his upper lip, but he was otherwise clean shaven in his prime. There was, in fact, nothing especially remarkable about his appearance, until you noticed the strange expression in his eyes. The unfortunate Jemmy suffered permanently from a startling and unmistakable squint, so pronounced that it was impossible at times to make out whether he was looking at you or your next-door neighbour. Legends built up on the matter of Jemmy's squint, the most persistent being the assertion that some batsmen encountering his penetrating stare for the very first time were so disconcerted and put off their stroke, as it were, that they were totally incapable of deciding if he was intending to bowl at them or the fielder at short-slip. His squint may have been very off-putting for some of his opponents, but it never seemed to interfere noticeably with his aim and accuracy. On the field of play, there was another equally striking feature about his appearance: Jemmy made a habit of wearing eye-catching shirts adorned with bold black and white stripes. For the rest, it may be added that he was not the most responsible of men, being rather happy-go-lucky by nature, and he was noted as a hearty eater, with a fondness for a tankard of "moyste and corny ale."

Jemmy's introduction to first-class cricket coincided with one of the most important and far-reaching alterations in the Laws of Cricket. With the prolonged and hard-fought battle to retain the round-arm action irretrievably lost in 1864, bowlers were now permitted to deliver the ball above the level of the shoulder. As we have already seen, the slow man James Southerton was one of those determined to exploit the new legislation to obtain greater freedom in the eternal struggle against all batsmen. Another was Jemmy Shaw. One of the finest fast bowlers among the professionals of his generation, Shaw was a fearsome left-hander, famous for his adoption of a high, rapid action. He possessed that much desired facility of hiding the ball from the batsman until the last possible moment. On arriving at the crease, his left arm came swinging from behind his back, the bowling hand briefly grazed his left shoulder, followed by a bewildering flurry of both arms, and in a trice the ball was on its way, pitching and rearing at the batsman often before the latter had completely shaped for the stroke. Jemmy placed little reliance on imparting much spin to the ball, but concentrated on the essentials of line and length, and he always bowled well within his strength. Unlike the less accurate George Howitt, he set no great store by the frequent use of the bouncer, preferring rather to send the ball

J. C. Shaw

Courtesy Roger Mann

through at the height of the knee and the bat handle. Around the early 1870s, when age began to take its toll, and he was feeling the strain of maintaining his speed for long spells, he resorted to "head bowling" by varying his pace and pitch and mixing in the occasional slower deliveries. These met with somewhat indifferent success, for Jemmy was no egghead and never satisfactorily worked out the problem of disguising his intentions.

Shaw's first-class career began in 1865 and ended in 1875. Since he never played in more than 17 matches in one year and often much less, it is hardly surprising that he failed to reach the magic figure of 100 wickets in a season. His best performance occurred in 1870, when, in only 12 matches and bowling in 23 innings, he claimed 96 victims at the splendid average of 10.31. In all, he totalled 636 wickets—plus 5 more for which no analysis is available—at an average of 14.43 runs in only 115 matches, and an average of over 3 wickets in every innings in which he bowled. He captured 5 or more wickets in an innings 59 times and 10 or more in a match 18 times. Like the 100 victims in a season, the feat of taking all 10 wickets in an innings also eluded him, though he came very close in the fixture with Gloucestershire, at Trent Bridge, on August 21, 22, and 23, 1871, when he returned figures of 9 wickets (including those of W. G., E. M., and G. F. Grace) at a cost of 86 runs. Against Surrey, also at Trent Bridge, on July 27 and 28 of the same season, he achieved his best match figures of 13 for 58 (7–28 and 6–30). There were times when he bowled with incredible economy, never more so than against Kent, once more on his home ground, on July 28 and 29, 1870. His figures in the visitors' first innings were 25 (four-ball) overs, of which 22 were maidens, and 4 wickets at the miserly outlay of 5 runs, the batsmen scoring off only 3 of the 100 deliveries!

Jemmy Shaw's most outstanding achievement against opponents of mettle was recorded at Eastwood Hall, on September 15, 16, and 17, 1870, when he was assisting Sixteen of Nottinghamshire against a team entitled "England." This name was not ill-chosen: with about one exception, the opposition consisted of the best professionals in the country outside of Nottinghamshire, but the match has not been rated as first-class. Unfortunate this was for Jemmy, whose figures were 10–20 (5 clean bowled) in the first innings and 5–33 in the second. From 1865 to 1876, when he was not engaged in first-class contests, he played for the All England Eleven, usually against local sides in "odds" matches. The bowling analysis for many of these matches, as mentioned previously, has seldom been preserved, and the scores are sometimes imprecise in failing to record the name of the successful bowler, or, in Jemmy's case, to distinguish between him and his unrelated namesake, Alfred Shaw. He probably took somewhere around 1,800 wickets, his best season being 1867, with a tally of 387 victims. In six first-class matches for the All England Eleven, he totalled 31 wickets at an average of 12.58.

The confrontation between W. G. Grace and Jemmy Shaw was staged in the period 1869–1875. Apart from county fixtures between Gloucestershire and Nottinghamshire, they were opponents in such matches as Gentlemen *v* Players (all 10 for which Jemmy was selected) and North *v* South. Appearing on opposite sides in 62 innings, they had many a titanic struggle, and though Jemmy did not bowl at W.G. on a few occasions, he managed to secure his wicket 20 times, including 9 clean bowled. In five matches, Jemmy dismissed the Champion in both innings, a feat he also achieved while assisting 22 of Scarborough as a Given Man against the United South of England Eleven, on the old Castle Yard ground, on September 1, 2, and 3, 1870.

It must not be imagined, however, that Jemmy had things all his own way. On the contrary, the Champion scored a century on their first encounter and added fourteen more in subsequent seasons, as well as making some other hefty contributions to his side's total. The balance, on the whole, was in W.G.'s favour. In three of their duels, the Champion went for a cipher in the first innings, only to retrieve his laurels with a massive retaliation in the second. Such an event took place for the first time when the North were playing against the South, at Canterbury, on August 9 and 10, 1869. Cock-a-hoop at his success in the first innings—8 wickets for only 19 runs, including clean bowling W.G. for a duck—Jemmy was brought down to earth with a shattering bump in the second. True enough, he got W.G. again, but only after the Champion had hit up a rapid 96, and Jemmy had perforce to be content with a solitary wicket while conceding 70 runs. "What do you think of him now?" was the gleeful question addressed to the crestfallen bowler. "I'll tell you what it is," replied the weary Jemmy; "I puts the ball just where I pleases, and then that gentleman puts it just where he pleases." We have here a perfect example of a Victorian euphemism: the journalist recording this conversation went to the length of adding, in brackets, "N.B. The word 'gentleman' did not occur in the original." Lord Harris was highly amused by this anecdote, substituting "beggar" for "gentleman" in his version of the conversation. There are no prizes for guessing the word Jemmy probably used to relieve his pent-up emotion.

The two other instances of the cheap dismissal followed by the revenge of W.G. both occurred in 1871. In H. H. Stephenson's benefit match, North *v* South, at The Oval, on July 31 and August 1 and 2, the Champion surrendered his wicket to Jemmy in both innings—for 0 and 268! The mode of dismissal in W.G.'s first attempt was lbw, first ball,

Lord Harris

and later, in print, the victim endorsed John Lillywhite's decision, saying, "and for once I am bound to say I think the verdict was right." This opinion deserves to be engrossed on fine parchment in letters of scarlet and gold. Was there ever another occasion when the Champion agreed with a leg-before decision against him? The other instance took place in yet another benefit match, this time in honour of that same John Lillywhite, who had given the great man out at The Oval. Opposing each other, at Hove, on August 14, 15, and 16, were Gentlemen and Players—the same encounter in which Mr C. I. Thornton did some big hitting—and W.G., bowled J. C. Shaw 0 in the first innings, made 217 in the second and grievously damaged Jemmy's promising match analysis beyond repair. The left-hander's 7 wickets for 72 runs was followed by 2 for 128, and this time he did not even have the satisfaction of getting rid of the Champion after his mammoth score.

In spite of his successes at one time or another, Shaw also came in for some rough treatment from W.G., who once punished him to the extent of scoring 20 runs off five consecutive deliveries. On only one other occasion—North *v* South, at Prince's Ground, on May 16, 1872—was Jemmy successful in trapping Grace leg before wicket. The umpire ruling in favour of the bowler was an ageing cricketer, whose career as a player began before the Champion was born. There were not, it must be freely admitted, too many officials as intrepid as John Lillywhite and the other veteran at Prince's who were prepared to brave W.G.'s notorious browbeating tactics. At times, Jemmy was plunged into the depths of despair, appealing in vain to Heaven whenever, as was almost always the case, his supplications for lbw were rejected, and the Champion would call out in that famous, squeaky, irascible voice, "Didn't pitch straight by half an inch!" Half an inch! How many umpires are there who could judge the line to half an inch? Eventually, realizing the futility of kicking against the pricks of misfortune and injustice, Jemmy would acknowledge defeat by giving W.G. an easy single, so he could try his luck with the other batsman. On at least one occasion, in a Gentlemen *v* Players match, he was solely to blame for his own disappointment, when he put down a simple return catch from Grace. Asked by one of his irate team-mates why he had failed to hold on to such a sitter, Jemmy put on a brave face, replying, "Oh, I like to see him bat!" Whenever he managed to take a wicket, the Champion's or any other batsman's, a remarkable change came over Jemmy. There were no more exaggerated histrionics, no dramatic leap, no punching the air, no mad dash down the pitch to receive his team-mates' back-slapping congratulations. Jemmy merely jammed his hands into his trouser pockets and stared vacantly into space, awaiting the arrival of the next batsman.

In Jemmy's time, there were a few specialists who fielded at short-leg, but should there be a passenger in the side, it was often felt that he would do the least harm in that position. Jemmy was often to be found stationed at short-leg, where he was, reputedly, prone to miss many catches. Yet, in spite of the instance of letting off W.G. mentioned above, he usually showed a much safer pair of hands to his own bowling. Of the 62 catches credited to him in first-class cricket, 34 were caught and bowled.

Jemmy was a right-handed batsman, though "batsman" is a misnomer if there ever was one, since his performance in that department of the game was even more inept than his fielding. It came as an agreeable surprise when he gave the scorers much to do, and this was, perhaps, partly a legacy of his employment as a professional coach, when all he was expected to do was bowl at his pupils. In all honesty, however, it must be frankly admitted that Jemmy's knowledge of even the bare bones of batting was virtually nil. Once, at Trent Bridge, his first county captain, George Parr, came across him trying out the feel of several bats by executing confident, imaginary strokes and enquired what kind he wanted. "Ah wants one as'll coot well," said Jemmy. "Coot well?" replied George; "much better get hold of one as'll stop straight 'uns, Jem!" Asked on another occasion how he came to be clean bowled, Jemmy delivered a sublime explanation of his dismissal, saying, "The ball coom back a bit and mar bat warn't *levvil*!" He made, it will be remembered, 9 runs on his first-class debut in 1865. Not until 1870 did he improve upon this. His highest score was 18 not out, and throughout his first-class career he reached double figures only 8 times. In 115 matches and 110 completed innings, he attained an aggregate of 467 runs at an average of 4.24. There have been worse records, though not many. Billy Buttress, with 3.82, was less successful, but take the case of William Slinn, of Yorkshire, another brilliant bowler, but as useless as Jemmy in the field or at the crease. Slinn spent most of his time playing as a Given Man for local teams against the itinerant elevens and appeared in only 19 first-class matches—two more than Buttress—ending up with a batting average of 2.00. The most fascinating statistic of Jemmy's prowess as a batsman comes from his performance for the All England Eleven in minor contests in 1872: matches, 9; innings, 12; times not out, 5; runs, 0; highest score, 0 not out; average, 0.00.

Fred Morley, who succeeded Shaw as the principal strike bowler for Nottinghamshire, was also a natural number eleven in the batting order of any team, and his lack of competence gave rise to one of those legends found so frequently in the mythology of cricket. Rumour said that, whenever Fred appeared and made his way out to the pitch in home matches, the Trent Bridge horse always automatically backed into position between the shafts of the roller. Fred had an exaggerated conception of his ability to score runs and once agreed to turn out in a match while pointing out that an injury would prevent him from bowling, but, in the event, his career average was not much better than Jemmy's, "although compared with J. C. Shaw he was almost a good batsman." It must, then, be acknowledged that Jemmy did not inspire much confidence as a run-getter and still less as an exponent of the technique of defensive batting, though there were, of course, a few times when he managed to resist all attempts to bustle him out. One of the most memorable occurred in a low-scoring match against Surrey, at The Oval, on August 10 and 11, 1874. Nottinghamshire needed 113 runs to win, and all seemed hopelessly lost when nine wickets were down for only 100. Surrey, licking their chops in anticipation and scenting the heady aroma of victory in their nostrils, saw Jemmy Shaw come out to join Samuel Biddulph, the visitors' wicket-keeper. To their astonishment and dismay, however, "J. C. Shaw was stubborn at the crisis," and succeeded in keeping his end up, while "Biddy" coolly knocked off most of the runs required (Shaw 1 not out).

Even more amazing was Jemmy's match-saving role in the contest with Gloucestershire, at Clifton, on August 22, 23, and 24, 1872. W.G. was out of the country, taking part in a tour of Canada and the USA with a team of amateurs, but his absence proved to be of little handicap to the home side, since his brothers E.M. and G.F. both helped themselves to centuries off some markedly ineffective bowling by the visitors. Fred Morley was the most successful (4–84), but Jemmy had a particularly bad time taking only 1 wicket and conceding 107 runs out of 309 from the bat! At the end of the second day, Nottinghamshire had reached 179 for the loss of 8 wickets and were perilously near the prospect of having to follow their innings (compulsory in those days with a deficit of 80 runs).

One of the not outs was Richard Daft, the Nottinghamshire captain, who was widely regarded as one of the best professional batsmen in England. The next morning, Daft went to take breakfast at the house of a friend in Bristol, where he was greeted with the news that Nottinghamshire would have to bat one man short. There then followed a tale which filled Richard with anger and finally made his hair stand on end. Anxious, perhaps, to avoid having to dwell on the ordeal to come, Jemmy Shaw had spent the evening liberally drowning his sorrows and playing cards with some of his team-mates. The inevitable arguments between these boon companions developed into full-blown quarrels, with Jemmy springing to his feet in high dudgeon and smashing all the glasses in a fit of alcoholic rage. Yelling that he would "go and do for himself," and flinging open the door, he had disappeared, minus his coat, into the darkness, and nothing more had been seen of him. Daft's thoughts were focussed immediately on the famous Suspension Bridge over the gorge at Clifton, a favourite resort of suicides. Happily, his gloomy forebodings were dispelled an hour or so later by the news that one of the Gloucestershire team taking a morning stroll across the Downs had discovered Jemmy fast asleep under a tree.

Jemmy regained consciousness and managed to arrive at the ground in time, but he took great pains to avoid his captain. Deciding that it would be more politic to postpone the necessary tongue-lashing until the innings was over, Daft said nothing for the time being and concentrated on the seemingly forlorn task of saving the follow-on. Shortly after the resumption of play, Fred Morley was bowled for 8, and it was Jemmy's turn to bat. By some incomprehensible stroke of fate he succeeded in staying at the crease, and an unbelievable stand was in the making. Naturally, Daft scored most of the runs, which was just as well, since his partner devoted himself almost exclusively to long-handle tactics. Would-be drives resulted in edges over short-slip's head; cross-batted swipes made contact only with the empty air. Interesting conversations developed in the middle of the pitch between overs, with Daft vainly beseeching his partner to calm down, and Jemmy, full of bravado, confidently maintaining that *he* was in no danger of losing *his* wicket. Not long after the follow-on was averted, Shaw was bowled for 9, with Daft undefeated (92). Their stand lasted one hour and forty minutes—probably the longest period Jemmy had ever been at the wickets—and the match ended in a draw. Throughout the rest of the day, the culprit died a thousand deaths in anticipation of the wrath to come. Daft, however, had a soft spot for his erring bowler and, feeling that he had suffered enough, contented himself with delivering a gentle homily mingled with a touch of heavy humour, saying, "It's lucky for you, Jemmy, that we saved the match to-day; and as I never saw you play half so well before, I should strongly advise you never to go to the expense of a bed again, but should always, if I were you, sleep in the open air." This tale of Jemmy's nocturnal escapade may have contributed to the development of a legend that a certain unnamed Nottinghamshire professional once avoided paying hotel bills in the vicinity of Lord's by sleeping out of doors in his cricket clothes during a spell of fine weather.

On another occasion, Richard Daft managed to rescue Jemmy from a highly embarrassing situation. They were both taking part in a minor match, the event being celebrated with an evening of music, singing, and good cheer. After several of those present had contributed their party pieces for the entertainment of the company, there was a loud, insistent call, supported almost unanimously, for Mr J. C. Shaw to perform a piano solo. There had evidently been a failure in communication somewhere, since Jemmy knew far less about playing the piano than he did about batting. Under the cover of the cheering, rapping on the table, and repeated demands for the expected musical treat, the squirming victim was driven to pleading with his old captain to rescue him from this predicament. Richard Daft was a good man to have on your side at the eleventh hour, and he soon proved himself equal to dealing with this emergency. Rising to his feet, he wasted no time in informing the assembled guests that "Mr. Shaw would have been most happy to have obliged them, but as the piano in the room was not a *left-handed* one, he greatly regretted his inability to do so."

Jemmy Shaw was evidently regarded with some favour at Cambridge University, since he was employed there for several years to bowl to the undergraduates at the beginning of the season. Nothing is known of his ability as an instructor, and in any case he was the last man in the world to demonstrate or give advice on the art of batsmanship. Was he expected to coach his pupils in bowling? If so, it was a question of trying vainly to make bricks without straw around 1874 or 1875, when Cambridge were desperately short of good bowlers. The day finally came when the Rev A. R. Ward, president for many years of the Cambridge University Cricket Club, hove in sight and bore down remorselessly upon Jemmy. It was rather like being subjected to a stately charge from a determined but slow-moving pachyderm. Son of William Ward, the famous amateur cricketer of a bygone age and a benefactor of Lord's, the reverend gentleman weighed around twenty stone in his early twenties and considerably more as he grew older, when he habitually wore a waistcoat with no less than 38 buttons—witness, C. T. Studd, who claimed that he had carefully counted them. Resolved, perhaps, to have a little fun at Shaw's expense, since, it must be admitted, the simple Jemmy was no intellectual giant, Ward addressed him with the following proposition: "Shaw, we are very weak in bowling, and we have arrived at the conclusion that you will have to become a member of this University. Do you happen to know your Greek testament?" Jemmy's jaw dropped. "What's *thaat*?" he blurted out aghast.

Jemmy, of course, never presented himself as a candidate for matriculation. Doubtless, such a conversation was all Greek to him, and doubtless his questioner was able to extract a little mirth out of his malicious jest, but it is nice to know that Ward eventually received his come-uppance a few years later. One day, when D.W. Gregory's Australian team were touring England in 1878, the brilliant, young

A. G. Steel

all-rounder, A. G. Steel (Cambridge University, Lancashire, and England) was sitting in the pavilion at Lord's. His companion was F. R. Spofforth, and neither was taking part in the match they were watching, but Steel had just been invited to assist the Gentlemen of England against the Australians the following week. The elephantine figure of the Rev Arthur Ward loomed on the scene. Now, it appears that Ward's knowledge of the population of Australia was extremely limited, and his mind was evidently restricted to vague memories of the team of black Aborigines that toured England in 1868. Arriving in the presence of the two spectators and recognizing Steel, who was in his first year at Cambridge, Ward opened the conversation, saying, "Well, Mr Steel, so I hear you are going to play against the niggers on Monday?" "His face," Steel wrote some ten years later, "was a picture when Spofforth was introduced to him as the 'demon nigger bowler'." Jemmy Shaw was avenged. Given his bulk and obesity, one could hardly say that the Rev Arthur Ward was made to look small, but had this anecdote been narrated in *Punch* at the time, it would certainly have been concluded with the legendary observation, "Collapse of stout party!"

Shaw's first-class career, which was spread over eleven seasons, shows an ascending curve reaching its apogee in 1870, and a comparable descent into decline and eventual oblivion. Top of the national bowling averages in his first season (1865), he came no lower than fourteenth in the next four years. "This splendid performer" occupied the eighth position in his marvellous year of 1870, claiming 96 victims at 10.31 and achieving his highest seasonal total of 5 wickets in an innings (11 times) and 10 in a match (4 times). Thereafter, until he finished with first-class cricket, he failed to attain a place in the top twenty of the averages. In 1871, his tally of wickets was still high (90), but they were obtained at a much greater cost (average 17.70). From then onwards, it was a sorry tale of a steady, perceptible decline from the lofty peaks of excellence. In 1872, his aggregate of dismissals decreased to 72, and his average increased to 20.86—a mediocre performance for anybody considered as a front-rank bowler in those days. One of the cricket annuals still characterized him as "One of the best bowlers (fast left-hand) out," but qualified this by adding "though hardly so successful of late." In the years 1872, 1873, and 1874, he played in 17 matches each season, the highest number in his whole first-class career, but he took fewer and fewer wickets, and finally, in 1875, the end came. At the beginning of the season, on May 6 and 7, he turned out for an England Eleven against Cambridge University—an annual event for several years in which he had participated previously by reason of his engagement as a practice bowler. Although he took only 1 wicket,

Jemmy had the unusual distinction of opening the England batting with W.G. and actually scored 15! The same pair also opened the bowling. He assisted Nottinghamshire against Derbyshire, at Trent Bridge, on May 17, 18, and 19, taking 2 wickets in each innings, and finally, against MCC, at Lord's, on June 14 and 15. W.G. was present at the obsequies and was "bowled Shaw" in both innings. The Champion's conqueror, however, was Alfred Shaw, not Jemmy, whose analysis in the first innings read 6–2–14–0. He was not given a turn with the ball in the second and, consequently, was denied the opportunity of one last contest with his old adversary. This match is remembered not so much for Jemmy Shaw's departure from first-class cricket, but for Alfred Shaw's magnificent bowling in the MCC second innings, when his 41.2 overs included 36 maidens, and he took 7 wickets for only 7 runs.

In reviewing the fortunes of Nottinghamshire throughout the cricket season of 1875, one of the annuals observed that, "The absence of J. C. Shaw from the ranks astonished not a few, but . . . when an old member of the eleven is evidently on the down line, the rising players naturally look for promotion." Useless with the bat and not much more than a liability in the field, Jemmy could no longer claim automatic selection for the County eleven, once his bowling powers were so obviously deserting him. Already established in the Nottinghamshire side were Martin McIntyre, an effective fast right-hander on his day, though at times unreliable in accuracy and especially in temperament, and Fred Morley, already regarded as one of the finest fast left-handers in the country. Jemmy was obliged to relinquish his place in the team to William B. Clarke, of Old Basford, who was outstanding in no department of the game, but was a competent bits-and-pieces man.

So, Jemmy Shaw retired from the arena of first-class cricket and maintained himself as best he might with match fees in minor affairs and professional engagements. He was employed by the East Lancashire Cricket Club on a semi-permanent basis (1877–1886) and, in this less arduous atmosphere, was still able to terrorize many of the batsmen confronting him at the crease. In 1884, Nottinghamshire granted him a belated benefit for the match against Yorkshire, at Trent Bridge, on July 17, 18, and 19. With the gate receipts and a subscription list, he received something in excess of £400, "a substantial profit" in those days.

Jemmy was not destined to savour the pleasures of a gentle retirement, recalling the glorious days of the past and his duels with the Champion, as he sat and enjoyed the warmth of the mellow sunshine. In the winter of 1888, he contracted pneumonia and died at New Cross, Sutton-in-Ashfield, on March 7, at the age of 51. How he kept the wolf from the door after the end of his engagement in Lancashire is a mystery. Possibly, he supported himself and his family on the proceeds of his benefit match for a time, but stark poverty had descended upon the Shaw household when his time for departure came, since he left an estate of only £8. Perhaps, even now, he is still bowling to the shade of W.G. on some celestial pitch, and it is to be hoped that Heaven lends a more sympathetic ear to his constant appeals for lbw. And perhaps, when Jemmy takes his turn at the crease, he no longer tries to keep his bat *levvil.*

CHAPTER NINE

Ephraim Lockwood *"Old Mary Ann"*

YORKSHIRE were in an awkward plight in the year of Grace 1868. For the needle match against Surrey, at The Oval, on August 24, 25, and 26, they faced the grim prospect of taking the field without their best eleven. Luke Greenwood, that good all-round man from Lascelles Hall, had been so seriously injured in a traffic accident at the beginning of the month that he was unable to play any more that season. A second misfortune befell the Tykes in the contest against Middlesex, at Islington, on August 14 and 15. During the home side's first innings, George Freeman, Yorkshire's champion fast bowler, wrenched his ankle so severely that he had to be carried off the field to receive medical attention. In Yorkshire's second innings, he hobbled out to bat at number 11, but he bowled no more in the match and, like Greenwood, he was absent for the remainder of the season. The gaps in the ranks of the bowlers could be filled to a certain extent, but there was also a vacancy for a batsman, since Mr Ashley Walker, the Bradford amateur, was prevented from taking part in the forthcoming match at The Oval.

The selection of a suitable replacement for Ashley Walker triggered off a prolonged and at times rather heated discussion among the blunt-spoken members of the Yorkshire team. Their captain, burly, bewhiskered Roger Iddison, advanced the claims of his own nominee, Milner Gibson, only to meet with some determined opposition. Family pride as well as some shrewd common sense stirred in the bosom of John Thewlis, a Lascelles Hallian like Luke Greenwood. Forget about Milner Gibson was the burden of his refrain, and give a trial to young Ephraim Lockwood instead. The latter, it soon transpired, was Thewlis's nephew. Now, Roger Iddison was not acquainted with Lockwood's cricketing ability, and the discussion was threatening to reach a deadlock, when Mr. Pedley, the Yorkshire "paymaster" for the occasion, said, "Is there anyone that knows this lad of yours, John?" Without hesitation, Thewlis suggested that they should ask Tom

Emmett for his opinion, and, to Uncle John's intense satisfaction, Emmett answered in his favour, saying, "Aye, Eph. Lockwood is a good 'un." This unconditional recommendation clinched the argument, and Iddison, wisely relinquishing his stance, offered no further opposition to the blooding of Thewlis's nephew. And so it came to pass that Ephraim Lockwood made his debut for Yorkshire, and nothing more was heard of the unfortunate Milner Gibson, who never appeared in first-class cricket.

Born at Lascelles Hall, near Huddersfield, on April 4, 1845, Ephraim Lockwood was one of that select band of cricketers in his native village who earned their living as hand-loom weavers. The time spent at the loom, it should be added, was so arranged as to encroach as little as possible on the hours they wished to devote to cricket practice. What some of the youngsters lacked in the way of orthodox cricketing gear was more than adequately counter-balanced by unbridled enthusiasm for the game. Lascelles Hall was a small, close-knit community, whose solidarity was cemented by much inter-marriage, and whose members, in their native pride and well developed sense of belonging, were given to displaying a certain reserve in the presence of outsiders. It is doubtful, however, if their demeanour ever approached anywhere near the blatant hostility expressed by those two miners featured in a famous cartoon in *Punch* in the 1850s ("Who's 'im, Bill?" "A stranger!" "'Eave 'arf a brick at 'im"). Like so many of the other male inhabitants of Lascelles Hall, so famous as a nursery of excellent cricketers, Eph. Lockwood partially forsook the loom in favour of seeking various professional engagements with clubs, and he was employed at Cheetham Hill, Manchester, at the time when he was summoned to play for Yorkshire at The Oval.

Of medium height in stature and weighing around 10 stone or so at the time of his debut, Ephraim's weight gradually increased to 12 stone or more during his first-class career. There was nothing particularly graceful about his movements or his figure: the impression of incipient plumpness and a certain breadth at the hips became more pronounced with the passing years, and eventually "his dimensions partook of the bulky." With bucolic features and outsize, clod-hopping feet, he bore no resemblance to a matinée idol or an Adonis. Clean-shaven at first, he later grew a moustache, which added a slight touch of dignity to his countenance, but detracted little from that essentially rustic appearance once associated in the popular mind with loose, white smocks and stray wisps of straw in the hair. Yet the guileless expression in his eyes and the unprepossessing appearance, not very far removed from the traditional conception of the innocent abroad, masked certain elements of Ephraim's real character. True enough, he was simple and good-

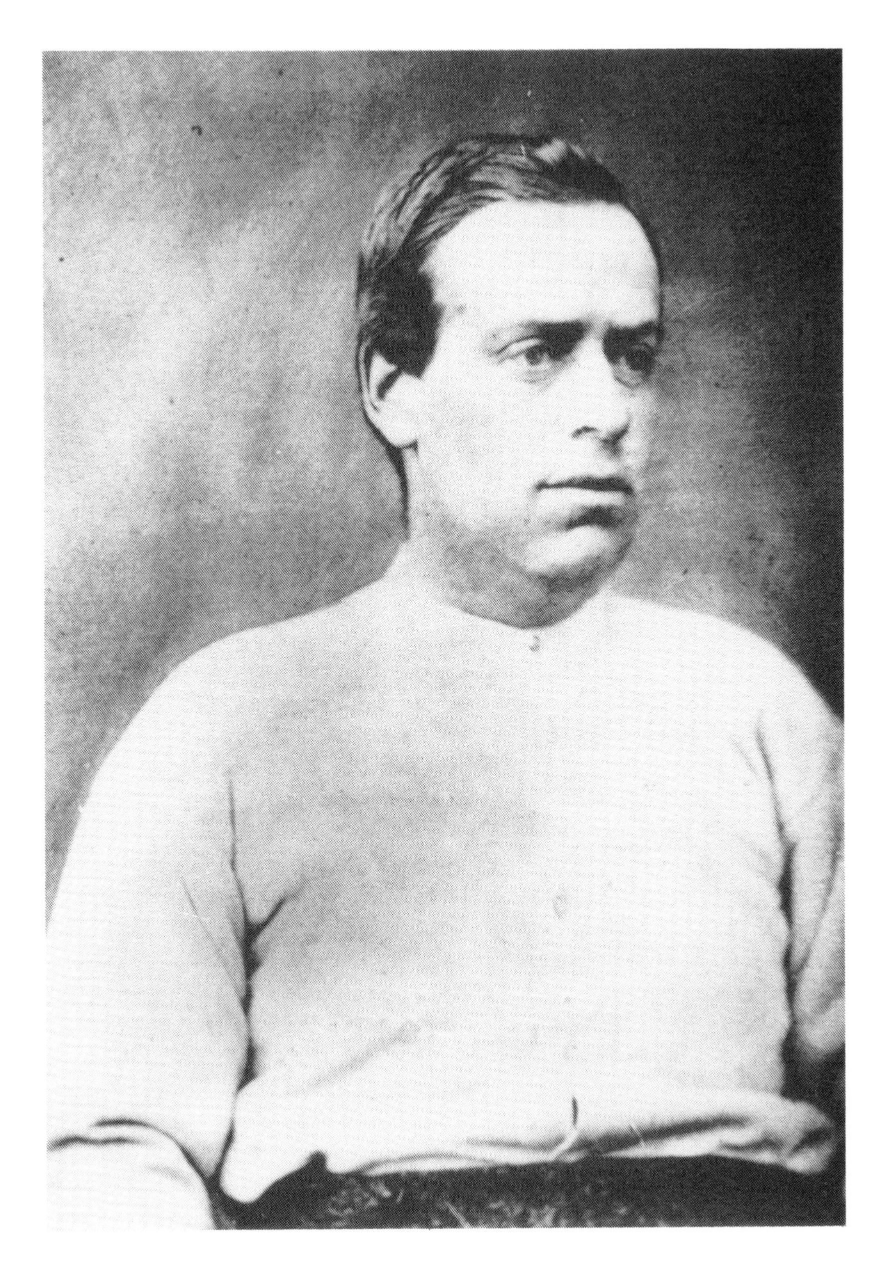

Ephraim Lockwood
"Old Mary Ann"

Courtesy Roger Mann

natured to excess, so that he was easily put upon by his team-mates, who had a tendency to treat him as the natural butt for their shafts of humour, but behind that unpromising exterior reposed a shrewd brain and a profound knowledge of cricket.

The telegram containing the invitation to play for Yorkshire nearly went astray, for Ephraim had just left Cheetham Hill to assist his village team in a two-day match at Yeadon. Fortunately, the message was forwarded to Huddersfield, and the novice packed his best cricketing gear into a parcel and, hat in hand, journeyed south by rail on the Sunday in time for the match at The Oval on the morrow—first-class matches in those days began on Mondays and Thursdays. On arriving at King's Cross, Eph. found Thewlis waiting there to greet him, and later, on their way to The Oval, Uncle John offered warm words of encouragement, saying, "If that does well i' this match it'll be a rare good thing for thee."

Having won the toss, Surrey took first innings and were restricted to a total of 195 by the depleted Yorkshire attack, with Tom Emmett nobly capturing 5 wickets at 13 runs apiece in 31 overs. The newcomer was given a brief, unsuccessful spell with the ball, conceding 20 runs in 6 overs, but Eph. hadn't really come south to do much in the way of bowling. Meanwhile, Roger Iddison had been puzzling over the Yorkshire batting order, and eventually he said to Uncle John, "Thewlis, have you any objection to your nephew going in first?" Thewlis, of course, had none, and the family partnership went out to face the Surrey bowling. When stumps were drawn, the Lascelles Hall pair were unbeaten, with Thewlis 51 not out and Lockwood 57 not out. Uncle John, no doubt, nursed his nephew along between overs at the start, but one wonders how Ephraim's morale stood up to the test, when Tom Emmett brought out a drink for him and whispered the stern, no-nonsense admonition, "Remember, tha's on thi merits."

The Oval crowd had seen Uncle John before, but they were all agog to know more about Ephraim. Wild rumours circulated, asserting that the newcomer must be a miner or a farmer's boy, and as the players left the field at close of play, some of the spectators rushed out on the ground to get a better look at this bumpkin, who had been scoring so many confident runs off the Surrey bowling. They were not impressed with what they saw. Amid all the hubbub and excited chatter, Ephraim distinctly heard one individual with a penetrating voice declaring in amazement, "Why, he's more fit to eat a penny cake than play cricket!"

It must be admitted that Ephraim created a sensation in more ways than one on that famous day at The Oval. It was not the custom in the 1860s for teams to turn out in uniform white clothing, at least from the waist upwards. Shirts of plain grey or patterned with spots or stripes were the normal wear, especially among the professionals, but Ephraim presented a rare and never-to-be-forgotten example of sartorial splendour for all the world to see. Above his flannel trousers, much shrunk in the wash, he wore "a shirt with red, black, and green squares like a church window." His stained-glass impersonation may have seemed a little out of the ordinary, but this type of eccentricity in matters of dress for a grand match in the metropolis was perpetuated a few years later by another scion of the Lascelles Hall Club. Gigantic John Ambler, who bowled fast and was in his element when smiting the ball "in rude fashion," appeared at Lord's, on May 6, 7, and 8, 1872, assisting 15 Colts of England against a powerful MCC side (including W. G. Grace and Alfred Shaw). Sweaters were not much in vogue at that time, so Ambler did Lord's proud by playing in a fur waistcoat. Those who have shivered in the chilly winds that often sweep pitilessly across the ground in early May will, perhaps, be prepared to concede that John Ambler showed eminent good sense in opting for the warmth of his Sunday best rather than a more conventional form of attire on that august occasion.

When play was resumed at The Oval on the Tuesday, the family partnership continued the good work by collaring the Surrey bowling again, and the total had reached 176—a Yorkshire record for the first wicket, which lasted for some time to come—before Ephraim was dismissed off a return catch to the bowler for 91. John Thewlis, "that sterling old cricketer," was eventually trapped into giving a catch to the wicket-keeper "after playing a sound 'cricketer's innings' of 108"—nothing flashy about Uncle John. This was his highest score in first-class cricket, and the first century notched for Yorkshire in a county match. Thanks to the batting of Thewlis, Lockwood, Iddison, and others, and the bowling of Emmett and George Atkinson, the visitors were victorious by an innings and 142 runs. The Oval, not surprisingly, became one of Ephraim's favourite grounds.

From the next season up to the end of 1883, Eph. was a regular and integral member of the Yorkshire team, and during this period he acquired two nicknames, one from his fellow players and another from some onlookers. To some he was, for obvious reasons, known as "Big Feet", and Eph. himself admitted that Lady Londesborough, wife of the generous nineteenth-century patron of Yorkshire cricket, used to say, "I'm sure that Lockwood would run *much* better if he wore smaller boots." An appellation used more universally by his contemporaries on the cricket field was invented by George Freeman during the course of a minor match in the early 1870s. One of the opposing batsmen cut one of George's deliveries in the direction of Ephraim standing at long-slip, who, with his large feet and ungainly run, was evidently slow to move to the ball. Freeman, in exasperation, shouted, "Come, look sharp, Mary Ann!" and, to the delight of his team-mates and Eph.'s own initial mortification, the name caught on. In the 1870s, the term "Mary Ann" was sometimes applied to effeminate individuals of unorthodox sexual proclivities. It is only fair to add that, however much Ephraim may have swayed at the hips when he ran, he was not cast in that particular mould. He was married twice, his second wife being a niece of Fuller Pilch, the famous batsman in the days of top hats and braces. The nickname "Mary Ann" clung to Ephraim throughout his career and beyond, becoming eventually, "Old Mary Ann," and sometimes just "Old Mary".

Ephraim's slowness in stopping the stroke off George Freeman was not characteristic of his usual performance in that department of the game. In the main, he was "a very safe but not a showy field," especially at point, operating "with great certainty," and once he achieved the quickest run out that Tom Emmett had ever seen—and Tom's career in first-class cricket lasted over twenty years. It happened in a match against Nottinghamshire, at Sheffield, in 1876, when Ephraim was bowling to Alfred Shaw. The latter advanced down the pitch to drive the ball hard along the ground. Ephraim not only stopped it, which would have been commendable enough, but held it cleanly and, seeing Shaw momentarily stranded in no man's land, flung the ball back over the flabbergasted batsman's head and broke the wicket. On rare occasions, "Old Mary" took a turn at keeping the wickets, but his performance in this role was rather patchy through lack of practice. In the Gentlemen *v* Players match, at Lord's, in 1877, he was the official wicket-keeper for the professionals and, rather appropriately, succeeded in stumping the Hon A. Lyttleton, his opposite number on the Gentlemen's side.

In spite of his lack of success with the ball on his debut, at The Oval, in 1868, Ephraim was a more than useful bowler for several years, capturing 206 wickets at an average of 16.78. Employing a high delivery and often varying his pace from slow to medium, he was most effective at spinning the ball whenever the ground was heavy. Usually regarded as a change bowler, he sometimes opened the attack, and in this role he recorded his best figures in an innings and in a match. Assisting the United North of England Eleven against the United South of England Eleven, at Bishop's Stortford, on June 10 and 12, 1872, he operated unchanged throughout both innings with J. C. Shaw as his partner—a nice contrast, with slow to medium right-arm at one end and fast left-hand at the other. The pitch, ruined by rain, suited "Old Mary" to perfection: he took 6 wickets for 47 runs in the first innings and 7 for 35 in the second, and 5 of his 13 victims were caught and bowled. A rain-sodden wicket was his ally once again, when Yorkshire encountered Nottinghamshire, at Bramall Lane, on August 28, 29, and 30, 1876—seemingly the same contest in which he ran out Alfred Shaw—and he returned a match analysis remarkable for its economy, delivering 53 overs, of which 43 were maidens, and capturing 2 wickets at a cost of only 14 runs. His figures in the first innings were outstanding—14 overs, 10 maidens, 4 runs, 2 wickets.

As a batsman, Ephraim was in many ways a model for all to observe and imitate. Though elegance and polish played no major role in his methods, that false friend flashy brilliance was even more alien to his technique. No man was more correct nor played with a straighter bat, and few of his contemporaries possessed the same powers of watchful patience as "Old Mary Ann." At home as either an opening batsman or in the middle of the order, and always regarded by his team-mates as the backbone of the Yorkshire batting, he was, without being intolerably slow, the personification of painstaking vigilance. Nobody could fault his immaculate sense of timing, and he was a past master at solving the knotty problems posed by a wet or bumpy pitch and pushing the total along, while his partners were rendered helpless by the treacherous conditions. He had the capacity to score all round the wicket and frequently tantalized the opposition by playing a seemingly half-hearted forward stroke to a "slow," which lofted the ball just over the heads of the frantic bowler and mid-off only to fall well short of the fielders in the deep. Another favourite was a hard leg-hit square of the wicket, but once he was foiled by the artful W.G., who laid a cunning trap with a characteristic touch of gamesmanship. Stealthily shifting his brother G.F. from long-leg to square, the Champion sent down a tempting half-volley, and "Old Mary" took the bait and was lost. As an exponent of the cut, however, Ephraim had no rivals. Precise timing and a quick turn of the wrist rather than brute force constituted the secret of his success as he chopped or patted the ball away with the face of his bat. Garnering an abundant harvest of golden runs when well set, he was the despair of opposing captains. No matter how much they adjusted the field, they were baffled by the uncanny skill with which he placed the ball surely through the gaps between short-slip, cover-slip, and point. Keen eyesight and a supreme confidence in his mastery of the stroke enabled Ephraim to cut balls even off the middle and off stumps with impunity.

Throughout his first-class career, "Old Mary Ann" scored 12,512 runs at an average of 23.60—a good record for the time. He made 1000 runs in a season four times, his best year being 1876, when his aggregate amounted to 1,261 (average 32.33), which included one century and nine half-centuries. In five other seasons, he totalled 900 or more runs, and it is probable that injuries and periodic spells of poor health played an important part in limiting his scoring. And, in the matter of bodily ailments, it is worth recording that he succumbed to something one would have imagined as verging on the impossible in our uncertain English climate: in 1873, he was prostrated by sunstroke! It could have happened to hardly anybody else but Ephraim.

When not assisting Yorkshire, "Old Mary" appeared in a wide variety of other matches, playing for North *v* South and for sides designated as "England" or "An Eleven of England." In the 1870s, he earned match fees by turning out for the All England Eleven, the United North of England Eleven, and Yorkshire United, many of the contests being minor affairs against "odds." His principal allegiance lay with the United North, and he holds the singular distinction of being the only player to appear in all the first-class fixtures undertaken by that particular itinerant eleven.

Ephraim made his debut for the Players against the Gentlemen, at Lord's, in 1869, and from 1872 to 1883 he was near to being ever present in the professionals' team, totalling 28 appearances. His aggregate was 1,179 runs at the rate of 21.83 per innings, a figure which is not so far below his career average in all first-class matches. At The Oval, his favourite ground, in 1877, he went in first with Arthur Shrewsbury, another usually careful batsman, and in the space of some three hours the pair put on 166 before Arthur was caught at the wicket for 78. Ephraim followed his partner not long afterwards, taken in the slips for 97. This was his highest figure in the series, and "his runs were got by faultless cricket." He marked eight half-centuries in all, though W.G. remembered with unsuppressed glee that Ephraim went for a pair at The Oval, in 1873, caught in the first innings and caught and bowled in the second by the Champion.

"Old Mary" fared much better against the Gentlemen the next season. In 1874, at The Oval—where else?—he opened the batting with Henry Jupp and became the first man for the Players to carry his bat throughout a completed innings, scoring 67 out of a total of 115. At his second venture, he reached 48. Sunday intervened, and then came the fixture at Lord's, in which Ephraim made 70 and 9. Opposed to him in both matches was a short, stout, thickset man, the wily, heavily bearded Scotchman, David Buchanan. The latter began his career as a fast left-arm bowler and continued in this style for nearly twenty years. Approaching the age of forty, he converted himself into a superb, slow left-arm trundler, able to break the ball both ways and control the amount of spin at will, though his command of length was not always consistent. He assisted the Gentlemen ten times, emerging as a veritable scourge of the Players, who were often tied up in knots by his

David Buchanan
"The professionals were his natural prey"
Courtesy Roger Mann

sly spinners. His tally of victims, in 19 innings, amounted to 87 (average 14.88); he claimed 5 wickets in an innings 9 times (best 9–82) and 10 in a match on 5 occasions (best 12–165). Eight times were the Gentlemen victorious in these ten encounters, and only once were they defeated. It may fairly be said that David considered that the professionals were his natural prey. He had accounted for Ephraim in both innings at Lord's, in 1872, and in the first innings at The Oval the following season, when "Old Mary" made his pair. To the end of his days, however, David nursed a grievance over the two contests of 1874. Early in the day at The Oval, according to his recollection, he enticed Ephraim into giving an absolute sitter to cover-point, but "The catch was unfortunately treated with too much nonchalance, and fell to the ground." So, instead of being dismissed for a mere handful of runs, "Old Mary" went on to carry his bat for 67. It was still worse at Lord's: off David's second delivery, he got a thin edge, but the wicket-keeper failed to hold on to the simple catch, and the lucky batsman was spared to take his score from 0 to 70. This was David Buchanan's final appearance for the Gentlemen, who experienced a rare defeat. Perhaps he gave up in sheer disgust at the poor support he received from his field, and in later years, rather churlishly, he refused to acknowledge that Ephraim was the finest cutter he had ever encountered.

In that same season of 1874, when Surrey were defeated by Yorkshire, at The Oval, on August 17, 18, 19, there was a nostalgic echo of the triumph of six years ago. Uncle John Thewlis opened the batting for the visitors, soon lost his partner for 0, and was joined by Ephraim coming in at first wicket down. This time, they put on 88, when Thewlis departed for 50, but his nephew carried on the good work by making 96. Uncle John retired from first-class cricket the following season; not so Ephraim, who still had plenty of years to come.

"Old Mary" made his initial first-class century in 1869—against Surrey, of course, at The Oval, on August 5, 6, and 7. He opened the batting with Joseph Rowbotham, and both of them reached three figures. The Yorkshire skipper at that time was still Roger Iddison, under whose leadership "Old Mary" made his debut in 1868. Roger relinquished the captaincy in favour of Joe Rowbotham in 1871, who retained it until 1875, by which time he was becoming rather too rotund for cavorting on a cricket field. Joe's successor was Ephraim, who held the office for two seasons (1876–77). From the point of view of tactics and a thorough knowledge of the game, this appointment could not be faulted. He captained the Players against the Gentlemen, at The Oval, in 1879, and against the Australians, at the same venue, in 1882. In this match against the tourists, he was "a distinct success," earning many compliments for the skill he displayed in his management of the bowling and his placing of the field, and achieving victory by an innings and 34 runs.

The be-all and end-all of captaincy, however, embraces more than the mere know-how of when to alter the positions of the fielders or work the bowling changes to the greatest advantage. The cerebral processes of the committee appointing Ephraim to skipper the Yorkshire side constitute a matter for earnest speculation. For a professional to captain an all-professional team successfully in those days, some special qualities were indispensable. Ephraim's make-up, unfortunately, was sadly deficient in the slightest spark of charismatic leadership, while his powers of peaceful persuasion were almost non-existent. During his first season, the results were fairly good on the whole, but it was a vastly different story in 1877, prompting one of the cricket annuals to observe, on considering the Yorkshire team's minimal achievements, that "It seemed to the casual observer that they did not work so well together as might have been the case, and there was certainly a lack of energy in the field that showed want of management somewhere." The problem was Ephraim's excessive good nature, coupled, perhaps, with the slight air of gormlessness that hung around him. W.G. made no bones about it, declaring that "Old Mary", as the Yorkshire captain, "lacked firmness in that position, pretty much owing to his desire to please everyone." Bowlers were accustomed to taking advantage of this and declined to go on again for another spell of punishment, in spite of "Old Mary's" prayers and supplications. This situation was all too patently obvious during the match against Gloucestershire, at Cheltenham, on August 17, 18, and 19, 1876, when the home side batted all the first day and much of the second. Their eventual total was 528, with W.G. carrying his bat through the innings for the colossal figure of 318, scored off no less than 8 bowlers, some of whom flatly refused to have another go at "the big 'un." As if to rub salt into the wounds, the Champion trapped "Old Mary" into hitting down his own wicket. The constant and unavailing struggle to establish some authority over ten rambunctious Tykes proved far too much for anybody of Ephraim's easy-going disposition, and his form in county matches deteriorated, though there was a noticeable improvement in other fixtures, when he could shed the overwhelming burden of responsibility. His successor in 1878 was Tom Emmett, who made a better fist of the job, and it remains a matter for conjecture why he was not appointed earlier, since he was senior to Ephraim in the team.

"Old Mary" never went on a tour to Australia, though his batting was much missed during 1876—77, when the party led by James Lillywhite, junior, played in the first two Test Matches between the two countries. He was offered a place in W.G.'s team in 1873–74, but "didn't fancy the outing at the time," and subsequently he turned down several invitations to go down under, one in 1881–82, when he was crippled with the pangs of persistent rheumatism (some of his friends twitted him with preferring to stay behind and get married!). Nor was he selected to represent England in the solitary home Tests of 1880 and 1882. Misfortune dogged his steps in the latter year, when he was opposed to the Australians nine times. He began well in the first three of five contests between Yorkshire and the tourists in June and July, and his overall record—top scorer on five occasions and an average of 23.38—was quite good. Unfortunately, he was very much under the weather in the middle of the season and suffered the indignity of marking a pair in two consecutive games. The Test Match at The Oval at the end of August had already been played when he recovered his health and his form.

There was, however, one invitation to go abroad with Ephraim did accept, though he wished later he had refused it. Towards the end of the English season of 1879, Richard Daft took his strong, all-professional Twelve on a short tour in North America, and Lockwood was one of five Yorkshiremen in the party, the remainder being members of the Nottinghamshire team. At all points of the game, the Twelve constituted an extremely powerful combination, worthy to represent England against much more formidable opposition than the teams of "odds" they encountered in Canada and the USA. Twelve matches in all were played, of which nine were won and three drawn. Ephraim, who was rested for two of the contests began reasonably well, scoring 30 in the first game and 18 in the second. Thereafter, his next seven innings brought him only 14 runs, and five times he failed to break his duck. He recovered eventually and rounded off the tour with two fine knocks of 60 and 88, which were sufficient to give him third place in the averages.

"Old Mary's" loss of form may certainly be attributed to distressing afflictions, both mental and physical. He was, to start with, a victim of homesickness ("I often wished myself at Lascelles Hall") and, in addition, he was a martyr to a never-ending form of enfeebling bodily discomfort. Anybody who, like "Old Mary," has a skin particularly allergic to insect bites and has experienced the venomous ferocity of North American mosquitoes, will readily feel for his plight. Wherever he went, "these troublesome insects" gave him no peace, especially at night time, and he was compelled to try and catch up on his sleep in the tents and dressing-rooms during the hours of daylight. One morning, when his room-mate George Pinder came down to breakfast, it was obvious that the Yorkshire stumper had been bitten several times on the face. The others began to poke fun at him, but Pinder soon interrupted them, saying, "You've seen nowt yet. Just wait till Ephraim appears." Not long afterwards, the latter sidled into the room, exhibiting a face more swollen and disfigured than ever. Realizing that, for the umpteenth time, he would be the butt of his team-mates' cruel humour, "Old Mary" sat down as far away as possible from them. A useless ploy, since his woebegone appearance aroused not sympathy but prolonged roars of derisive laughter.

It was possibly on the same morning, as luck would have it, that arrangements had been made for a group photograph of the team to be taken. "Old Mary's" affliction was rendered worse by the condition of his left eye, which was so puffy that it was almost closed. The photographer took endless pains to conceal his predicament as far as possible, placing him at the left of the line seated on the ground and looking somewhat towards Tom Emmett at the opposite end. In order to maintain the sufferer's head in the required position, the photographer produced a special instrument to prop it up and then returned to the camera. A split second before the picture could be taken, John Selby called out, "Can't yer gie Lockwood a prop for that eye?" The team dissolved in helpless laughter, though whether "Old Mary" joined in the mirth is not recorded.

Ephraim's chosen companion throughout most of the tour was his Yorkshire team-mate, George Pinder. Although the latter was not entirely averse to taking a rise out of his chum at times, they were inseparable and took many a stroll together. Their progress, however, was rather eccentric, since Ephraim always walked along several steps behind Pinder, rather after the fashion of some married couples, yet this separation never seemed to interfere with the lengthy conversations they managed to carry on with each other. Such a form of companionship still exists in modern times: on the very day I was writing these words, I observed a man going past the window, followed at a short interval by his wife.

On one of their free days, Daft's Twelve were taken to see Niagara Falls. Some of the team enlivened the proceedings at the viewing area by playing practical jokes on each other, but for once "Old Mary" contrived to avoid them. Standing to one side, inevitably with George Pinder, he contemplated the awe-inspiring spectacle in stony silence. Pinder, however, was more moved by the scene, exclaiming in delight and asking his companion what he "thought on't." "Well," replied Ephraim after a short pause, "Ah think nowt on't; Ah'd rather be i' Sheffield." This *bon mot* has been repeated over the years with slight variations, the most important being the substitution of "Lascelles Hall" for "Sheffield," the later version being interpreted as proof of the perpetrator's naivety, philistinism, and homesickness. Those who prefer the earlier wording might think that, in mentally juxtaposing the sublime splendour of Niagara Falls with the then well known smoke and grime of Sheffield, Ephraim was uttering a straight-faced witticism.

The visit to Niagara Falls took place on a Sunday, and in the evening Richard Daft and the secretary of the team decided to go to church. On their way there, they bumped into Lockwood, who on this occasion was accompanied not by Pinder but Tom Emmett. The two Yorkshiremen were talked into attending divine service, and at the conclusion of the sermon the plate was brought round for a collection. Now, Ephraim, like some other Yorkshiremen, was evidently rather careful with his "brass." As the plate came nearer to him, he closed his eyes and appeared to be in a deep, peaceful slumber, maintaining this posture until any danger of having to lighten his purse had passed. All in all, it seems a thousand pities that Ephraim did not go on even one other tour. What a wealth of anecdotes has been lost to us!

The Roses Match, at Bramall Lane, on July 24, 25, and 26, 1882, was designated as "Old Mary's" benefit match. It was not a roaring success in more ways than one. Rain on the first two days restricted the hours of play and limited the number of spectators, notwithstanding the beneficiary's popularity with the Yorkshire crowd. The gate money amounted to only £278, but this was bolstered to nearly £600 by a very good subscription list. Ephraim's own contribution to the match was of little moment: he did not bowl, held no catch, and was dismissed for a single in his only innings, but then "at this period of the season Lockwood himself was neither in good form nor in good health." In fact, the benefit came off in those weeks, when "Old Mary" performed so badly against the Australians and forfeited any last chance of representing England in a home Test.

In the following season, Ephraim scored the last and most famous of his eight centuries in the contest with Kent, at Gravesend, on August 16 and 17, 1883. Thanks to his contribution with the bat and some good bowling from others, Yorkshire gained an easy victory by an innings and 94 runs. He went in at number 5 around 1.00 p.m. and remained at the wickets for about four hours and a-quarter, giving no chance and marking 208, which included no less than 23 fours. It was the highest individual score in first-class cricket that year. His first partner was the famous Yorkshire stonewaller, Louis Hall, who recollected that "Old Mary" went through a rather sticky patch in the first fifteen minutes, but then settled down to play a vintage Lockwood innings. Hall's dead-bat defence was breached with the total at 76, and his place was taken by the amateur, Edward Lumb, whose technique was not dissimilar to Hall's. A protracted stand ensued, with Lumb, like Hall, lost in admiration at the way Ephraim was cutting boundary after boundary off balls on the middle and off stumps. And his own opinion of his performance? "Self-praise," he said later, "is no recommendation; all the same I may be allowed to say that it was the finest innings I ever saw."

The opening match of 1884, against Gloucestershire, at Moreton-in-Marsh, on May 8, 9, and 10, was a disaster for Ephraim, who collected a pair. At the end of May, he received an injury to one of his fingers, and although he returned to the County Eleven the following month, he was lamentably out of touch. In July, he turned out for an Eleven of England against the Australians, at Huddersfield—virtually his home ground—and in September he assisted Yorkshire against MCC, at Scarborough. He failed to reach double figures in either of these games, and, as far as inter-county fixtures were concerned, he had been shunted from the Yorkshire Eleven in the middle of June. Ephraim was rather cagey and tight-lipped about the reasons for his dismissal. When asked about it subsequently, he avoided the touchy subject with a terse reply of "Perhaps I made one mistake." In his final county match, against Nottinghamshire, at Bramall Lane, on June 16 and 17, he was involved in an unpleasant incident. Fielding, as usual, at point, he held a catch close to the ground, but the umpires ruled in favour of the batsman, a decision which "produced a reprehensible demonstration from the spectators." Possibly Ephraim incurred the wrath of the powers that be by expressing dissent with the officials, but that is mere conjecture. Suffice it to say that, in subsequent seasons, he assisted Yorkshire only once more—in a minor match of moderate importance.

Lord Hawke admired "Old Mary's" skill as a batsman and could not complain of his conduct ("He fairly enjoyed his glass, but never forgot himself," so drink was not the cause of dismissal). His lordship was fascinated by the sight of Ephraim indulging in the pastime of bathing in the sea at Scarborough during the period of the Cricket Festival. As was the custom in those days, he would hire a bathing machine—a sort of hut on wheels—and the services of an attendant. There was no danger of being swept out into the deep, since Ephraim was always securely attached to the machine with a rope under his armpits. With infinite caution, and grasping a cake of soap in one hand, he used to wade out until the water reached his waist, lather himself thoroughly, and take a bath "with some bobbing dips and profuse splutterings." And so, Ephraim made full use of the expenditure on the hire of the bathing machine and avoided the extra cost of taking a bath at his lodgings. He was, as we have seen, always careful with his "brass."

After his retirement from the first-class game, Ephraim continued to play cricket at his beloved Lascelles Hall and occupied himself with the management of a business dealing in sporting goods at Huddersfield, where, having outlived many of his team-mates, he died on December 19, 1921, aged 76. Long before that, in the 1890s, he was approached by two journalists eager to obtain his reminiscences. A modest man, easily moved to embarrassment, he was at first reluctant to talk about himself, but his inherent good nature prevailed, and he was persuaded to grant the interviews. He dilated on his experiences, recalling not only his triumphs and misfortunes but also an incident in which, for once, he was the instigator rather than the victim of a practical joke. It occurred during the course of a Gentlemen *v* Players match, at The Oval, in the early 1880s. Ted Peate, the Yorkshire bowler, thoughtlessly left his watch on the dressing-table in his hotel room and, to make matters worse, forgot to close the door. Passing by shortly afterwards, Ephraim slipped into the room and pocketed the watch ("for safety!"). Discovering his loss later, Peate could not remember exactly when he had last seen the watch, but eventually concluded that it must have been stolen at The Oval. The news of the "theft" was noised abroad, and after W. G. Grace and Lord Harris had expressed their sympathy, Peate decided to go and report the matter to Scotland Yard. Keeping a perfectly straight face, Ephraim offered to accompany him, together with two or three others, who were also in on the joke. Police investigations were initiated, of course to no avail, and finally, after about a fortnight, the joker quietly took his victim on one side and returned the missing article. Peate, renowned for his own well developed sense of humour, was fortunately able to see the funny side of the deception, just as Eph. had anticipated. Otherwise, he recollected in telling the tale, he wouldn't have taken the watch—or perhaps he would have purloined somebody else's instead. "Besides," he added, "Yorkshiremen *will* do frivolous things sometimes."

Ephraim's departure from the cricket field was commemorated in a sympathetic valedictory notice by the Hon R. H. Lyttelton in one of the cricket annuals. This perceptive appreciation affirmed the deservedly high reputation "Old Mary" had earned, regretted the bouts of poor health that had affected his form, and spoke of his extraordinary skill "on sticky and difficult wickets." His performances for Yorkshire had been good, his achievements for the Players and the North even better. "The true Yorkshire stolidity about his play" and his superb mastery of the cut were, of course, not forgotten, and Lyttelton, in conclusion, delivered an accurate assessment of Ephraim's rightful place in the cricket of his time: "He was altogether a batsman who in his prime was in the first eleven of England."

CHAPTER TEN

R. G. Barlow *"Patience Personified"*

Richard Gorton Barlow took great pride in his second name. He was descended, he claimed, from the Gortons, an ancient and impoverished family, whose dwindling patrimony had been consumed, in Dickensian fashion, by the machinations of the Court of Chancery. Nevertheless, the name in Barlow's eyes was a mark of distinction to be guarded jealously and preserved with honour throughout his own generation. His residence at Old Trafford around 1890 bore the name of "Gorton House," where he treasured the mementoes and records of all his achievements on the cricket field.

Barlow was born at Barrow Bridge, Bolton, on May 28, 1851, and in his boyhood showed early promise as a left-handed all-rounder. At the age of about thirteen, he experienced a momentous event destined to exert a lasting influence over his future career. Taking him on one side, his father drew his attention to "the awkwardness and stiffness which left-handed bats so often display" and urged young Dick to become a right-handed batsman. One is reminded instantly of the time when left-handed penmanship was regarded with marked disfavour, and unfortunate pupils were compelled to convert themselves into right-handed scribes, sometimes to the detriment of their psychological functions. There is no apparent evidence that Dick Barlow was injured mentally in any perceptible manner, such as developing a tendency to stammer, but the transformation produced nothing remotely resembling stylish elegance or fluent stroke-play in his batting. Dourness and impregnability characterized his performance at the crease.

Leaving school at the age of fourteen, Barlow worked for a time at a printing office, but found that the long hours interfered with his cricket practice. Next he became an iron moulder, and when his family moved from Bolton to Staveley in 1865, he continued in this occupation at the local Iron Works. The change of residence suited young Dick, since cricket flourished in that part of Derbyshire, and he was soon selected to play for the first eleven of the Works Club. Having made a name for himself in local circles, he confidently embarked on a new career as a professional cricketer, his first engagement being at Farsley, near Leeds, in 1871. In the same season, he made his debut in first-class cricket.

In later years, a pleasant legend was invented to explain how Barlow came to the notice of the Lancashire Committee. This anecdote, clearly based on hindsight and a knowledge of Barlow's technique of batting, was retailed with relish by W. G. Grace and others. Barlow, it was alleged, was employed as a porter at a remote station in Lancashire, where few trains stopped, and in the long intervals the station-master and his staff used to play cricket. One day, it happened that a keen supporter of Lancashire cricket found himself stranded at the station and condemned to a wait of three dreary hours before the arrival of the next train. Approaching the station-master, the unhappy passenger enquired how he could pass the time. "You can join us in a game of cricket, if you like," was the reply. "Come and have a bowl at our porter; he's been batting for six weeks, and we can't get him out!" The story was repeated over the years with variants as to the length of Barlow's innings. In one version, the stranded traveller is identified as A. N. Hornby, the Lancashire captain, who was so enthralled at the discovery of such a valuable anchor man that Barlow was there and then drafted into the County Eleven.

Let us pause for a moment to consider a curious variant to this story, which is attributed to J. B. King, the famous bowler from Philadelphia, who once included in an after-dinner speech the tale of the vicissitudes he encountered while travelling on an express train in England. The train stopped at a wayside halt to take on coal and water, but it failed to start after this was completed. King went to enquire about the delay and came across a game of cricket in progress, with the station-master batting and the porter bowling—a nice reversal of the roles. Another half-hour passed, and finally King ventured to ask the porter when the express train would leave. "I can't really say, sir," answered the weary porter. "It might go at any time." Then, as an idea occurred to him, he asked King if he could bowl, and King admitted that he had done so once or twice in his life. With his first ball he clean bowled the station-master. Grasping his saviour by the hand, the porter exclaimed, "Thank God, sir! I've been bowling at him for a fortnight! Thank God for doing that!" Then, reverting to his official duties, he blew a shrill blast on his whistle and paused for a moment to regain his breath. "The express," he announced, "leaves immediately."

To return, however, to the original legend of the obdurate railway employee addicted to the tactics of the barn-door game, it is but justice to add that W.G. was prepared to admit the story might not be true ("I don't vouch for it"). At the same time, he felt that Barlow might well have been capable of keeping up his wicket for six weeks. Alas! it was most certainly a fiction, as Barlow was at pains to point out when he came to publish his reminiscences, *Forty Seasons of First-class Cricket*. His introduction, he explained, followed more orthodox lines. In June 1871, while playing for Staveley against the All England Eleven, he made a favourable impression on William Hickton, a Derbyshire man who had been turning out for Lancashire for several seasons. On Hickton's advice, Barlow applied for a trial at Old Trafford, came through with flying colours, and was selected to play against Yorkshire, at Sheffield, on July 17, 18, and 19. Barlow refers to the Staveley match more than once in his book, but his memory may have played him tricks. The match probably came off in 1869, not 1871. There is, however, no doubt about the date and circumstances of his first-class debut.

Having won the toss, Lancashire took first innings, and A. N. Hornby asked Barlow where he usually went in. The callow youth answered naively that he went in first. With a touch of irony wasted on his raw recruit, Hornby then enquired if he would like to open the batting in this match, and Barlow in all innocence said he didn't mind. Hornby smiled and went away to write out the order, putting Barlow down at number 7. Not long after going in, he sustained an injury to the little finger of his right hand and was compelled to retire hurt, but he resumed his innings the next day, scoring 28 not out. The early Yorkshire batsmen went fairly cheaply, but a stubborn partnership for the ninth wicket held the visitors' attack at bay. One of the Lancashire professionals, the splendidly named Cornelius Coward, who had had some batting practice against Barlow that morning, urged the captain to give the youngster a turn with the ball, and Hornby agreed. The advice could not have been better: with his initial delivery in first-class cricket, young Dick clean bowled the Yorkshire number 10. A most promising debut—28 not out in his only innings, match figures of 4 wickets for 44 runs, and one catch. By the mid–1870s, Barlow had become a regular member of the County side, and his fame began spreading beyond Old Trafford.

A lithe, athletic figure, of medium height and weighing around 11 stone, Dick Barlow was a handsome man with light-coloured eyes and dark hair. For several years in the 1880s, he wavered over the matter of hirsute appendages, wearing at times a moustache and beard, while at others he reduced the beard to luxuriant sideburns by shaving his lower lip and chin. Eventually, he settled for abandoning the razor and sported a full beard, which gave him a distinct resemblance to an old-fashioned naval officer. Fastidious in all things, he was noted for

R. G. Barlow
"Patience Personified"
Courtesy Roger Mann

the neatness and cleanliness of his turn-out, both on and off the field. A healthy man, he paid much attention keeping himself in good trim with regular daily exercise. A teetotaller and a non-smoker, an advocate of a plain diet and a devotee of the virtues of taking several cold baths a week, he would have been a godsend to the editor of the *Boy's Own Paper*. Cricket was not his only sport: he also made his mark in football, playing as goalkeeper for several seasons in the north and acting on occasions as a referee, officiating in that historic match of 1887, when Preston North End defeated Hyde by 26 goals to nil. Serious and seemingly rather lacking in a developed sense of humour, he was justifiably proud of his achievements and made exhaustive records of his doings with bat and ball. He kept a careful watch on his personal details published in one of the cricket annuals, reporting each change of address and adding half-an-inch to his height and four pounds to his weight. His passion for accuracy was extended even to his batting: preferring to rely on himself rather than the scorers and score-boards, he always kept a count of his runs throughout an innings. This feat of mental arithmetic was not so stupendous as it sounds, since Dick was no whirlwind at the wickets.

Barlow's smartness as a fielder gave rise to comment ("more energetic than most of his brother pros"). Keen and willing to fill any position, he would cheerfully go into the deep, but point was the post at which he excelled. At the outset of his career, his opportunities for bowling were rather limited, but after a few seasons of being regarded merely as a change, he became an integral member of the Lancashire attack. Left-arm, around medium pace, with a perfectly fair action, he displayed complete mastery of line and length and varied his spinners with the occasional delivery that came with the arm. His accuracy enabled him to keep down the runs on hard, true ground, but he was most effective on a crumbling or drying pitch. In the early 1880s, the Lancashire bowling resources were the envy of most of the other counties. The captain commanded a galaxy of five first-rate bowlers of varying deliveries: the talented amateur all-rounder A. G. Steel, a slow man able to turn the ball both ways; Alec Watson, a canny Scot, dispenser of off breaks after the fashion of Surrey's James Southerton, and sometimes known as "The Southerton of the North"; George Nash, slow left-arm, from Buckinghamshire; John Crossland, a recruit from the Nottinghamshire coal-mines, right-arm *very* fast, favouring horrendous yorkers; and Dick Barlow. This array of talent nevertheless caused A. N. Hornby some knotty problems. The increasing demands of the legal profession drastically curtailed Mr Steel's opportunities for appearing in first-class cricket; Watson's action was suspect; Nash, it was widely believed, threw every ball he delivered; and Crossland, with his terrifying pace, was the most notorious "chucker" of all. "When I began to watch cricket," said one writer, "it was an adage about the Lancashire attack that Crossland, Nash and Alec Watson all threw, after which, as a change, Barlow went on to bowl." Other counties complained, two of them even cancelling the annual fixtures, and soon Nash was quietly shunted, while Crossland, deemed by MCC to have broken his residential qualification for Lancashire, vanished also. In consequence, Barlow was called upon to assume an overwhelming amount of the bowling, and the quality of his batting inevitably suffered under the stress of this additional burden. Shortly, however, Barlow and Watson—the latter surviving all adverse criticism—received the assistance of a rising star in Johnny Briggs.

Once, during the course of an innings of 117 for Lancashire *v* MCC, at Lord's, in 1885, Barlow hit 3 fours in one four-ball over. So out of character was this feat that it was considered worthy of special comment. A search through the reminiscences of Dick's contemporaries fails to reveal exact details of how "Patience Personified" made his runs or whether he employed any favourite scoring stroke. He was the perfect "barn-door" batsman, renowned as one of the arch-exponents of playing what was known in those days as "the old man's game." Every fibre of his brain and body was devoted to the preservation of his stumps. Endowed with unlimited powers of concentration and an infallible judgement of length, he specialized almost exclusively in forward defensive play and was always "a sore trial to the best bowler," often hitting the ball with a sort of half-cock stroke. W. G. Grace, who does not seem to have had any great liking for Barlow, described his play as "monotony incarnate," but Dick was the perfect foil for his mercurial county captain, A. N. Hornby, one of the quickest run-getters of his or any age, with a distinct inclination for taking a single off the first ball he received. For a decade or more, these two opened the Lancashire batting, and as the "run-stealers" immortalized in Francis Thompson's poem they kept the score ticking along merrily, with Hornby—hatless and sometimes padless also—sprinting up and down the pitch and Barlow answering his captain's call. Apart from one occasion in a Roses match, at Old Trafford, on August 3, 4, and 5, 1882, when Barlow astonished the Yorkshiremen and the spectators by out-scoring his partner for a while, it was Hornby who was chiefly responsible for hitting up the runs, while Dick's own score remained largely stationary. There were several instances of this phenomenon, but probably the most famous occurred in a fixture with Nottinghamshire, at Trent Bridge, on May 15, 16, and 17, 1876. The first Lancashire wicket fell with the total at 45, consisting of Hornby out for 44 and 1 bye, and Barlow in fact was batting for nearly an hour

A. N. Hornby

R. G. Barlow

"The Run-stealers"

before opening his account. There were, naturally, occasions when the captain's notions of scoring by shock tactics could not fail to place the partnership in jeopardy, and more than one disaster was the result. Sometimes Hornby ran himself out; more often he ran Barlow out. According to one legend, whenever the professional was the victim, he was regularly presented with a sovereign as a token of apology and consolation.

Barlow attained a four-figure aggregate only once in his first-class career—1,138 runs in 1882 and approaching the double with 92 wickets—and made only four centuries. A somewhat modest achievement, you would say, but let us at least consider as a means of comparison the batting record of his famous Lancashire parrtner, who had to do very little in the way of bowling. Although Hornby was comfortably ahead in the matter of first-class centuries (16 all told), he succeeded in scoring 1000 runs in a season only twice. Barlow's highest score was the 117 he hit up for Lancashire against MCC, at Lord's, on July 20 and 21, 1885—"hit up," since he was at the wickets for just over three hours and marked 10 fours. This, however, was a rate of scoring he rarely attained. The typical Barlow is more truly represented by his record of carrying his bat throughout a completed innings no less than ten times in first-class cricket—a feat surpassed by only a handful of other batsmen. There is a certain macabre satisfaction to be derived from reading over the details of these marathon efforts, each in its own way a gem of obdurate batsmanship and a study in immobile concentration. Consider that match against Nottinghamshire in 1876, when Hornby was out for 44, at which time Barlow's score was 0 not out. He went on to carry out his bat for 34, having tormented the bowlers—among them Alfred Shaw and Fred Morley—for 225 minutes! It "was not a showy innings," said one of the cricket annuals, "nor was it a fast display of batting." The same publication described his innings against Kent, at Maidstone, on August 19, 20, and 21, 1889, as "a proof of his unwearying care." Barlow went in first and carried his bat for 51, which included 23 singles. His vigil lasted five hours, and this is generally believed to be the slowest half-century ever scored in county cricket. He was undefeated four times in 1882. Against the Australians, at Old Trafford, on June 1, 2, and 3, he "carried out his bat for a faultless and most patient 66"—his highest score in this respect—and was rewarded with the sum of nearly £15 from a collection taken in the pavilion.

In all this saga of stubborn resistance, Barlow's most memorable feat—statistically—occurred at Trent Bridge, on July 8, 1882, in a gallant but vain attempt to rescue Lancashire from defeat. In the first innings, he had made 8 in 75 minutes, but this, by his standards, was fast scoring compared with his performance in the second. Opening, as usual, with A. N. Hornby, he was batting for 70 minutes before opening his score, having lost five partners. When the last wicket fell, he had been at the crease for over 150 minutes, making 5 not out, all of them singles! There was another side to the story of Lancashire's second innings. Apart from two overs, the Nottinghamshire bowling was shared between Alfred Shaw, slow-medium, and Wilfred Flowers, off breaks. Wily Alfred noticed a worn patch at one end of the pitch and devised a cunning plan. To Flowers was entrusted the task of exploiting this spot, while Shaw, knowing Barlow would be playing "the old man's game," tried to keep Dick opposite to him as much as possible and keep him pegging away with his forward defence. Flowers took 7 wickets for 35 runs, Lancashire were dismissed for 69, and Nottinghamshire won the match by 37 runs.

Throughout his long career (1871–1891), Barlow was more than once the victim of what be termed unusual dismissals. At the start of his first innings in the annual fixture between MCC and Lancashire, at Lord's, on June 11 and 12, 1883, he played the ball towards mid-off, where it was stopped by an amateur called J. S. Russel. There was no chance of a run, and Barlow left his crease to do a little gardening, believing that the ball would be considered "dead". Russel thought otherwise and, seizing the opportunity to dispose of a burdensome opponent cheaply, he returned the ball not to the bowler but to Mordecai Sherwin, the massive wicket-keeper, who whipped off the bails. It was an unfortunate way of being run out, and "The matter," said one of the cricket annuals, "gave rise to some comment."

In an earlier match at Lord's (North *v* South, on June 10, 11, and 12, 1878), Barlow was dismissed in a much more unusual fashion and earned a place in the record books. He had a rather irritating habit of nudging the ball away after he had played it, and would sometimes try to amuse the crowd by pretending to set off for a run. On this particular occasion, he blocked the ball, tapped it a second time, and performed his comic turn. He was, no doubt, merely joking, but the jest was ill-timed, since the fielder at point uttered a stentorian appeal, and with much reluctance Dick trudged off to the pavilion, put out for having "hit the ball twice." He always maintained that he had no intention of running, and the matter still rankled with him many years later. "I say now," he wrote, "as I said then, that I consider the appeal was a very unsportsmanlike one, and was only made by one of the fielders, who doubtless wished to get me out of the way, as I had been batting some time." Barlow had made 20, and the fielder, not surprisingly, was W. G. Grace. Dick had his revenge the next day by clean bowling the Champion.

There was a touch of farce about the most bizarre dismissal suffered by Barlow. Around 1878, he was playing in a minor match for Whitehaven against the United South of England Eleven, and misjudged a second run. Sprinting to regain the crease, he grounded his bat, which, unfortunately, stuck in the soft turf, and the handle flew up, struck him on the head, and knocked him out. At the same time, Ted Pooley, the United South wicket-keeper, gathered the ball, removed the bails, and ran him out. Barlow lay unconscious on the pitch, and, in the time-honoured phrase, somebody "forced brandy down his throat." Long afterwards, Ted Pooley—a seasoned toper if there ever was one—gleefully recalled this arbitrary treatment administered to a somewhat ostentatious teetotaller. It might be argued, however, that Barlow got his priorities right. When he came round, the blow on the head and the unwelcome dose of brandy took second and third place, and his first question was, "I am not out, am I?"

Regarded in his prime as one of the best all-rounders of his age, Barlow scored 11,217 runs in first-class cricket, yielding an average of 20.61—a most satisfactory achievement in the 1880s. Had he never scored a run, however, he would still have been worth his place in most elevens solely on account of his fielding and bowling. His left-arm, medium-pace deliveries were credited with 951 victims for an average 14.50. Three times he took 100 wickets in a season, his best being 130 (average 13.18) in 1884, and he captured 5 wickets in an innings 66 times and 10 wickets in a match 14 times. His best bowling in an innings was 9 for 39, for Lancashire *v* Sussex, at Old Trafford, on June 24 and 25, 1886, and his best match figures 13 for 48 (7–16 and 6–32) for an England XII *v* XII of Cambridge University, at Cambridge, on May 10 and 11, 1880. Miserly in the matter of conceding runs, he recorded some remarkable analyses. For Lancashire against Kent, at Old Trafford, on June 20 and 21, 1878, in the second innings he delivered 7 maidens in 9.3 (four-ball) overs, and took 5 wickets for only 3 runs. In the Roses Match, at Huddersfield, on August 8 and 9, in the same season, his figures in the first innings were 27.1–16–22–8. Most spectacular of all was his performance for Lancashire against Derbyshire, at Derby, on June 27 and 28, 1881. His analysis in the first innings was 10.1–9–3–6, the first five wickets, which included a hat-trick, being captured without conceding a run!

Barlow achieved the hat-trick four times in first-class cricket, a record surpassed by only seven other bowlers. He took great pride in accomplishing this feat for the Players against the Gentlemen, at The Oval, in 1884. His victims were an illustrious trio—W. G. Grace, J. Shuter, and W. W. Read. Dick's final hat-trick occurred most opportunely in his Benefit Match against Nottinghamshire, at Old

Trafford, on August 5, 6, and 7, 1886. Disposing of the last two batsmen with successive deliveries in the first innings, he dismissed Arthur Shrewsbury with the first ball he bowled in the second. Since he also scored 50 in his only knock, and over 26,000 persons passed through the turnstiles during the three days, Barlow could look back on a highly satisfactory benefit.

It is more than possible that relations between Barlow and W. G. Grace were not always entirely harmonious. The former, as we have seen, considered the Champion's appeal for "hit the ball twice" as being very unsportsmanlike—though, all things considered, W.G. was probably justified in the action he took, according to the letter of the law. An additional cause of resentment lay in Grace's treatment of "Patience Personified" in print. In his book, *Cricket*, published in 1891, W.G. gives pen portraits of many of the first-class cricketers he had encountered. To Dick he allots barely half a page, but devotes much more space to some of the lesser lights. A magisterial rebuke for this curmudgeonly attitude appeared in the *Manchester Guardian* and is quoted at length by Barlow in his reminiscences. Grace's portrait of Dick in a later book was more extensive, but it still lacked enthusiasm when discussing his style of batting. Be that as it may, W.G. might have been motivated by some subconscious hostility on other grounds. A conqueror of fast men, the Champion was more vulnerable to those of slow or medium pace, and he had many a tussle with left-handers in particular. Of all that long line of bowlers who took W.G.'s wicket, one of the most successful was Dick Barlow, who dismissed him twenty-five times in first-class cricket.

The doughty deeds performed by Barlow for Lancashire alone throughout his long service would have been sufficient to earn him lasting fame, but his career was by no means confined to county cricket. Between 1876 and 1886, he assisted the Players against the Gentlemen nineteen times, though his record in the series was not outstanding. For several seasons, he was chosen regularly to represent England against Australia, appearing in seventeen Tests, in which he scored 591 runs (average 22.73) and took 34 wickets (average 22.55). He had the rare distinction, shared with only one other professional (George Ulyett) and two amateurs (W. G. Grace and A. G. Steel), of being selected for all seven home Tests in 1882, 1884, and 1886. No large score stands against his name, but on more than one occasion he performed his allotted task of playing "the old man's game" by wearing down the bowling at one end while the runs came from the other. At Old Trafford, on July 5, 6, and 7, 1886, he played two gritty, match-saving innings of 38 not out and 30 and, for good measure, took 7 wickets for 44 runs in Australia's second innings. Another exceptional performance

George Ulyett

with the ball occurred earlier in the Oval Test of 1882: taking full advantage of a sodden pitch, he returned figures of 5 wickets for 19 runs in the tourists' first innings. When the home side began their reply, Barlow was W.G.'s partner for the first wicket, after which he opened the bowling, when the Australians took their second innings, thus achieving another of those way-out records joined to his name. "This match, by the way," wrote Dick, "enables me to make a statement—not boastfully, but as a fact of interest. I was selected to both bat and bowl first for England (also for the Players *v* Gentlemen the same year). That is what no other representative English cricketer has been called upon to do in England."

Dick Barlow toured Australia three times (1881–82, 1882–83, 1886–87) and accomplished a highly satisfactory record as a batsman in all first-class matches, with averages ranging between 30.07 and 21.18. Most successful on his first visit, he gave the Australians a vision of things to come in the opening first-class fixture against New South Wales, at Sydney, on December 9, 10, 12, and 13, 1881, when he spent about four hours in scoring 75. "As I was walking back to the pavilion," Dick recalled, "a gentleman stepped over the rails, and with ceremonious politeness handed me an old cricket-belt with the remark, 'I thought we had the champion sticker in Alec Bannerman, but you win the belt. Take it.' I took it, and have it to this day." This assertion that the Lancastrian was an even greater exponent of the "barn-door game" than the notorious Australian stonewaller appears to have been taken at its face value as a compliment by Barlow. Not so his captain, Alfred Shaw: in Alfred's account of the episode, Dick's "gentleman" becomes "a local wag." It was on this first visit down under that Barlow obtained his highest score in Test Matches (62 at Sydney, on February 17, 18, 20, and 21, 1882). During the course of his three tours, he played in all ten Tests and did not miss a single match in any of the other fixtures.

On his second visit to Australia, Barlow was one of the principal actors in what was described as "The only unpleasant circumstance during the whole tour." It occurred in the Third Test, at Sydney, on January 26, 27, 29, and 30, 1883. W. L. Murdoch, captain of Australia, complained about the peculiar pattern of Barlow's spikes, alleging that they were cutting up the pitch when he ran over the crease after delivering the ball. The England skipper (Hon Ivo F. W. Bligh) ordered Dick to remove them, but at the same time he pointed out that precisely the same objection could be made to F. R. Spofforth's bowling. "The Demon" produced his boots, which were equipped with spikes only in the heel. Compelled to admit that their effect was similar to Barlow's, he nevertheless denied that he was damaging the pitch

F. R. Spofforth
"The Demon"

intentionally. An appeal to one of the Australian umpires evoked a curious decision: the official ruled that, because Spofforth denied that he was damaging the turf on purpose, it was fair play! England were disposed of for 123 in their second innings, thanks mainly to Spofforth, who took 7 wickets for 44 runs. In doing so, he cut up the pitch very badly. Seldom can there have been a better illustration of the old biblical prophecy that "He that diggeth a pit shall fall into it." Australia were summarily defeated, dismissed for 83 by only two bowlers, one of them capturing 7 wickets for 40 runs. This was Dick Barlow's best bowling performance in an innings in Test Matches, and the feat was celebrated in no uncertain manner by a group of enthusiastic England supporters. "Some of the spectators carried me shoulder-high," Dick remembered, "and were so demonstrative that they almost pulled me limb from limb. A collection of over £20 was made for and presented to me, along with a beautiful silver cup and several other articles, for this bowling performance."

As an all-rounder among the professionals of his day, Dick Barlow had few rivals apart from William Barnes of Nottinghamshire and Willie Bates of Yorkshire. The latter, however, was never selected to assist England in a home Test. Throughout his many years of service to Lancashire, Barlow accomplished some mighty deeds, but there were occasions when his form temporarily deserted him. In 1884, circumstances required him to do so much bowling that his batting collapsed. In other matches, when there were more bowlers available to share the load, he did better, and for the North of England against the Australians, at Trent Bridge, in the first three days of September, he accomplished a remarkable match double (the second of his career) and was primarily responsible for the North's gigantic victory by 170 runs. The North withered away in their first innings, dismissed for 91, with Dick (at number 5) scoring 10 not out. The Australians fared little better, reaching a total of 100, and Dick's analysis, as second change, was 6–3–6–4. Spofforth, it is said, was anticipating a massacre with grim glee, exclaiming, "Give me the ball, and they won't get 60." He was wrong. Although the North were in danger of collapsing again at the beginning of their second innings, a long partnership between Wilfred Flowers and Barlow put an entirely different complexion on the game. Flowers made 90, and "Patience Personified," defying the Australian attack for 270 minutes, notched 101 runs "without blemish," scoring only 5 fours. This, incidentally, was his maiden century in first-class cricket. In their second innings, the Australians were put out for 76, and Dick, bowling unchanged, returned an analysis of 27–13–42–6. His match statistics, therefore, were 111 runs for once out, and 10 wickets for 48 runs. "Such a performance in a match of this importance," wrote one journalist, "has never been recorded, and a subscription was made and presented to him, along with a few other presents (including a silver claret-jug and a diamond breast-pin), whilst he was enthusiastically cheered." The wages of a professional cricketer at that time were hardly excessive, but there were always the "perks" to be had on the side for an outstanding performance, and Dick received a generous amount of them.

Barlow assisted Lancashire for twenty-one seasons, making his debut (1871) and final appearance (1891) in a Roses Match, and it may fairly be claimed that his employers had excellent value for their money. He scored two centuries for the County, both, curiously, within a few days of each other at the end of July 1885—117 against MCC, at Lord's, and 108 against Gloucestershire, at Old Trafford. On this second occasion, he produced a typical Barlow performance, batting throughout the whole of the first day, reaching 103 not out, when stumps were drawn. W.G. was a member of the opposing teams in both matches, and doubtless the memory of fielding out while "Patience Personified" was at the wickets for a grand total of 510 minutes accounted in some measure for the Champion's somewhat acidulous remarks on the Barlow system of batting. Dick headed the Lancashire batting averages in 1875, 1882, and 1885, and carried his bat ten times throughout a completed innings exclusively for the cause of the Red Rose. He came top of his County's bowling averages in 1881, 1882, and 1884, while against Surrey, at Old Trafford, on July 12, 13, and 14, 1883, he achieved the first match double of his career, scoring 71 and 39 not out, and taking 5 wickets for 27 runs in the first innings and 5 for 92 in the second.

From about 1887 onwards, Barlow's powers were on the wane, and he was no longer being selected to appear for the Players against the Gentlemen, nor for England against Australia. He continued to assist Lancashire for a few more years, but in its 1892 issue one of the cricket annuals remarked in sorrow, "The time has arrived for Barlow to give up the place he so long and so honourably held . . ." By then, in fact, Dick had already been omitted from the side. Alec Watson, his team-mate and old bowling partner, once made a strange observation while discussing the remuneration of professional cricketers. Commenting on the principle of winter pay, Watson said that "there was no chance of any such good fortune in our days. It was a hard task to keep county cricket going at all then. Why, the Lancashire Committee have had to leave Barlow out because they could not afford to pay him." Watson did not elaborate this statement, so it is not clear whether he was referring to some point in the course of Dick's career or its termination. Whatever the reason for Barlow's departure from the

Alec Watson
"The Southerton of the North"

County side at the age of forty, he was convinced he could have continued playing for another season or two. Such, also, was the opinion of his old adversary, W. G. Grace ("He was left out of the Lancashire team long before he had lost all form"). The Champion and the "Lancashire Stonewall" may not have always seen eye to eye, and one's batting technique was diametrically opposed to the other's. They had little in common beyond a mutual love of the game, but one record they shared: neither was ever dismissed for a pair in first-class cricket.

Nor was W.G. the only person to consider that there was still plenty of cricket left in Barlow. The latter was approached by several other counties, one of them offering him a three-year contract, but as far as Dick was concerned, the prospect of playing for any county other than Lancashire was unthinkable. He became instead a first-class umpire, operating on the county circuit for twenty-one years, and his second career was marred only by a prolonged argument with Ranji, who once disagreed vehemently with one of his decisions. On June 1, 2, and 3, 1899, he stood in the First Test, at Trent Bridge (W.G.'s final Test!). Between whiles, he appeased his hunger for active participation in the game by turning out for Royton in the Central Lancashire League (1891–1897). Subsequently, he played four seasons for Blackpool, where he had built a suitable house for his retirement.

As a sideline during his playing days with Lancashire, Barlow had set himself up as a dealer in sporting goods at Manchester, and after his move to the seaside resort he continued in this occupation, operating from his home. With his umpiring and his business interests he led a full life, and any time left over was devoted to the organization and decoration of his house. The Barlow residence was a veritable museum of cricketana, a sort of Memorial Gallery in miniature, reflecting the highlights of the owner's connection with sport. The walls of the hall and other rooms were almost covered from floor to ceiling with a profusion of photographs; an armoury of bats, including one battered old favourite with which Barlow had scored 4,000 runs, adorned the wall of the bathroom; innumerable trophies, presents, and mementoes, all of them souvenirs of the owner's exploits, were on display in different rooms; the tiles in the front sitting-room featured a coloured representation of Lord Sheffield's cricket ground and portraits of himself, A. N. Hornby, and Dick Pilling, the Lancashire and England wicket-keeper. The gas lamp in the hall bore the names of A. G. Steel and other famous players, but the most prized item of the whole collection was the stained-glass window in the vestibule door. This unique treasure, now happily preserved in the pavilion at Old Trafford, was another portrayal of Barlow, Hornby, and Pilling on the field of play.

Barlow died on July 31, 1919, leaving an estate of over £1,500, and his grave was marked with a remarkable headstone, which he had designed himself. Beneath the inscription recording a brief, bare outline of some of the dead hero's achievements appears a representation of a bat falling to the ground in front of a wicket broken by a ball and the rubric "Bowled at Last," a proof that Barlow was not entirely devoid of a wry sense of humour.

An obituary described Barlow as "a quiet, chatty, neighbourly man" in private life. Within the four walls of his household, he was said to have been something of an autocrat and, disappointed in his conception of domestic bliss, he sought consolation elsewhere for a time, becoming the father of an illegitimate son, who was ultimately responsible for the preservation of the famous stained-glass window. Family matters, one feels, may have been of secondary consideration in Barlow's eyes. Cricket was first and foremost his own true love. "In conclusion," he wrote in his reminiscences, "I don't think that any cricketer has enjoyed his cricketing career better than I have done; and if I had my time to come over again I should certainly be what I have been all my life—a professional cricketer."

CHAPTER ELEVEN

William Barnes "Barney"

LIKE Jemmy Shaw, the fast left-hander and one of the most famous of W. G. Grace's early adversaries, William Barnes was a native of Sutton-in-Ashfield, in Nottinghamshire. Born on May 27, 1852, he came out early as a professional cricketer by accepting a position with the Garrison at Winchester when he was approaching his twentieth birthday. Employed at Leicester the following year, he then spent the next two seasons at Trent Bridge, where he was engaged by the Nottinghamshire Amateurs. The time and the place were ideal for "Barney," and, attracting the favourable attention of the authorities, he was drafted into the County Eleven in 1875. Like Jemmy Shaw, he was admitted to the senior side without undergoing a trial in the colts. By this time, Jemmy's day was done, and the two famous sons of Sutton-in-Ashfield were never team-mates in a first-class match. "Barney" made his debut in the home fixture against Gloucestershire, on July 29, 30, and 31, without, however, setting the Trent on fire, but better things were to come. It was a momentous year for Nottinghamshire, since 1875 also marked the first appearance of Arthur Shrewsbury and William Henry Scotton.

A tall man, standing 6 foot or thereabouts, and weighing not much more than 12 stone, Barnes was not particularly athletic in either his appearance or his movements and seemed to make little effort to derive any noticeable advantage from his physical attributes. His stoop-shouldered, shambling gait would have driven a Guards drill sergeant to the verge of apoplexy, relieved only by an outburst of savagely sarcastic imprecations. Of "Barney's" moustache, however, any military martinet would have secretly approved, perhaps even going as far as to utter a few words of grudging praise. The virgin growth was more than adequate; the mature development thickened as it grew downwards over his mouth, concealing in part the loss of several teeth; the final version, assuming a drooping, handlebar shape and sometimes controlled with an application of wax, was a thing of splendour.

Combined with his natural pallor, it lent an almost baleful cast to his countenance and the little that could be seen of his smile.

"Barney" was a complex being, a mixture of opposites. As earthy as any professional cricketer of his time, he nevertheless revealed some of the traits normally associated with the amateur's approach to the game. There was something of the Cavalier as well as the Roundhead in his conception of his beloved sport. You could not imagine him being anything else but a cricketer, so extensive was his devotion during his active life. Rare indeed were the times when he did not derive an overwhelming satisfaction in the pursuit of his chosen vocation. Statistics and averages meant little to him, and the word "sedate" was commonly excluded from his vocabulary. Country-house cricket—or what he called "park cricket"— was his ideal, and at times he was heard to express his disappointment that a lack of adequate financial resources prevented him from indulging this whim. Perhaps it was just as well. Though normally genial, he was not entirely the most easy-going of men, and his ability to maintain a harmonious relationship while rubbing shoulders with the gentry he would have encountered in such surroundings is open to doubt. A strict adherence to the principles of punctuality was hardly one of his outstanding virtues, and his demeanour was sometimes adversely affected by moodiness and a lack of self-control, particularly when he had succumbed to the temptations of what the more abstemious Victorians were wont to term "the Demon Drink." Once or twice, these failings escaped to break through the surface in spectacular fashion and cast a brief blight on his brilliant career, but as a general rule they were subordinated to his inborn merry temperament and his supreme passion for cricket. When in a good frame of mind, which was usually the case, he often regaled his team-mates with a flow of wry remarks, spoken in a drawling manner with the broadest of Nottinghamshire accents and memorable more for the quaintness of the delivery than for any lasting subtlety of wit.

Barnes was a great all-rounder, one of the greatest in the history of Nottinghamshire cricket, and certainly one of the greatest of his age. He was far above average as a fielder, particularly when positioned near the wicket, since he did not possess that long, accurate throw essential to a specialist in the deep nor a speedy pair of heels. The swiftness of his reflexes, however, was not entirely wanting at a time of crisis. At Lord's, on June 6, 7, and 8, 1881, when he was assisting Under Thirty against Over Thirty, an injury to the nominated wicket-keeper deprived "the young 'uns" of his services in their opponents' second innings. The chore of replacing the custodian was delegated to Billy Barnes, who was doubtless not slow in appreciating the humour of the situation. Nobody could have expected him to match up with the best wicket-keepers of the day, but he was far from disgracing himself. True enough, he gave W.G. a life by putting down a catch, but he conceded only 2 byes—the lowest figure in all four innings. In addition, off the trundling of two celebrated slow bowlers, he trapped three batsmen out of their ground, the first of his victims being the Champion, who was "easily stumped." In his more orthodox role on the field in first-class matches, he held 342 catches.

As a bowler, "Barney" probably suffered from too much competition and more certainly from a lack of opportunity in his early days. Usually regarded at first as a useful change, he claimed more attention by dint of perseverance, and he performed some outstanding feats whenever he found the conditions were favourable to him. There were times when he achieved a state of pre-eminence, and if the circumstances had warranted it, he would have left a more permanent mark as a superlative bowler. His pace, fast-medium, combined with a high action, made the ball cut back from the off and rise from the turf with an awkward, alarming kick, and on a hard, bumpy ground he was a holy terror to dainty, squeamish batsmen. A crumbling, damaged pitch yielding an uneven bounce was his delight. Sharing the bowling honours with Ted Peate, the Yorkshire slow left-hander, in the fixture between Gentlemen and Players, at Lord's, on July 6 and 7, 1885, "Barney" was in his element. On the second day, cracks and small holes appearing in the surface at the Nursery End produced an unplayable blitzkrieg of bumpers, break-backs, and shooters. Of twenty-one batsmen dismissed throughout the last day, no less than fifteen succumbed to the vagaries of the pitch at that wicket. "Barney," whose share of the booty was 4 for 48 in the first innings, was far more destructive in the second, accounting for 7 of his opponents, including W.G. clean bowled, at a cost of only 58 runs.

Altogether, in his first-class career, beginning in 1875 and lasting until 1894, "Barney's" tally of wickets just passed the 900 mark, at a fraction over 17 runs apiece. He never succeeded in attaining 100 victims in one season but came twice within very close striking distance, taking 97 wickets in 1885 and again in 1888. In the latter season, too, he recorded his best bowling performance in an innings and a match in the contest between Gloucestershire and Nottinghamshire, at Cheltenham, on June 14, 15, and 16. The visitors went to the wickets first and were not dismissed until the following morning for a total of 215. On a pitch affected by rain, the home side were put out for 112 and 75, and the chief architect of their humiliating defeat by an innings and 28 runs was Billy Barnes. At his first essay, he delivered 49 overs, including 27 maidens, taking 8 wickets for 64 runs, and his figures in the second were 31–22–25–5. When you add to this magnificent

William Barnes

Courtesy Roger Mann

achievement his score of 51, top for his side and in the match, and his 3 catches (E. M. Grace once, W.G. twice), you can readily appreciate "Barney's" outstanding merits as one of the leading all-rounders of his or any other age.

It was as a batsman, however, that Barnes established his principal claim to greatness. Like Percy Holmes, of Yorkshire fame between the two World Wars, he would sometimes enter the fray minus a batting glove on his left hand, either as an act of defiance or a desire for greater freedom in his grip. His posture at the wicket, with his shoulders slewed round to give him a version of the two-eyed stance, would have attracted little favourable comment in more modern times, and many a pair of hands would have been wrung in horror at the sight of his legs and feet. The right toe, not always planted parallel to the crease, occasionally showed a tendency to stray in the direction of the slips, while the left one was so aligned as to be pointing towards mid-off or almost straight down the pitch. He held his bat very high up on the handle, and this, together with his height and long reach, gave him an overriding advantage in scoring on the off side. His fierce leg-hitting was unorthodox in that he usually struck the ball square with a vertical rather than a horizontal bat, but many of his runs came from cuts, late cuts, and cover drives. Above all, an acknowledged expert at the square drive, his arms seemed to extend like a telescope when he dispatched the ball like a rocket to the boundary, making little attempt to conceal his satisfaction as his features settled into a grim Mephistophelean smile. No stylist in the true sense of the word, he practised a style that he had made his own. A little uncertain now and then at the beginning of his innings, he occasionally lost the battle of wills with the bowlers, no more so than the time when he was assisting the Players of England against the Australians, at Crystal Palace, at the end of September 1880. Going in at number 1 on a dead, sodden ground, he was easily the top scorer with 39 in the first innings, but he yielded the ascendancy to his adversaries by allowing himself to be cramped and tied down by a succession of over-pitched deliveries that effectively neutralised his long, forward reach. Capable of exercising infinite patience while playing himself in, he possessed an excellent defence and could keep his end up and graft for the precious runs as well as any of his celebrated contemporaries. Grafting for long drawn-out periods, however, was far removed from his natural game, and once his confidence was firmly established and the total was ticking over, he blossomed into the personification of carefree stroke-play. An atmosphere of dullness and stagnation was rarely permitted to reign whenever "Barney" was at the crease. Widely acknowledged to have been one of the most exciting and attractive run-getters of the 1880s, especially when batting on a firm, hard pitch, he loses little in comparison with any of the other Titans of his time.

While viewing in retrospect the cricket season in which Billy Barnes and Arthur Shrewsbury made their debut for Nottinghamshire, the 1876 edition of one of the annuals expressed approval of the promise and progress of the two newcomers, but added a rider, remarking that Barnes had it in his power to become first-class. In the event, both rose to the top of the ladder of success, but on figures alone Shrewsbury has by far the more impressive record as a batsman. His aggregate, average, and number of centuries were all a good deal higher than "Barney's," but it must not be forgotten that they were boosted by the benefit of a longer career and a larger number of not out innings. Of even greater significance was the fact that, being no kind of a bowler at all, Arthur was able to concentrate exclusively on his batting, whereas the amount of vigorous trundling that fell to "Barney's" lot would have inevitably had some effect on his batting. Far more patient and watchful by temperament, Shrewsbury was the greater run accumulator—he scored 10 double hundreds—but there was much more conspicuous zest and enjoyment about Billy Barnes's batting and a patently obvious desire to go for the bowling and force the rate of scoring. In certain circumstances, such as the make-up of the rest of the team, you could envisage the possibility that, on occasions, "Give me 'Barney' " might have taken preference over W.G.'s "Give me Arthur."

In his first-class career, Billy Barnes attained an aggregate of 15,425 runs, with 21 centuries and an average of 23.19—statistics which could not fail to impress his contemporaries, when the condition of some pitches still left something to be desired in the way of a shirt-front surface and an even bounce. Five times he scored 1,000 runs in a season, and on the first occasion, in 1880, with a total of 1,220, he was the first Nottinghamshire batsman to achieve this goal as well as being the only cricketer to reach a four-figure aggregate (W.G. could manage no more than 951 runs that year, though his average was superior to the professional's). "Barney's" best run-getting year was 1883, when he was about at his peak as a batsman, reaching a tally of 1,308. He passed the thousand mark for the fourth time the next season, but then fell below this level for several years. Ill-health may have contributed to this retrogression, for "Barney" had a tendency to suffer from internal ailments, such as dyspepsia. A notable and welcome return to the summit of former excellence was manifested in 1889, when what might be termed the late afternoon of his career was stealing into sight. Although "a mere shadow of his former self" when the rains came and the grounds turned treacherous in August, he totalled 1,249 runs, averaging 34.69, and occupying the fourth place in the national table for the batsmen. These constituted the highest seasonal average and the best position he ever achieved throughout his career, and never again did he come within reasonable striking distance of either.

Barnes made his maiden century in his third season of first-class cricket, when he was assisting Nottinghamshire against Kent, at Canterbury, on June 14, 15, and 16, 1877. Going in at number 7, and scoreless in his first innings, he carried out his bat in the second for 109—"a very good display, made without a chance and in good style; his chief figures were thirteen fours." His last ([illegible]), a brief glow in the gathering gloom, occurred at Hove, on June 8, 9, and 10, 1893. Soaring between these lofty peaks was many another splendid achievement, crowned by his highest score of all in the contest between Sussex and Nottinghamshire, at Hove, on July 21, 22, and 23, 1887. In an innings lasting about four and a-half hours and displaying a complete mastery of the home side's attack—nine bowlers were put on—he emerged as the top scorer with 160 runs in the book. As usual, his figures contained a notable number of boundaries, in this instance 22 fours.

In 1879, Barnes was engaged as a member of the MCC ground staff, and he continued to hold this appointment until 1898. With his all-round skills perpetually in demand against strong opposition, he was frequently selected to appear in important fixtures. Five of his centuries were scored in MCC matches, his best being 140 not out against Yorkshire, in a drawn game at Lord's, on June 1 and 2, 1885. In a majestic partnership with William Gunn lasting about four hours and forty minutes, the two Nottinghamshire professionals took the MCC total from 72 for 3 to 402 for 4! Only two days' play had been allocated to the match, since June 3 was Derby Day, otherwise "Barney" might have made a sizeable addition to his own contribution, with the Yorkshire attack, apart from Ted Peate, wilting under the weight of such heavy and unrelenting punishment.

"Barney's" service to his employers at Lord's was not confined to playing in first-class fixtures and bowling in the nets: he performed several astonishing feats in some of the minor contests. A special entry in *Wisden* drew the readers' attention to his doings in three matches in the week ending August 15, 1885, when he succeeded in piling up an aggregate of 396 runs in four consecutive innings, yielding an average of 99. As if this were not enough, he also found the time and the energy to take 11 wickets at 18.10 runs apiece. His most spectacular achievement in contests at this level was staged at Lord's, on June 1 and 2, 1882, when MCC were entertaining Leicestershire (not a first-class county at that time), though the visitors could have found little in the way of entertainment, as far as the cricket was concerned. After Leicestershire had been put out for 152, MCC lost their first two wickets for only 19 runs. At this point, "Barney" was joined by another ground professional, Billy Midwinter, the only cricketer to play for Australia against England and for England against Australia.

A tall, handsome, powerfully built all-rounder, who in 1878 succumbed to the blandishments of W.G. and abandoned his Australian team-mates at Lord's in order to turn out for Gloucestershire at The Oval, Midwinter had the physique to emulate Australia's G. J. Bonnor but often neglected his natural advantages. For a big man, he was surprisingly diffident in his stroke-play, but every so often he would attempt a mighty hit, "accompanied by a curious hiss through his teeth," and would instantly revert to his normal, more sedate technique. On this particular occasion, however, with Leicestershire cast in the role of martyrs, the Anglo-Australian stepped out of character. In a stand lasting nearly five and a-half hours, the total was increased from 19 to 473, representing a scoring rate of over 80 runs an hour. Barnes, carefree to the extent of giving several chances, was the first to leave, followed almost immediately by his partner. The latter made a faultless 187, presumably with much curious hissing, seeing that he hit 1 six ("the ball bounding from the roof of the grand stand clean out of the ground"), 1 five, and 12 fours. "Barney's" Satanic smile was doubtless even more in evidence: his 266 included 1 six, 4 fives, and 26 fours!

Billy Barnes was well nigh an automatic and permanent choice for the Players against the Gentlemen for over a decade. Making his first appearance in the series at Lord's, in 1879, and his last at Scarborough, in 1892, he totalled 30 matches, a figure exceeded by very few of his contemporaries. During this period, he missed only two fixtures. In 1881, Alfred Shaw and Arthur Shrewsbury organized a strike by seven of the professionals, of which Barnes was one, against their masters at Trent Bridge. For this reason, all these Nottinghamshire men were excluded from consideration for the Players' team at The Oval, though three of them, including Barnes, were given places in the side for the Lord's match. The only other contest he missed was the one at Hastings, in 1891. One of the few cricketers of his time to reach four figures, he totalled 1,263 runs at an average of 27.45, which places him high up in the table of aggregates and averages attained by those who turned out for one or the other side in the series during the nineteenth century. He scored 6 fifties, but his best innings was 130 not out, recorded quite late on in his career in the fixture at Lord's, on July 8 and 9, 1889. He entered the fray at first wicket down with the total at 13 and remained at the wickets while 267 runs were added to the score, and his innings, which lasted about three hours and fifty minutes and contained 9 fours, was flawless apart from one chance, which was put down by the fielder at long-slip. His bowling was equally as praiseworthy as his batting: he captured 72 wickets at an average of 13.34, taking 5 in an innings five times and 10 in a match twice, his best figures occurring in that previously mentioned contest on a damaged pitch at Lord's, in 1885. For all-round performance in the whole series from beginning to end, Barnes's record is really only surpassed by those of W. G. Grace and Wilfred Rhodes, though one or two others come close.

W.G. had good reason to remember those hideous conditions at headquarters on that occasion, but the equivalent fixture two years later remained even fresher in his memory. The state of the ground was in Barnes's favour once more, and he recorded match figures of 10 wickets for 58 runs (6–23 and 4–35), dismissing the Champion off a catch in the first innings and clean bowled in the second. In the contest at The Oval immediately afterwards, the conditions sided with "Barney" yet again, and he took 9 wickets for 116 runs, disposing of W.G. in the second innings. So, in the narrow space of only five days' play, he registered another notable all-round performance, scoring 36 and 42 and getting rid of 19 batsmen for only 174 runs. In these stern and at times fiercely fought contests between amateur and professional, he disposed of the Champion five times, nor did W.G.'s wicket necessarily always remain inviolate in other matches, since, all told, the Nottinghamshire all-rounder dismissed him on fifteen occasions.

Although Billy Barnes did not enter the ranks of first-class cricketers until 1875, his name was one of the first to come into contention whenever teams were selected to represent England against the Australians in home Tests. He and two Nottinghamshire team-mates who were also members of the ground staff at Lord's—which was probably advantageous to their cause—were the only professionals picked to assist England in the first ever home Test Match, at The Oval, on September 6, 7, and 8, 1880. Put on as a change bowler for a brief spell in the visitors' second innings only and taking the final wicket at a cost of 17 runs, "Barney" was picked primarily to play as a batsman, a lone figure in the glittering galaxy of gentlemen, whose names preceded and followed his in the order of going in. Lord Harris, England's captain in this encounter, decided that "Barney" should bat at "second wicket down, and that distinguished position was not beyond his merits." He played a useful innings of 28 and contributed his not inconsiderable mite to England's victory by 5 wickets.

From 1880 to 1890, England contended against Australia at home in 13 Test Matches, and Barnes was omitted from the side for only two of these—at Lord's, in 1884, and at Old Trafford, in 1886. Battling against one of his periodic bouts of indifferent health in the early part of 1882, he nevertheless staged a remarkable recovery, scoring 1,194 runs, with three centuries. His form, however, unfortunately forsook him in the crucial contest on August 28 and 29, when Australia defeated England by 7 runs, and "the Ashes" were born. He took 1 wicket in Australia's second innings, but failed to get into double figures with the bat, marking 5 at his first attempt and 2 at his second, prompting the remark in one of the cricket annuals that "when nerve and defence were sadly needed in the great match at the OVAL he was found wanting." There is a certain lack of justice in this damning judgement, and it would be grossly unfair to single out the Nottinghamshire professional as the sole culprit in the lamentable collapse of England's hopes and pride, seeing that eight batsmen in the second innings were able to manage only 18 runs between them. Barnes was by no means the sole member of the side to fall victim to an attack of nervous apprehension while awaiting his turn to bat. Of the Lancashire amateur A. G. Steel, dismissed for a blob at this critical time, it was said that his "teeth were all in a chatter." And, it was added rather unkindly, "Barnes's teeth would have been chattering if he had not left them at home."

"Barney" never really came off with any consistency in Test Matches in England, though he could not complain of any lack of opportunity. His aggregate was 237 runs at the disappointing average of 14.81, and he played only two innings of outstanding merit. At Lord's, on July 19, 20, and 21, 1886, when the ground had been rendered hazardous by rain, he scored 58, sharing a partnership of 161 runs for the fifth wicket with Arthur Shrewsbury, who went on to make 164, his highest score in Tests. England were victorious with only one innings, as they were again at The Oval, on August 13 and 14, 1888, when Barnes was in excellent form, scoring 62 and putting on 112 runs for the fifth wicket (again!) with little Bobby Abel. As a bowler also, he gave an excellent display of his all-round talents, with 2 for 18 in the first innings and 5 for 32 in the second, marking his best performance with both bat and ball in the same match, as far as home Tests are concerned. The fact remains, however, that much of the fame he earned as an international cricketer came from his exploits in Australia.

"Barney" took part in four tours, but one wonders how he managed to pluck up the courage to undertake the second one after his initial experiences. His first trip abroad took place at the end of the 1879 season, when he was included in Richard Daft's team visiting North America—the same one when Ephraim Lockwood was not impressed with Niagara Falls. For some of the party, much of the tour was quite a joyous affair, but others were not so fortunate, and when you read the reminiscences of some of our early tourists, particularly the details they give of their reactions to the storm-tossed oceans, you are amazed as to how a few of them survived to tell the tale. In the absence of effective stabilizers, several of Daft's party, including the captain himself, spent a miserable time on the Atlantic, but the most wretched of all was Billy Barnes, who lay in his cabin on the rack of sea-sickness throughout the voyage. So severe were the spasms he suffered that the ship's doctor was compelled to swathe him tightly in towels to prevent him from damaging the muscles of his stomach. Pale and woebegone when he at last set foot on dry land, he had lost so much weight that his clothes hung in generous folds around his attenuated frame. The programme consisted of "odds" matches, and "Barney," understandably, stood down for the first. He made his highest score (59) in the second, and missed none of the others, managing to come fourth in the batting averages, though he "was never quite at home." When the voyage back to England was almost over, he was heard to declare that the green countryside at the mouth of the Mersey was the grandest sight he'd set eyes on since his departure from Nottingham!

In view of these experiences of 1879, you would have been convinced that he would have never ventured forth again, but the intrepid "Barney" accepted an invitation to tour with the Hon Ivo F. W. Bligh's team visiting Australia in 1882–83. Whether it was on this occasion or another is impossible to say, but on one of his trips to the Antipodes, "Barney" is supposed to have caused a profound impression upon the mayor at the port of disembarkation. This local dignitary was in the middle of his speech of welcome to the team, when his gaze suddenly fell on Barnes. Mindful of what he evidently considered most appropriate for this formal event, "Barney" had donned his Sunday best. The ravages of sea-sickness were plainly to be seen in the ghastly, almost ghostly pallor of his features, which formed a striking contrast with the sombre clothing he was wearing—long black coat, black trousers, black tie, and black hat. Add the black mourning hat-band and gloves, and you would have had an exact replica of an undertaker's mute. On learning the identity of this grisly apparition, the mayor approached, held out his hand, and the following brief conversation ensued:

> "I am very pleased to make your acquaintance, Mr Barnes. I hope I see you well?"
>
> To him, with a sociable grin which emphasized the absence of many grinders, responded the Notts man:
>
> "Well, thank'ee, Ah'm not feeling over cliver this morning."

This, presumably, was "Barney's" conception of sophisticated small talk, and I suppose that once again he had left his teeth behind.

In one of the minor matches of Ivo Bligh's tour, Barnes performed an unusual feat. While bowling on uneven ground in the contest against 22 of Bendigo, at Sandhurst, on November 22 and 23, 1882, he sent down a shooter, which crashed into the wicket, making the bails fly all the way down the pitch to the bowler's end. Yet, by some extraordinary freak, the stumps remained in a perpendicular position and, apart from the missing bails, looked as though the ball had missed them completely. This, unfortunately, was about the only exploit of "Barney's" which could lay any claim to being out of the ordinary. He had, in fact, a wretched tour, since on top of the lingering effects of sea-sickness he had difficulty in coping with the climate and "was altogether out of form in Australia." This applies, moreover, to all departments of the game. Usually a safe and most reliable man in the field, he was guilty of missing catches several times. In this, he was by no means the only culprit: the general standard of fielding displayed by some of the Hon Ivo's men was nothing short of abominable. Seven of the seventeen fixtures in the programme were first-class and, in contrast to the Yorkshire all-rounder Willie Bates, who produced several sterling performances, "Barney" could do little right, coming ninth out of twelve in the batting averages (11.30) and seventh out of eight in the bowling table (23.53). He did very slightly better as a batsman in the four Test Matches, though a long way below what had been expected of him, and the less said about his bowling the better. All in all, it was a tour which he would have been thankful to consign to oblivion, while cherishing a fond hope that he might be blessed with a more favourably disposed fortune in the future. The four professionals in the Hon Ivo's party set sail for England in advance of the gentlemen. For part of the voyage, at least, the sea was smooth, which would certainly have been of some consolation not only to "Barney" but also to fast left-hander Fred Morley, a simple soul who had originally thought up an ambitious plan for making his way home ("No more ships for me. I'll return by the overland route").

"Barney," happily, was destined to make full amends on the next tour to Australia, in 1884–85, organized by the combination of James Lillywhite, junior, Alfred Shaw, and Arthur Shrewsbury. The first two took little part in the cricket, being concerned with umpiring and managerial duties, while Shrewsbury acted as the playing captain of the side. Most of the contests were played against teams of "odds," but eight were first-class, including five Test Matches, of which the Englishmen won three and lost two. Apart from one hitch, the whole tour was one long and almost uninterrupted triumph for Billy Barnes, who enjoyed better health and took infinite care not to disturb the equilibrium of his internal organs as much as possible. On at least one occasion, when making his way from one game to another, he was adamant in electing to travel the long way round on dry land to his destination rather than expose himself to the hazards of a much shorter trip by sea. His form was so consistent that he stood at the top of the batting averages in both first-class and minor matches, and he headed the list of bowlers in the table of statistics for the former. In the opening Test, staged at Adelaide, in the middle of December 1884, he made an excellent contribution to England's victory. Going in at number 4 in the first innings, he made a stand with Scotton that took the total from 107 to 282. Although four chances went begging,"both men played finely, each in his own style." Eventually, when he had made 134 in a stay of nearly five hours, "Barney" was yorked by G. E, Palmer (Scotton was in six hours for 82!). Barnes had his revenge in Australia's second innings, when he clean bowled Palmer for no score, taking 3 wickets for 51 runs.

Another personal triumph was recorded in the next international contest, which came off at Melbourne, in the first week of the new year. Having made his highest score and only century in Test Matches, "Barney" achieved his finest match figures as a bowler, claiming 9 wickets for 81 runs (3–50 and 6–31). For the feat of obtaining the best analysis among the seven English bowlers put on, he received a prize of £5, donated by a "generous supporter of cricket." One extraordinary feature of this bowling performance concerns the modes of dismissal—two bowled, three caught, and *four caught and bowled*!

A virtual passenger in the Third Test—of which more in a moment—Billy's sterling merits as an all-rounder and currently the most valuable member of Shrewsbury's side were further demonstrated in the last two contests, at Sydney and Melbourne respectively, in March, with scores of 50, 20, and 74, and 7 more wickets for 123 runs. His record for the rubber, virtually on the basis of four matches, was 369 runs at the, for those or any other days, very high average of 52.71, and 19 wickets at a cost of 15.36 each.

In one of the principal obituaries published shortly after Barnes's death, the writer drew attention to his subject's popularity with fellow cricketers and spectators alike, asserting at the same time that the Nottinghamshire favourite was "Not, perhaps, as amenable to discipline as the average school-girl." In the atmosphere prevailing in English cricket in the late twentieth century, he would, I think, have become permanently persona non grata with the TCCB. A classic illustration of his failing marred the Third Test, at Sydney, on February 20, 21, 23, and 24, 1885, when Australia's victory by only 6 runs owed much to the behaviour of Barnes. It appears—for what reason has never been satisfactorily explained—that he fell into a quarrel with Arthur Shrewsbury, and although the condition of the pitch was perfect for his type of bowling, he refused to go on. Retribution followed swiftly in England's first innings: "Barney" was ignominiously dismissed by a stumping off the first delivery he received, when the ball rebounded from the wicket-keeper's pads into the stumps. Perhaps this incident served only to harden his heart, for he persisted in his refusal to bowl when Australia went in again. At his second attempt with the bat, he failed again, scoring only 5. "It is to be regretted," wrote one journalist, "that a cricketer of Barnes' experience and skill should so far forget himself and his side as to let personal pique affect the result of a contest" (Shades of George Tarrant against Middlesex in 1866!). Happily, as we have seen, the rancour was not carried over to the next Test, when "Barney" was back to his best again.

Barnes made his last visit to Australia in 1886–87 as a member of another team organized by Lillywhite and Shaw and captained by Shrewsbury. Only two Test Matches were arranged, both resulting in victories for the visitors. In the first, at Sydney, at the end of January 1887, "Barney" was out of luck in his first knock, but was second top scorer with 32 in the next. He opened the England bowling in both innings, taking 8 wickets for 47 runs and marking his best analysis in Test Matches (6–28). An untoward incident occurred after the conclusion of this contest, with most unfortunate consequences. I do not know for sure if "Barney" had been celebrating unwisely and indulging to excess in his favourite beverage, but he became involved in a flaming row with Percy McDonnell, the Australian captain, whom he had dismissed for low scores (clean bowled and leg before). Bitter words were exchanged, tempers were lost, and it came to blows—or rather, one blow. Barnes swung a wild punch at McDonnell's face but missed his mark and smashed his right hand into the wall behind. "Judging by the serious nature of the injury which Barnes's hand received," said Alfred Shaw, "it must have been fortunate for McDonnell that he did not receive the blow on the face." Percy survived, and took part in the next Test, but "Barney" did not, and he was an absentee for most of the remainder of the tour. Since Lillywhite and Shaw had not really made the trip as players, the team was, in effect, reduced to ten men, and the services of one Reginald Wood were enlisted. Wood, a native of Cheshire, had assisted Lancashire as an amateur half a dozen times before emigrating to Australia, and the thought that one day he would play for a team identified as England against his new homeland can hardly have been uppermost in his mind until now. He turned out in the Second Test, at Sydney, making 6 and 0, and was then lost to international cricket. As for "Barney," he made no more trips abroad,

P. S. McDonnell

but he assisted England in five more home Tests in 1888 and 1890. In 21 encounters with Australia, he achieved a very commendable all-rounder's record, scoring 725 runs at an average of 23.38, and taking 51 wickets, averaging 15.54.

Recovering from the injury to his hand, "Barney" did well with both bat and ball in 1887, though, in a sense, he fell between two stools, scoring 957 runs and taking 90 wickets. He did, however, succeed in making three centuries, which included the highest he ever scored. His batting declined noticeably in 1888, sliding from 33 to 18.41, but he compensated for this to a certain extent by taking 97 wickets for the second time in his career. The next two years yielded an even greater contrast. Achieving his second highest seasonal aggregate of runs and his highest ever average in 1889 but doing little bowling, he slumped in the most spectacular fashion in 1890. Characterized as "the most conspicuous failure of the year" and "the greatest disappointment" among the professionals, his lamentable lack of form was manifest in an aggregate of only 409 runs at an average of 11.05, though his bowling proved useful at times (46 wickets, average 15.15). The flame of his genius flared up intermittently in the following season, especially at Trent Bridge, on June 11, 12, and 13, when he played a prominent part in the decisive defeat of Yorkshire by an innings and 25 runs. Nottinghamshire's most successful bowler in the visitors' first innings, with 4 wickets for only 16 runs, he went on to defy the Yorkshire attack for nearly five hours in making 104 without giving an actual chance. Easily the top scorer in the match, he was rewarded with a collection of over £11 for this epic performance. It must, however, be acknowledged that this was hardly the most sparkling example of his run-getting, seeing that his century contained only 3 fours.

From then onwards, there was a deterioration in Barnes's batting. Yet, though a veteran in years of service and greying at the temples, he showed no desire to give up the game, and in the contest with Sussex, at Hove, on June 8, 9, and 10, 1893, he was vouchsafed one more opportunity to demonstrate his ancient skills to the rising generation. One of three Nottinghamshire centurions—the others were Shrewsbury (164) and William Gunn (156)—he played a characteristic innings, scoring 102 in just under three hours and hitting 13 fours. His career as a first-class cricketer, however, was ebbing away on the tide. From the middle of May to the beginning of July 1894, he appeared in three MCC matches and assisted Nottinghamshire nine times. During this period, his benefit match came off at Trent Bridge, on June 18, 19, and 20, when Nottinghamshire drew with the Gentlemen of England (minus W.G.) in a contest "productive of high-scoring." The beneficiary, who scored 32 and took 1 rather expensive wicket, received

£350—a reasonable though not entirely excessive sum, considering his popularity, even by the standards of the time. Dropped from the County Eleven after one match at the beginning of July, he was recalled for the away fixture with Leicestershire at the end of the month, but scores of 0 and 4 ensured his final omission from the team.

Nottinghamshire had a poor season in 1895, with the losses column far outweighing the list of victories, and more than one journalist rushed into print with the suggestion that Barnes should be reinstated in the side. This gratuitous advice was ignored, since the Committee at Trent Bridge had had more than enough of "Barney." They had no desire to lay themselves open once again to the depressing prospect of having to deal with his drinking habits and his lack of punctuality.

I find it hard to accept as undeniably and completely authentic a story, which nevertheless makes some attempt to create an impression of the errant Nottinghamshire all-rounder's character and testifies to the fame he had acquired to such an extent that anecdotes were related about what he *might* have done in certain circumstances (compare a certain F. S. Trueman). The story tells that "Barney" turned up late and in his cups for a Nottinghamshire match at Lord's, but he confounded all critics by scoring a rapid, faultless century. Notwithstanding this magnificent performance, he was hauled before the Committee back at Trent Bridge shortly afterwards to receive a stern reprimand for his conduct. After hearing them out in silence, "Barney" tendered his apologies but ventured to point out that, having made a century before luncheon when he was intoxicated, it would pay the Committee to get him drunk before every match!

A similar anecdote was narrated by the Yorkshire batsman, John Tunnicliffe, whose abstemious demeanour was the very opposite of "Barney's." This incident took place at Lord's also, and again the actual match is difficult to identify. After treating all the other professionals in the dressing-room to a series of hilarious jokes, "Barney" went out and took several wickets. Since the MCC side contained some good batsmen, the successful bowler believed that he would not have to go in for a long time. Consequently, at luncheon, he displayed a marked preference for liquid rather than solid refreshment. As it happened, MCC suffered a minor collapse, and late in the afternoon he emerged blinking in the daylight and made his way out to the pitch. "With his slouching, sliding kind of walk," said Tunnicliffe, "it was difficult to tell whether he was sober or not." The Yorkshireman was soon left in no doubt. As "Barney" drew level with him, he gave a knowing wink, whispering, "John, there are several balls knocking about, and I think it safest to go for the middle one." Contrary to Tunnicliffe's expectations, there was no imminent catastrophe—in fact, there was no catastrophe at all. With a lavish array of his favourite off-side strokes, the veteran easily passed the half-century and more, and nobody else, other than Tunnicliffe, not even the hawk-eyed Lord Hawke (pun unintentional), was any the wiser about the batsman's true condition. Clearly, "Barney" had made an unerring choice when he opted for the middle ball, but then, as W.G. said, his "faculty for getting out of scrapes was remarkable."

Off the field, Billy Barnes followed the occupation of publican (what else?), being the landlord of *The Angel Inn*, at Mansfield Woodhouse, in his native county. There, around the end of February 1899, he fell ill, and he died some three weeks later, on March 24. He passed away in fairly affluent circumstances, leaving an estate of £1,549.

E. V. Lucas, the well known author, had an enduring love of Nottinghamshire cricket and the famous players of the Victorian age. Writing just before World War II, he cast his mind back to former days, and he dwelt on the pleasure to be derived from watching William Barnes in action. The latter, for whom patience was not often a virtue, would have been considered much too frivolous and irresponsible to have earned even a grudging acceptance into the ranks of the more sober-minded players of the 1930s. Lucas pursued his fantasy, thinking also of Barnes's great contemporary, Arthur Shrewsbury. What magnificent batsmen they both were, but how different in temperament and style—"Shrewsbury played like a classic, and Barnes like a romantic!" And if only you could envisage the possibility of calling one of them back from the past, which one would you choose? Lucas had no doubts on that score. "Thinking over the innings of the past which I have seen and would see again," he declared, "I believe I would recreate 'Barney' at his most reckless before any other player."

CHAPTER TWELVE

Edmund Peate *"The Best Left-hander in England"*

ARTHUR Thomas Edward Trelor was scarcely a name to conjure with in first-class cricket. His record was, to say the least, rather undistinguished. Playing for Middlesex against Oxford University, in 1872, he made 10 in his two innings and conceded 27 runs for 1 wicket. The County refrained from calling upon his services again, so Trelor turned his mind to other means of earning a living. In spite of the increase in the number of first-class matches, itinerant teams travelling round the country were still attracting some interest, and lately a new dimension had been added to the national pastime. Viewing this trend with a favourable eye, Trelor (sometimes spelt Treloar) set himself up as the impresario of the Imperial Clown Cricketers.

Clown Cricket was an irrational form of entertainment peculiar to the Victorian age. A bizarre and frankly incompatible union of the circus ring and the cricket field, it enjoyed a modicum of ephemeral popularity in the 1870s before subsiding into well deserved obscurity. It was, in its own way, a harmless enough diversion for an uncritical audience and, on the credit side, it provided summer wages for a few needy individuals anxious to obtain a billet.

Around 1875, Trelor had some vacancies in his company and accordingly advertised for professional cricketers. One of the successful applicants was Ted Peate, a youngster from Yeadon with ambitions to appear before a public beyond the immediate confines of the Leeds district. The troupe, he found, consisted of eight cricketers, eight talking clowns, and eight acrobats. Ted, of course, was assigned to the first group, but was willing and eager to have a go at the other roles, resplendent in gaudy paint and tights. He did "a bit of talking" sometimes and on one occasion rashly tried to imitate one of the acrobats in hanging upside-down by his toes. This well-meaning attempt had painful consequences, so, nursing his bruises, Ted decided to limit his activities to the cricket side of the entertainment and the cracking of a few jokes. All went well with the troupe thereafter, until the manager made the woeful and unmitigated error of staging a performance at Sheffield, where genuine cricket was almost a religion. Failing to appreciate this travesty of their favourite sport, the local "grinders" rose to their feet and expressed their disapproval in unmistakable terms. The wretched, would-be entertainers were driven from the field by a host of menacing spectators, who gave vent to their disgust with a chorus of boos and jeers, and followed this up by hurling a shower of missiles, including clods of earth ("well mobbed and sodded" was Ted's recollection of that memorable scene).

Born at Holbeck, Leeds, on March 2, 1855, Edmund Peate was barely out of his infancy when his family moved to Yeadon, one of the most famous nurseries of Yorkshire cricket. As he approached manhood, he came under the watchful eye of several seasoned professionals and was soon regarded as a promising prospect possessing more than ordinary merit. Cricket, he eventually decided, would be his living, if he could make the grade. The genuine article, that is. There would be no more engagements with Trelor's company, though the episode left its permanent mark, since Ted retained a clownish streak throughout his life. Going out into the world once more, he obtained employment with the clubs at Batley and Carlisle before accepting a post at Manningham. Club professionals in those days were usually engaged first and foremost for their bowling skills, and at this stage of his career Ted was a *fast* bowler. A warp twister in the textile trade at Yeadon in the winter months preceding his appointment at Manningham, he found the time during working hours to exercise his arm in a shed. Dissatisfied with the prospects of pace bowling, he practised assiduously, experimented, mastered the art of line and length, and converted himself into a *slow* bowler. Apart from one match with the Manningham Club, he never bowled fast again.

In August 1878, Peate assisted 18 of Yeadon and District against the Australian touring team and contributed to the local side's victory by taking 4 wickets. Shortly afterwards, at the end of the season, he had a momentous encounter that was largely instrumental in bringing him to the notice of the Yorkshire Committee. He went to Scarborough to watch a game in the Cricket Carnival (later Festival). The Yorkshire Gentlemen were one man short for their match against the local club, and the Rev E. S. Carter asked round the pavilion if anybody would care to fill the vacancy. Ted volunteered his services, and, having first ascertained that he could bowl, Mr Carter invited him to join the side. The circumstances could hardly have been more propitious. As the Gentlemen's wicket-keeper, Mr Carter was in a perfect position to observe the qualities of his recruit. He was favourably impressed, and later he asked Ted to give him details of his performances with

Manningham. These Mr Carter forwarded to the County Committee, recommending his discovery as a likely candidate for higher honours.

Mr Carter was not without some influence in the higher echelons of Yorkshire cricket, and Ted was selected to undergo a trial with the colts at the beginning of the 1879 season. Coming through this ordeal with flying colours, he was promoted into the senior team, making his debut against Nottinghamshire, at Trent Bridge, on June 9, 10, and 11. In a dreary match ruined by almost non-stop rain, he took 2 wickets for 31 runs in 39 overs. Apart from a brief spell towards the end of July, the predominantly wet weather persisted throughout much of the summer, and Ted, retaining his place in the team, revelled in the damp pitches whenever play was possible. His best bowling in an innings was 6 wickets for 14 runs and his best match figures 12 for 77. At the end of the season, his tally was 75 wickets at an average of 12.44 in 15 matches. According to the general opinion, he would probably do great things in the future, provided he could command more developed powers of spin and increase the pace of his delivery; otherwise, he would incur harsh treatment on firmer pitches favouring the batsmen.

Slightly under 6 foot tall and weighing close on 12 stone, Peate was no physical fitness fanatic, and later he put on excess weight at an alarming rate. He had the misfortune to suffer from defective vision and, even at the height of his career, he would normally wear glasses off the field and could be seen reading from a book held close before his eyes. This *might* have been partly a leg-pull, since Ted was one of several humorists in the Yorkshire team, though in later years he took to wearing his glasses more frequently. He had a slightly comical expression and a somewhat ragged moustache that threatened to defy all efforts at grooming, until eventually it grew long enough to droop in waxed points past the corners of his mouth.

Left-handed in all things, Peate had no pretensions to being an all-rounder. His imperfect eyesight was a serious handicap in the field and at the popping crease. A mediocre fielder in his early days, he taught himself to become more reliable without ever attaining or even aspiring to the standard of brilliance. Having little appreciation of defensive tactics, he was a natural lower-order batsman of the hoick-it-away variety and, in the judgement of W. G. Grace, Ted "did not trouble himself much about his batting average." He never scored a century, though he came pretty near to it on one famous occasion. In one department of the game, however, he was without any exaggeration superb. Yorkshire had not possessed a genuine slow–medium left-arm bowler of any quality for well over a decade, and of all the renowned virtuosos of that spell-binding art he was irrefutably one of the greatest, though his reign was all too brief—less than ten years at the top.

Edmund Peate

Courtesy Roger Mann

In the early days, when Peate worshipped at the shrine of speed, he always delivered the ball with a high-arm action. During those portentous months spent in the process of conversion from fast to slow, he took as his model one of his mentors, Amos Marshall of Yeadon, a left-arm medium-pacer, who played little first-class cricket but turned out several times for the Yorkshire United County Eleven in 1874. When the metamorphosis was complete, Peate emerged from the chrysalis as a sort of throw-back to a previous generation: his elevated over-arm delivery had become round-arm, almost on a level with the shoulder. Bowling sideways-on round the wicket with an easy, unlaboured action and a low trajectory, he could keep going for long spells, a facility unfortunately exploited to the uttermost by some of his captains. One of the arch-apostles of length-bowling, he soon pinpointed his opponents' weaknesses and sought to outwit them with subtle variations of pace and flight, dropping the ball on an imperceptibly different spot with each delivery ("There is a length which no batsman can play, and I used to study to find it"). He had a slight, natural break and could turn the ball both ways, but claimed that he never relied much on break and spin as essential to his powers of deception, though he was perhaps over-modest in this respect. Persistent and always probing to gain the upper hand over his adversaries, he was rarely collared except by batsmen such as A. G. Steel, the Lancashire and England amateur. An accomplished slow–medium bowler himself, "Nab" Steel knew that the best method of overcoming Peate's wiles was to counter-attack by rushing out and driving the ball before it could pose any threat. This kind of treatment and a series of missed catches were apt to have an adverse effect on Peate's morale. There were, however, not many keen-eyed Steels about, who were willing to take such risks and get away with it.

Conditions looked favourable for the batsmen at the beginning of the 1880 season, but the dry, quick pitches vanished from June onwards, though the weather was not so bad as it had been in 1879. Peate, it was observed, had managed to increase his pace and break slightly without sacrificing his mastery of line, length, and flight. He took 138 wickets at a cost of little more than 12 runs apiece, and he went on to top 100 victims in each of the next five seasons. The late twentieth-century obsession with covered pitches and an ever-present pair of fast or fast–medium bowlers to open the proceedings was unheard-of in Peate's day. A captain would usually begin with his best bowlers, the pace being of secondary importance, and in many of the Yorkshire matches at this time the attack often started off with a famous partnership—Ted Peate (slow–medium left-arm) at one end, and Willie Bates (off breaks) at the other. In the limited-overs version of cricket so popular to-day, Bates would have been included in the team largely for the brilliance of his aggressive batting, whereas Peate might well have found it difficult to command a place at all, except as the drinks waiter.

Generally speaking, a bowler of Peate's type prefers a sticky wicket to a dry one, and on these grounds it has sometimes been implied that his immediate and startling success arose from operating constantly on a series of damp pitches. This is only partly true, since there were many occasions on which he performed with great merit on a dry surface. The batsmen found the conditions much more to their liking in 1881—dry in May, hot and dry in June and July, with the rain setting in only in the following month. A comment on Peate's progress throughout the season in one of the cricket annuals makes interesting reading: "Curiously enough, the wet weather in August interfered with his success, instead of giving him an advantage." Nevertheless, Ted's tally of victims for the season rose to 173 at an average of still less than 13 runs per wicket, and he achieved the best match figures of his career by taking 14 for 77 (6–47 and 8–30) against Surrey, at Huddersfield, on June 2 and 3. Yorkshire had a gigantic victory by an innings and 217 runs. Batting throughout the whole of the first day with some sterling efforts in the first half of the order, including two centuries, the innings closed at 388 for 9, with numbers 7 to 10 collapsing for only 10 runs. Number 11 was Peate, who, thinking he would not be wanted until the next morning, had left the ground early and consequently missed his turn with the bat. Presumably, he was pardoned for this offence when he bowled so magnificently the next day, unchanged throughout both innings in partnership with Allen Hill (fast right).

By now, Peate had fully justified his claim to represent the Players against the Gentlemen, taking part in the fixtures at The Oval and Lord's. A loose and crumbling pitch at headquarters made conditions ideal for the slower bowlers in the amateurs' first innings, and Peate took full advantage of it. He had played against W. G. Grace in county matches in the two previous seasons, clean bowling him on their first encounter. Now, at Lord's, in 1881, he surpassed himself, tying up the Champion in knots. With three successive deliveries, each spinning viciously off the treacherous turf, Ted beat the bat and the stumps as well before succeeding in penetrating W.G.'s defence. From 1881 to 1886, Peate was a regular choice for the Players. He played in 11 matches and took 39 wickets at the, for him, somewhat excessive cost of 25.53 each.

The Champion, it was sometimes alleged, was more comfortable against fast bowling rather than slow. Among all his famous adversaries, Ted Peate was one of the bowlers he found most troublesome and "puzzling." The left-hander's strike rate was commendable:

opposed to W.G. in a total of 58 innings—though not necessarily bowling at him in all of them—he dismissed the Champion 14 times (9 bowled, 5 caught). One memorable exploit was recorded in Yorkshire's match against Gloucestershire, at Bramall Lane, on July 31 and August 1 and 2, 1882, when he clean bowled both of the opening batsmen, E. M. and W. G. Grace, for no score in the first innings.

Grace, however, was not the only famous batsman to be shackled by the bonds of Ted's wizardry. One of the Australians was driven to despair by his utter failure to overcome the spell cast upon him and determined to practise and improve his technique in the seclusion of his bedroom. With bat in hand, he essayed a series of strokes against imaginary deliveries, first back ("That's the way to play you, Peate"), then forward ("Not this time, Peate, my boy"), and finally, releasing all his pent-up frustration with a mighty leg-hit ("How do you like that, Peate?"), he smashed the toilet set on the wash-stand into smithereens. His new-found confidence swiftly evaporated the next day on facing the flesh-and-blood Peate—clean bowled first ball. Ted was told that the "hero" of this performance was the Australian captain, W. L. Murdoch, but the name of G. J. Bonnor, the legendary big hitter, has also been proposed. Either would fit the bill, though Murdoch has a slight edge overall (dismissed 17 times in 45 innings, Bonner 13 in 42). In 1882, though, there was a much greater disparity: Bonnor was Peate's victim 3 times, Murdoch 11! The latter, incidentally, shared W.G.'s opinion that Ted was a more difficult bowler to face than either Peel or Briggs, both first-rate left-handers whose careers overlapped Peate's.

In the winter of 1881–82, Peate went on his only visit to Australia and New Zealand as a member of the team got up by James Lillywhite, junior, Alfred Shaw, and Arthur Shrewsbury. Throughout the whole tour, he took over 200 wickets at a single-figure average, but many of the matches were played against "odds." In first-class fixtures, he was not so successful, averaging 18.40 for 30 wickets, but only one other bowler had a better record—his Yorkshire partner, Willie Bates, whose 30 wickets cost 17.33 each. Seven bowlers in all were put on, and almost 40% of the overs delivered were credited to Peate—a striking example of a man being bowled into the ground.

The weather pattern of 1881 was not repeated the following year, when there was "a great dearth of sunshine, and, worse still, a superabundance of rain." Peate, not surprisingly, experienced the most successful season of his first-class career, in spite of being laid up with a sprained ankle early in July and a badly cut knee in September. Playing in 30 matches, he claimed 214 wickets at an average of 11.52, taking 5 wickets in an innings 21 times and 10 in a match 8 times. He also recorded his first performance of the hat-trick, when Yorkshire humbled Kent, at Bramall Lane, on June 12 and 13. When recalling this triumph, Ted remarked that he had upset the House of Lords and knocked out Irish Home Rule in three balls. His victims were Lord Harris, Lord Throwley (once described as "not a real lord . . . only a Discount"), and the professional, E. O'Shaughnessy. As official recognition of this feat, he was awarded talent money. In addition, he was presented with a silver mount for a walking-stick, shaped like a hand holding a revolver. To his friends Ted would announce with mock solemnity that this trinket was "a facsimile of a mailed fist, presented to me by the German Emperor."

One of Ted's most remarkable exploits of the season occurred at Old Trafford, on September 14, 15, and 16, when the North of England easily defeated the Australians. He opened the bowling in both innings with Jack Crossland, the Lancashire fast man, whose searing yorker was considered a blatant throw by all but Lancastrians. There was little to help Ted in the pitch, which was perfectly hard and true, but his bowling "was the feature of the match." His figures were 5–54 in the first innings and 5–51 in the second, and one knowledgeable writer went on record with his belief that he had never seen a better performance by Peate. W. L. Murdoch, by the way, lost his wicket to Peate in both innings (bowled and lbw), while Bonnor was dismissed each time by Crossland.

The North's victory was a sweet revenge for the catastrophe at The Oval, on August 28 and 29, when Australia beat England by 7 runs in the single Test Match of the season. The visitors made only one change in their side for the contest at Old Trafford, but only four of the triumphant North had also appeared for England, a fact which might be construed as a criticism of the selectors. Peate was the last batsman to be dismissed at The Oval, and, in spite of his magnificent bowling—4 wickets in each innings for only 71 runs—it has sometimes been implied that, by getting out as he did, he was to blame for England's defeat. Well, Ted was not exactly chosen to play for his batting, so who else could be considered at fault? One prime candidate was Mr A. P. Lucas, who, in missing a vital catch at long-on, permitted 17 more runs to be added to the score. Another was W. G. Grace, who infuriated the Australians, particularly F. R. Spofforth, with a blatant piece of gamesmanship, which backfired by strengthening the tourists' will to win. And, finally, several England players—genuine wielders of the willow—who allowed Spofforth and H. F. Boyle to establish a moral ascendancy over them and weakly capitulated.

Mr C. T. Studd, one of the most gifted amateurs of the day, performed the double of 1000 runs and 100 wickets in 1882—only

W.G. had done this previously—and he had already taken two centuries off the Australians' bowling earlier in the season. In the crucial match at The Oval, however, he had an unhappy time. Clean bowled for a duck by the saturnine Spofforth in the first innings and equally unsuccessful with the ball, Studd was dropped down the batting order from number 6 to number 10 in the second. Needing 85 to win, England had made 53 when the fourth wicket fell. The weather was miserably cold, the remaining batsmen began to suffer from the jitters, and when their turn came to go in, they submitted tamely to the domination of Spofforth and Boyle. A succession of maidens ensued, runs were scarce, and more vital wickets were lost. When the eighth fell off the last ball of an over from Spofforth, Charlie Studd cast off the blanket he had been wearing round his shoulders to keep off the shivers. It is fair to assume that he, like the others, was feeling rather nervous. Standing impotently at the non-striker's end, he witnessed England's death throes. With the first delivery of what proved to be the final over of the match, Boyle trapped Billy Barnes into giving a simple catch to point. Enter Ted Peate, who, it is said, had been plied by his team-mates with fortifying sips of champagne, currently known by the euphemism "tonic." He lashed away the first ball he received for 2, calling upon Studd for an impossible third run which was refused. Missing the next, he was clean bowled by the last delivery of the over.

This incident gave rise to an anecdote which has been repeated ad nauseam. On being rebuked for his rashness (too much "tonic"?) and failure to keep his end up and leave the run-getting to his more talented partner, Ted is supposed to have answered, "Ah couldn't troost Mester Stood!" On being asked the same question a few days later at Scarborough by one of the selectors of the England team, he replied with a dead-pan expression that he thought he was the better bat. The now accepted wording of the anecdote probably originated in a terse conversation between Lord Harris and Peate within minutes of the end of the match. His lordship, also a member of the selection committee, demanded to know why Peate "had been so on the jump" and trying to get his partner "to run for the most ridiculous things." There was no hesitation in Ted's rejoinder: "Ah warn't afeerd for mesen; Ah were afeerd for Mester Stood; Ah knew Ah could play old Spoff!" The sort of humorous reply to be expected from a Yorkshireman, but was there an element of truth? Charlie Studd had failed against Spofforth in the first innings and had not exactly been exuding confidence in the dressing-room. Motivated, perhaps, by his assessment of the situation, Ted tried to persuade his nervous partner to go for a risky third run to prevent him from having to face Spofforth in the next over—and, any way, Charlie would have had a chance to make some runs off the two

C. T. Studd

Courtesy Roger Mann

remaining balls from Boyle. A dangerous and temporary solution to an immediate problem, but one which, given luck, might have produced the desired result. Maybe what Ted actually said to Lord Harris was, "Ah knew *Ah* could play old Spoff!"

It is far from easy to live up to the reputation of having taken 214 wickets in one season, and by that uncompromising yardstick Ted was less successful in 1883, accounting for a mere 120 victims. To do him justice, though, it should be remembered that this figure was exceeded by only one other bowler. This falling-off, a disappointment to Ted's many admirers, was set down "not to a loss of form, but to a lack of advantages." To begin with, Bates and Peate had been joined in the Yorkshire side by a third slow bowler, Bobby Peel—destined to be Ted's eventual successor for county and country—making it "difficult for the captain to work the changes properly." Of greater significance was the weather, since England experienced the rare luxury of basking in the finest conditions for several years, producing hard, true wickets for about three months in all. On one occasion, however, in the contest between Yorkshire and Surrey, at Holbeck, Leeds, on July 23 and 24, the pitch was "very soft and treacherous," and Peate was heard to remark that the match would be over before the luncheon interval on the second day. Yorkshire won the toss, batted first, and made 116. There was no need for them to go to the wickets again. Surrey were dismissed for 31 in little more than an hour and, when stumps were drawn, 5 of their batsmen in the second innings had been dispatched for 33. Their final total was 82, the rout being completed not long after the resumption of play, leaving Yorkshire victorious by an innings and 3 runs. In Surrey's first innings, Ted delivered 16 overs, of which 11 were maidens, and recorded the best figures of his career—*8 wickets for only 5 runs*, statistically one of the finest performances ever achieved by a bowler. Holbeck, of course, was his birthplace, but Ted was bitterly disappointed in his hopes for any tangible reward from the spectators for his extraordinary feat. In reply to a suggestion that a collection should be taken in recognition of his bowling, a Holbeck man said bluntly, "Oh, be ———, he has ruined our gate; I shall object to the hat going round!" And that, Ted remembered, was the only reward he received from Holbeck.

One of the games of 1883 in which Peate was unsuccessful was the Roses Match, at Old Trafford, on July 5 and 6, but he did not let it affect his sense of humour. One of the talking points in the world of cricket at that time was unfair bowling, and Lancashire, it will be remembered, possessed more than one "chucker," the principal offender being Jack Crossland, Peate's principal partner in the North of England's trouncing of the Australians, in September 1882. Edward

Roper, an amateur, who at different times played for both Lancashire and Yorkshire, was on this occasion assisting the former and found himself batting against Peate, who, Roper recalled, "was always full of fun and jokes." The umpires in those days, all old professionals, were unwilling to blight a fellow-player's career, so Crossland and the others were never "called." Standing at Peate's end was George Wootton, once a pace bowler for MCC and Nottinghamshire, and Ted said to him, "Look here, George, you umpires are not worth twopennorth of gin, you daren't no-ball anybody. The first ball of the next over, I declare to you, I will throw at Mr Roper, and I'll bet you anything you like that you daren't no-ball me." Came the moment, and Ted's word was as good as his bond. He made a deliberate shy at the batsman, and since the umpire remained silent and passive, Mr Roper hastily blocked the ball. Then, to the huge delight of all those within earshot, Peate turned to Wootton, exclaiming loudly, "There, it shows what you umpires are all worth!" To me, personally, this does not sound much like the exact words you would expect to be used in those circumstances, but perhaps Mr Roper was merely giving a polite version of Peate's monologue, shorn of its expletives.

By 1884, the Hon. M. B. (later Lord) Hawke had assumed the captaincy of Yorkshire, and legend says he was warned that the all-professional team consisted of "ten drunks and a chapel parson." Peate was neither a religious man nor a total abstainer. He was, said Hawke, "a really charming fellow," but it is possible that the future peer and some members of the Committee did not entirely approve of him and marked him down as a candidate for shunting. This process, it might be said, was already put into operation shortly before the opening matches of the 1884 season when for neither the first nor by any means the last time, the powers that be in Yorkshire adopted a policy that was as tactless as it was short-sighted. At the beginning of the season, the Committee incurred some adverse criticism for the system they employed in the selection of players. Two youngsters, G. P. Harrison and Irwin Grimshaw, were given a contract to appear in all matches. "Shoey" Harrison, a fast bowler with a slightly suspect action, had made his first-class debut in 1883 with such notable success that he was chosen to assist the Players against the Gentlemen, at Lord's. Here he suffered some severe punishment at the hands of W. G. Grace, but at the end of the season he had managed to secure 100 wickets at an average of 13.26 in all matches. Grimshaw, who had made his first-class debut in 1880, was regarded as a promising batsman, though his record in 1883 was only moderate. On the surface, these operations did not seem too unreasonable, at least as far as Harrison was concerned. The Committee then went on to administer a severe slap in the face to two of the more established professionals by engaging Ted Peate for no more than three matches initially, as though he were required to serve some sort of probation, and by offering nothing but the Colts' match to the long-serving Tom Emmett. Metaphorically wagging an admonitory finger at the Committee, one of the cricket annuals observed that "Such proceedings could not fail to breed a spirit of discontent and dissatisfaction." As things turned out, most of the bowling for Yorkshire fell to the lot of Peate and the veteran Emmett, whose performance was all that could be desired. "Shoey" Harrison, a perfect example of the one-season man, lost his pace as well as his place in the side, and did little in later years. Irwin Grimshaw achieved some merit as a batsman in 1884, scoring 710 runs at an average of 21.51, but he soon faded and was out of the picture after 1887. You could not, therefore, have too much faith in the Yorkshire Committee's judgement or powers of perception at that time.

In 1884, England experienced one of the most glorious summers for over a decade, even more so than the previous year, with the prevailing conditions weighted heavily in favour of the batsmen. Determined, perhaps, to rehabilitate himself in the eyes of the Yorkshire Committee, Ted Peate was compelled to summon forth all his bowling skills with the minimum of assistance from a spinner's pitch. He came through with flying colours, emerging as the leading wicket-taker of England, with 137 victims at an average of 13.63. Success came his way more than once against the Australians. In a low-scoring contest at Bradford, on June 9 and 10, on one of the few occasions in the season when the ground was damp and unreliable, Ted returned match figures of 10 for 62, accounting once for Bonnor (because of an injured finger, Murdoch was unable to play!). He made a signal contribution to England's overwhelming victory, at Lord's, on July 21, 22, and 23, by bowling "wonderfully well" in the first innings and recording his best Test analysis of 6 for 85. A month earlier, however, when representing the North of England, at Old Trafford, on June 19 and 20, the country's best left-hander surpassed his exploits in the equivalent fixture of 1882. Bowling unchanged on an unresponsive pitch throughout both the tourists' innings, he achieved one of the most remarkable feats of his career, prompting the following commendation in one of the cricket annuals:

> The main cause of the English victory was Peate's bowling, and all things considered, it is doubtful whether the Yorkshireman has ever accomplished a better performance. The Australians seemed altogether unable to hit him, and in the two innings he took 10 wickets at a cost of only 51 runs. His achievement was the more remarkable as the ground was hard and fast.

Peate's complete figures for the two innings were 40.1–24–28–5 (total 91) and 37.2–25–23–5 (total 107); only two other bowlers were put on (Barlow, Barnes, and Bates were not required!), and Peate was unchanged throughout. So much for the tales of perpetual rain at Old Trafford and the allegations that Ted was only successful on a damp pitch.

In yet another encounter with the Australians, Ted was selected to assist the Players of England, at The Oval, on July 31 and August 1. The home side, unfortunately, were below their full strength, and the visitors won easily by 9 wickets in circumstances that provoked a riot. When the luncheon bell rang at two o'clock, the Australians were only 11 runs short of victory. In order to avoid inflicting a stark financial loss on the caterers, the Australian captain (Murdoch) agreed to adjourn, making the condition that no further charge for admission should be levied. This proviso was not communicated to an unruly mob, who staged a prolonged demonstration in front of the pavilion. George Giffen, the Australian all-rounder, happened to appear in the doorway and was given a cheer. Shortly afterwards, he was joined by Peate, who received a similar greeting. C. W. Alcock, the Surrey secretary, tried to persuade Giffen to pacify the crowd. Having no faith in his own powers of oratory, the South Australian declined, and the desperate Alcock turned to Peate, pleading for his assistance. Ted's reply was terse, blunt, and to the point: "Naw, thank you, sir; Ah coom 'ere t' play cricket, not t' quell a riot." The turmoil continued after the interval, but eventually order was restored by the arrival of police reinforcements, and the game reached its inevitable conclusion. The Players had made only 71 in their second innings, to which Ted, as second top scorer, contributed 19 before yielding for the second time in the contest to "old Spoff." His bowling in this match "was up to his best standard" (5–55 and the only wicket—Bonnor's!—in the second innings).

On the county circuit, too, Ted had his triumphs. Against Gloucestershire, at Moreton-in-Marsh, on May 8, 9, and 10, his analysis in the second innings was 6 for 13, including the second hat-trick of his first-class career. His first victim of the three was E. M. Grace, who hit down his own wicket. At Gravesend, on August 14 and 15, he took 8 wickets for 63 runs in Kent's first innings. In the fixture with Surrey, at Dewsbury, on July 24, 25, and 26, he did little in the way of bowling but marked his highest score in first-class cricket. Batting at number 8 in Yorkshire's second innings, he made 95, including 16 fours. He had three lives, one before he had scored. Another occurred when he struck the ball up to such an immense height that, as Ted recalled, "the Surrey team were able to hold a

G. J. Bonnor and F. R. Spofforth

committee meeting to decide who should attempt the catch." The task was entrusted to E. J. Diver, reputed to be Surrey's safest catcher. Unfortunately for Diver, he made a miscalculation: the ball fell three yards behind him, and Ted merrily continued to wield the long handle.

On one occasion in the 1880s, Peate made a brief acquaintance with the highest level of political life in England. At the end of a day's play at The Oval, he went for a stroll round London, accompanied by one of his team-mates, George Ulyett. The latter was, if anything, an even greater leg-puller than Ted. They made their way to Whitehall and were intrigued by the sight of a huge crowd and an array of carriages. Curious as to the cause of this activity, the Yorkshire pair turned into Downing Street and discovered that Mr Gladstone was holding an official reception at number 10. Feigning deafness, Ulyett strode straight past the expostulating flunkeys with Ted following hard on his heels, saying, "My friend is deaf; I must follow him." By this stratagem, the two gatecrashers got as far as the reception room, where they encountered a famous Lancashire cricketer among the bona fide guests. Gawping at them in amazement, the amateur hastily enquired what they were doing there and how they had managed to get in. Casting off his pretence of deafness, Ulyett rose splendidly to the occasion, replying, "Oh, we thought it was a place of entertainment"—in which, perhaps, he was not so far wrong—"so we thought we would just look in." Concluding that the time had come for them to make an exit, the uninvited guests retreated into Downing Street, marvelling that the arrangements for guarding the Prime Minister's official residence were so ineffective.

It may be fairly argued that, with his performance throughout 1884, Peate had won back his stripes, especially since the weather had not been his ally for any length of time. I do not think that Ted was much of a man for praying, nor do I know whether he hoped for a return of those conditions prevailing at the outset of his career, but if so, his supplications fell on deaf ears. The characteristic features of the season of 1885 were good wickets and favourable weather, on the whole. With his figure verging on the appearance of being a little too well-upholstered, he was probably beginning to feel the strain of day-in day-out cricket, considering the amount of bowling he had to do. He had his moments, at Lord's, for instance, when he marked his best analysis (5–51) for the Players against the Gentlemen, while at Cambridge, early in the season, his figures in the second innings were vintage Peate (39–30–12–5), which ought to have impressed the Hon M. B. Hawke, the undergraduates' captain, seeing that he succumbed to Ted's trickery for 3 and 0. His best performance statistically came late in the year, at Harrogate, on September 10, 11, and 12. Playing for an Eleven of England against Alfred Shaw's Australian team, he produced a semblance of his old form in the second innings, sending down 13 overs, of which 6 were maidens, and claiming 6 wickets for only 17 runs. While admitting that his final figures for the season were very good, and conceding that "he had still few, if any, superiors," one of the annuals observed that he was "hardly as deadly as he had been in previous years." One of only five bowlers to capture 100 wickets or more, he failed, however, to attain a place in the top twenty of the national averages, in which he had appeared without a break since 1880. His tally of victims declined from 137 in 1884 to 115 in 1885, and his average rose by over 3 runs each to 16.91. The number of times he took 5 wickets in an innings fell from 13 to 8, while he secured 10 in a match only once. In addition to physical degeneration, Ted had other troubles: a victim of the overwhelming success achieved in earlier years, he was also coming under the threat of a dangerous rival in the Yorkshire side in the person of Bobby Peel.

As things turned out, 1885 was destined to be Peate's last full outing in first-class cricket. The cycle of generally fine summers continued unabated in 1886, and bowlers of his type were compelled to seize the rare opportunities that came their way, mainly in the first few weeks of the season and only occasionally afterwards. Fortune granted Ted one final fling in the grand manner in what was surely one of his favourite fixtures. The Australians were in England once again, and their usual contest against the North took place on a rain-soaked pitch, at Old Trafford, on May 31. In a drawn match, restricted by the elements to one day's play, three innings were completed and the fourth begun. The visitors, at their first attempt, were put out for 45, which turned out to be the highest total of all. In reply, the North could make only 34, the highest score coming from Ted, who defied "old Spoff," marking 8 not out. The tourists, dismissed for 43 in their second innings, succeeded in dispatching one of the North's openers before close of play. Mr A. N. Hornby, the home captain, employed only two bowlers throughout the match—Ted Peate and Alec Watson, the Lancashire off spinner ("The Southerton of the North"). The condition of the pitch probably presented the former with an easier task, but his statistics were even better than those he had achieved in the equivalent fixture in 1882 and 1884, when he had to exert all his craft on ground that suited the batsmen. At Old Trafford, in 1886, he returned match figures of 12 wickets for only 50 runs (8–23 and 4–27). Murdoch was not participating in this tour, but one of Ted's victims in each innings was Bonnor!

Peate was nothing like so successful against the Australians elsewhere. Selected, largely on reputation, perhaps, for the First Test on his favourite ground of Old Trafford, on July 5, 6, and 7, he went wicketless in the first innings (0–30) and, in the second, conceded 45 runs in claiming only one victim—Bonnor again, and for the last time! This was Ted's final international match. The demands of Yorkshire prevented him from appearing in other representative contests, such as the Players *v* the Australians, at Trent Bridge, on June 21, 22, and 23, and Gentlemen *v* Players, at Lord's, on July 12, 13, and 14. At The Oval, immediately afterwards, he assisted the Players for the last time and failed to take a wicket. By now, the tragic decline from his former eminence was all too patently obvious. His last match against another county occurred in the fixture with Nottinghamshire, at Bramall Lane, on August 9, 10, and 11. Thereafter, his affiliation as a member of the Yorkshire team was tenuous—against MCC at the Scarborough Festival in 1886 and at Lord's early the next year, and finally against Liverpool and District, on June 23, 24, and 25, 1887.

In weighing up Yorkshire's rather indifferent record for 1886, one of the annuals observed that "It was thought advisable to leave Peate, who had been one of their chief mainstays as a bowler for some years, out of the team . . .". As to the immediate reasons for his sudden omission from the team for the remainder of August 1886, the official County archives, I am informed, are silent. On figures alone, it is not easy to comprehend, seeing that Peate was the second most successful bowler against Nottinghamshire with 4 for 29. Did he celebrate this modest return to form unwisely and possibly step out of line with the Hon M. B. Hawke, his skipper? The latter was certainly responsible for the sacking of the once great left-hander, though he does not dilate upon his exact motives in his memoirs. He averred that Peate bore him no grudge—rather surprising, considering the future baron had abruptly deprived him of part of his means of livelihood—and went on to quote with relish Ted's comment on Willie Bates's decision to take a wife at the height of the cricket season ("Baates is a fool! 'E's gone and got married id middle o' soomer. 'E should have got married id middle o' winter so that 'e could pay 'is oondivided attention to it").

Perhaps it was sheer lack of commitment that brought about the dismissal of "The Best Left-hander in England," for it was evident that Ted was no longer fit enough for the wear and tear of three-day cricket. He had his share of physical infirmities: his eyesight was getting poorer, and an old injury to one of his knees now permanently affected his mobility on the field. For these misfortunes he could hardly be held responsible, but in another way he was his own executioner. Since the days when he had first appeared for Yorkshire, his girth and weight had increased to such a considerable degree that, in more modern times, he would have been a prime candidate for a lengthy sojourn at a health farm. A steady intake of ale may have contributed to this condition, but the principal cause was apparently something different. He had an excellent appetite, which was even unaffected on board a ship on a heaving ocean, and there can be little doubt that his addiction to the flesh-pots brought about his undoing. One of his friends was adamant in his belief that "it were ower eatin' as did Ted Peate!"

Life, happily, did not come to a dark end with Peate's departure from the Yorkshire team. Some time before this sad event, he had gone into business at Leeds as a dealer in a wide variety of sporting goods, and around 1890 he held the appointment of custodian of the ground at Headingley. He played much cricket with incomparable success in one-day matches, especially at Yeadon and later Skipton. His popularity never waned, and whenever his "rounded figure and spectacled face" appeared on any ground, he was instantly recognized by the public. During the time he was at Headingley, he returned briefly to first-class cricket, appearing for a North of England Eleven against the Australians, on September 1, 2, and 3, 1890. Although "old Spoff" was not there, nor Bonnor with the flailing bat, there was one nostalgic echo of past times in the person of W. L. Murdoch, once more leading the tourists. Murdoch was almost certainly out before Ted came on in the first innings, nor did he fall victim to the blandishments of the rotund left-hander on his other visit to the wickets. Ted took 1 for 22 in each innings, performing more economically in the second.

At Bedale, on May 9 and 10, 1895, in a match played for the benefit of the local veteran George Anderson, Peate assisted 18 of North Yorkshire against a Yorkshire Eleven, which included nine who appeared for the County, most of them as regulars, that season, and two old hands recently retired from first-class cricket. One of the three amateurs in the Yorkshire Eleven with a zest for swinging his bat was the source of intense chagrin to the left-hander in the space of one over. Lunging wildly at the first delivery, the batsman was way out of his crease, but the ham-fisted wicket-keeper muffed a golden opportunity to stump him. The next was nicked gently to shot-slip, who proved no safer than the wicket-keeper. An identical stroke off the third went to the same fielder, who this time managed to hold on to the ball. When his opponent stood his ground and rather belatedly began massaging his leg, Peate wasted no time in telling him he was out to a catch. The batsman had other ideas, however, demanding to hear the umpire's decision, and the official, on hearing the formal appeal, replied, "Not out, of course, can't you see the gentlemen rubbing his leg?" So furious was Ted at this chicanery that his next delivery, bereft of any line and length, was hoisted right out of the small ground. When the umpire awarded six runs, the luckless bowler exclaimed, "What! six for that!

G. J. Bonnor W. L. Murdoch

Two of Peate's favourite victims

Why, I could spit over the blooming fence." (I doubt if "blooming" was the word actually used at this moment of stress, but let it pass). Apart from this, Ted had an excellent match, taking 5 good wickets in the first innings and 1 of the 2 to fall in the second, when his victim was George Ulyett, his team-mate of his Yorkshire and England days and his companion in the escapade at number 10 Downing Street.

On one occasion in the years following Peate's retirement, it is said that Yorkshire were found to be short of a bowler, and the Committee invited him to rejoin the ranks and play in certain matches. After several consecutive days of practice to see if his game leg would stand the strain, he broke down and sorrowfully had to decline the honour. It was, perhaps, just as well that the attempt to bring about Ted's recall was abortive, since come-backs sometimes turn out to be nothing but a disaster, especially for sportsmen, and he had after all nothing really to prove. His bowling record was and still remains phenomenal. In only eight seasons, the first and last of which were not complete, one overseas tour, and the three matches played in 1887 and 1890, he took 1,076 wickets at an average of 13.48, claiming 5 or more in an innings 94 times and 10 or more in a match 27 times. There are very few better records from his time.

Raw, cold weather marked the beginning of the new year of 1900, and Willie Bates contracted a severe chill while attending the funeral of old Uncle John Thewlis, whose service with Yorkshire had ended in the mid-1870s. Bates, whose health was not of the best, developed a fatal inflammation of the lungs and expired on January 8. Ted Peate was not long in following his erstwhile bowling partner. On a chilly night at the beginning of March, he attended a performance at a local theatre and was stricken down shortly afterwards with congestion of the liver. Chafing at his confinement to the sick-room, he insisted on getting up too soon. Pneumonia set in, and he died at his home on March 11, 1900, the fourth Yorkshire cricketer to pass away in the space of less than three months.

Ted Peate's successors in the Yorkshire and England teams up to the outbreak of the First World War were Bobby Peel and Wilfred Rhodes. Which one was the greatest of this magnificent trio? David Hunter, the famous Yorkshire stumper, who in his time kept wicket to all three in first-class or other matches, had decided views on the matter. In David's expert opinion, Peel was superior to Rhodes, but, he insisted, "Peate was the finest left-arm bowler I ever saw."

SELECT BIBLIOGRAPHY

The principal publications consulted are the following:

1. Collections of Scores, Annuals, and Reference Works

Bailey, Philip, Philip Thorn, and Peter Wynne-Thomas, *Who's Who of Cricketers* (Feltham: Newnes Books, 1984).
Cricket Scores and Biographies, 15 vols.
Cricket Matches 1860–1863, First Class Cricket Matches 1864–1866, and succeeding volumes covering the period 1867–1894, comp. and pub. by the Association of Cricket Statisticians.
Frindall, Bill, comp. and ed., *The Wisden Book of Test Cricket 1877–1984* (London: Guild Publishing, 1985).
—— comp. and ed., *The Wisden Book of Cricket Records* (London: Guild Publishing, 1986).
A Guide to Important Cricket Matches Played in the British Isles 1709–1863, A Guide to First Class Cricket Matches Played in the British Isles, and various county booklets, comp. and pub. by the Association of Cricket Statisticians.
The Guide to Cricketers, ed. Frederick Lillywhite.
James Lillywhite's Cricketers' Annual.
John Lillywhite's Cricketers' Companion (later *John & James . . .*, and finally *James Lillywhite's Cricketers' Companion.*
John Wisden's Cricketers' Almanack.

2. Newspapers

Bell's Life in London
The Cambridge Chronicle and University Journal, Isle of Ely Herald, and Huntingdonshire Gazette
The Cambridge Independent Press
The Daily Telegraph
The Field, the Country Gentleman's Newspaper
The Illustrated London News
The Illustrated Sporting News
The Illustrated Times
The Leeds Daily News
The Leeds Mercury
The Manchester Guardian
The Sheffield Daily Telegraph
The Sporting Life
The Sportsman

The Times
The Yorkshire Herald
The Yorkshire Post

3. Journals and Periodicals containing articles and miscellaneous material

Baily's Magazine of Sports and Pastimes
Cricket: A Weekly Record of the Game
Cricket Chat
The Cricket Field
The Cricket Quarterly
The Cricket Statistician
The Cricketer
The Journal of the Cricket Society
Labour History
The Playfair Cricket Monthly
Wisden Cricket Monthly

4. Books

Altham, H. S., and E. W. Swanton, *A History of Cricket* (2 vols., London: George Allen & Unwin Ltd., 1962)
Alverstone, The Rt. Hon. Lord, and C. W. Alcock, eds., *Surrey Cricket: Its History and Associations* (London: Longmans, Green, and Co., 1904)
Ashley-Cooper, F. S., *Edward Mills Grace Cricketer* (London: Chatto & Windus, 1916)
—— *Nottinghamshire Cricket and Cricketers* (Nottingham: Henry B. Saxton, n.d. [1923])
—— *Cricket Highways and Byways* (London: George Allen & Unwin Ltd., 1927)
Barker, Ralph, *Ten Great Bowlers* (London: Chatto & Windus, 1967)
Barlow, Richard Gorton, *Forty Seasons of First-class Cricket . . .* (Manchester: John Heywood Ltd., n.d. [1908])
Bettesworth, W. A., *The Walkers of Southgate: A Famous Brotherhood of Cricketers*, ed. by E. T. Sachs (London: Methuen & Co., 1900)
—— *Chats on the Cricket Field*, with Explanatory Notes by F. S. Ashley-Cooper (London: Merritt & Hatcher, Limited, "Cricket Office," n.d. [1910])
Birley, Derek, *The Willow Wand: Some Cricket Myths Explored* (London: Queen Anne Press, Macdonald and Jane's, 1979)
Bowen, Rowland, *Cricket: A History of Its Growth and Development throughout the World* (London: Eyre & Spottiswoode, 1970)
Brookes, Christopher, *English Cricket: The Game and Its Players through the Ages* (London: Weidenfeld and Nicolson, 1978)
Caffyn, William, *see* "Mid-on"
Catton, J. A. H. ("Tityrus"), *Wickets and Goals: Stories of Play* (London: Chapman and Hall Ltd., 1926)
Coldham, James D., *Lord Harris* (London: George Allen & Unwin, 1983)
Collins, W. E. W., *Leaves from . . . An Old Country Cricketer's Diary* (Edinburgh and London: William Blackwood & Sons, 1908)

Daft, Richard, *Kings of Cricket: Reminiscences and Anecdotes with Hints on the Game* (Bristol: J. W. Arrowsmith; London: Simpkin, Marshall, Hamilton, Kent & Company, Limited, n.d. [1893])
—— *A Cricketer's Yarns, to Which Have Been Added a Few Genealogical Tables of Nottinghamshire Cricketing Families*, ed., with an Introduction, by F. S. Ashley-Cooper (London: Chapman and Hall, Ltd., 1926)
FitzGerald, R. A., *see* "Quid"
Gale, Frederick, *Echoes from Old Cricket Fields, or, Sketches of Cricket and Cricketers from the Earliest History of the Game to the Present Time* (London: Simpkin, Marshall, and Co., 1871; rpt. Wakefield: S. R. Publishers Ltd., 1972)
—— *The Game of Cricket*, 2nd ed. (London: Swan Sonnenschein & Co., 1888)
Gibson, Alan, *The Cricket Captains of England, A Survey* (London: Cassell Ltd., 1979)
Giffen, George, *With Bat and Ball: Twenty-five Years' Reminiscences of Australian and Anglo-Australian Cricket* (London: Ward, Lock and Co., Limited, 1898)
Gordon, Sir Home, Bart., *Background of Cricket* (London: Arthur Barker Limited, 1939)
Grace, W. G., *Cricket* (Bristol: J. W. Arrowsmith; London: Simpkin, Marshall, Hamilton, Kent & Co., Limited, 1891)
—— *The History of a Hundred Centuries*, ed. by W. Yardley (London: L. Upcott Gill, 1895)
—— *"W.G.": Cricketing Reminiscences and Personal Recollections* (London: James Bowden, 1899)
Green, Stephen, ed., *Backward Glances: An Album of 60 Early Cricket Photographs 1857–1917* (Newport, I.W.: M. G. Richards, n.d. [1976])
Hadfield, John, *A Wisden Century 1850–1950* (London: Sporting Handbooks Ltd., 1950)
Harris, Lord, *A Few Short Runs* (London: John Murray, 1921)
Harris, Lord, and F. S. Ashley-Cooper, *Lord's and the M.C.C.: A Cricket Chronicle of 137 Years, Based on Official Documents, and Published with the Knowledge and Sanction of the Marylebone Cricket Club to Commemorate the Centenary of Their Present Ground* (London: London & Counties Press Asociation, 1914; rpt. London: Herbert Jenkins Limited, 1920)
Hawke, Lord, *Recollections & Reminiscences* (London: Williams & Norgate, Ltd., 1924)
Hawke, Lord, Lord Harris, and Sir Home Gordon, Bart., eds., *The Memorial Biography of Dr. W. G. Grace* (London: Constable & Company, Ltd., 1919)
Holmes, The Rev. R. S., *Surrey Cricket and Cricketers 1773 to 1895* (London: "Cricket" Offices, 1896)
—— *The History of Yorkshire County Cricket 1833–1903* (London: Archibald Constable and Co. Ltd., 1904)
Hyndman, Henry Mayers, *The Record of an Adventurous Life* (London: MacMillan and Co., Limited, 1911)
Ledbrooke, A. W., *Lancashire County Cricket: The Official History of the Lancashire County & Manchester Cricket Club 1864–1953* (London: Phoenix House, 1954)

Lewis, W. J., *The Language of Cricket, with Illustrative Extracts from the Literature of the Game* (London: Oxford University Press, 1934)
Lillywhite, Fred., *The English Cricketers' Trip to Canada and the United States* (London: F. Lillywhite; Kent & Co., 1860; rpt., Introduction by Robin Marlar, Tadworth, Surrey: World's Work Ltd., 1980)
Lubbock, Alfred, *Memories of Eton and Etonians, Including My Life at Eton, 1854–1863, and Some Reminiscences of Subsequent Cricket, 1864–1874* (London: John Murray, 1899)
Lucas, E. V., ed., *A Hundred Years of Trent Bridge* (Privately Printed for Sir Julien Cahn, 1938)
Lyttelton, The Hon. R. H., *Cricket* (London: Duckworth & Co., 1898)
Lyttelton, The Hon. R. H. and others, *Giants of the Game: Being Reminiscences of the Stars of Cricket from Daft down to the Present Day* (London: Ward, Lock & Co., Limited, n.d. [1899])
Martineau, G. D., *The Valiant Stumper: A History of Wicket-keeping* (London: Stanley Paul, 1957)
"Mid-on" [R. P. Daft], ed., *Seventy-one Not Out: The Reminiscences of William Caffyn* (Edinburgh and London: William Blackwood and Sons, 1899)
Midwinter, Eric, *W. G. Grace: His Life and Times* (London: George Allen & Unwin, 1981)
Mulvaney, John, and Rex Harcourt, *Cricket Walkabout: The Australian Aboriginal Cricketers on Tour 1867–68*, revised ed. (London: MacMillan London Limited, 1988)
"Old Ebor," *see* Pullin, A. W.
Parker, Eric, *The History of Cricket*, The Lonsdale Library of Sports, Games & Pastimes, XXX (London: Seely Service & Co Limited, n.d. [1950])
Pullin, A. W. ("Old Ebor"), *Talks with Old Yorkshire Cricketers*, 2nd ed. (Leeds: "The Yorkshire Post," 1898)
—— *Talks with Old English Cricketers* (Edinburgh and London: William Blackwood and Sons, 1900)
—— *Alfred Shaw Cricketer: His Career and Reminiscences*, recorded by A. W. Pullin ("Old Ebor") (London: Cassell and Company, Limited, 1902)
—— *History of Yorkshire County Cricket 1903–1923* (Leeds: Chorley & Pickersgill Ltd, The Electric Press, 1924)
Pycroft, The Rev. James, *The Cricket-field, with Some Notes by H. H. Stephenson*, ed., with an Introduction, by F. S. Ashley-Cooper (London: St. James's Press Co, Ltd., 1922)
—— *Cricketana* (London: Longman, Green, Longman, Roberts, & Green, 1865)
—— *Oxford Memories*, in John Arlott, comp., *The Middle Ages of Cricket* (London: Christopher Johnson, n.d. [1949]) [Contains extract, "Cricket Recollections"]
"Quid" [R. A. FitzGerald], *Jerks in from Short-leg* (London: Harrison, 1866)
Ranjitsinhji, K. S., *The Jubilee Book of Cricket*, 6th ed. (Edinburgh and London: William Blackwood and Sons, 1898)
Read, W. W., *Annals of Cricket: A Record of the Game Compiled from Authentic Sources, and My Own Experiences during the Last Twenty-five Years* (London: Sampson Low, Marston & Company Limited, 1896)
Roper, Edward, *A Sportsman's Memories*, ed. Fred W. Wood (Liverpool and Prescot: C. Tinling & Co., Limited, 1921)

Routledge, Edmund, *Handbook of Cricket* (London: George Routledge and Sons, n.d. [1866?])

Rutter, Edward, *Cricket Memories: Rugby—Middlesex—Free Foresters* (London: Williams and Norgate, Ltd., 1925)

Selkirk, George H., *Guide to the Cricket Ground* (London and Cambridge: MacMillan and Co., 1867)

Shaw, Alfred, *see* Pullin, A. W. ("Old Ebor")

Spratt, A. W., *A Short Account of the Career of the Eminent Cricketer Robert Carpenter* (Cambridge: Cambridge University Press, 1897)

Steel, A. G., and the Hon. R. H. Lyttelton, and others, *Cricket*, 2nd ed., The Badminton Library of Sports and Pastimes (London: Longmans, Green, and Co., 1888)

Taylor, Alfred D., *Annals of Lord's and History of the M.C.C.: A Concise Record of the Club's Progress Gleaned from Authentic Sources from the Date of Its Formation to the Present Time* (Bristol: J. W. Arrowsmith; London: Simpkin, Marshall, Hamilton, Kent & Company Limited, n.d. [1903])

Thomas, Peter, *Yorkshire Cricketers 1839–1939* (Manchester: Derek Hodgson Publisher, 1973)

Warner, Sir Pelham, *Lord's 1787–1945* (London: George G. Harrap & Co. Ltd., 1946)

—— *Gentlemen v. Players 1806–1949* (London: George G. Harrap & Co. Ltd., 1950)

West, G. Derek, *The Elevens of England* (London: Darf Publishers Limited, 1988)

Williams, Marcus, ed., *The Way to Lord's: Cricketing Letters to The Times* (London: William Collins (Willow Books), 1983)

—— ed., *Double Century: 200 Years of Cricket in The Times* (London: William Collins (Willow Books), 1985)

Wilson, E. R., in P. F. Warner, *Cricket: A New Edition*, The Badminton Library of Sports and Pastimes (London: Longmans, Green, and Co., 1920)

Wood, Frederick, *Beeton's Cricket Book* (London: Frederick Warne and Co., n.d. [1866])

Wright, L. G., *Scraps from a Cricketer's Memory* (Derby: Derbyshire County Cricket Supporters' Club, 1980)

Wynne-Thomas, Peter, *Nottinghamshire Cricketers 1821–1914* (Haughton, Retford, Notts: The Author, 1971)

—— *England on Tour: A Record of All England Cricket Tours Overseas, with Accounts, Results and Statistics* (London: The Hamlyn Publishing Group Limited, 1982)

—— *The Hamlyn A–Z of Cricket Records* (London: The Hamlyn Publishing Group Limited, 1983)

—— *'Give Me Arthur': A Biography of Arthur Shrewsbury* (London: Arthur Barker Limited, 1985)

—— *The History of Hampshire County Cricket Club* (London: Guild Publishing, 1988)

Index